TELEVISION, IMAGINATION, AND AGGRESSION:

A Study of Preschoolers

TELEVISION, IMAGINATION, AND AGGRESSION:

A Study of Preschoolers

JEROME L. SINGER
DOROTHY G. SINGER
Yale University

LEA LAWRENCE ERLBAUM ASSOCIATES, PUBLISHERS
1981   Hillsdale, New Jersey

Lawrence Erlbaum Associates, Inc., Publishers
365 Broadway
Hillsdale, New Jersey 07642

Library of Congress Cataloging in Publication Data

Singer, Jerome L
  Television, imagination, and aggression.

  Bibliography: p.
  Includes index.
  1. Television and children—longitudinal studies.
  2. Imagination in children. 3. Aggressiveness in
children. I. Singer, Dorothy G., joint author.
  II. Title.
HQ784.T4S56   791.45'01'3   80-36810
ISBN 0-89859-060-4

Printed in the United States of America

Contents

Preface

This book presents a detailed account of a two-year study relating preschool children's home television-viewing patterns to their spontaneous behavior, play, aggression, and language use in nursery school settings. It also describes an attempt to modify children's viewing patterns and behavior through interventions with parents and special training procedures. Questions of the possible theoretical significance for child development of the role of imagination and of the massive impact from the television medium on the broadening experience of the preschool child are also addressed.

This study is the first to track preschoolers over a year's time while obtaining data on TV as well as overt behavior. We have subsequently repeated this effort with a larger sample of children drawn from a lower socioeconomic class background, but it will be some time before that data is fully analyzed. On the whole the more recent study yields rather similar findings with respect to play patterns, TV-viewing, and aggressive behavior so that we feel some confidence in reporting the earlier study now. Results of a concurrent study using many similar methods carried out in South Africa by Dr. Diana Shmukler lend further support to some of our findings. Research on TV-viewing and aggression in elementary school children carried out by Drs. Leonard Eron and Rowell Huesmann in Chicago is also providing comparable data. It is our hope that this report can spur others to follow up on many of the implications of those results using comparable naturalistic methods.

We believe this book will be of special interest to behavioral scientists and graduate students in the fields of child development and communication research. We have also tried to present material that can be of use to early childhood educators, to psychiatrists, social workers, and other mental health professionals concerned with the origins of imagination and with the impact of television. In a sense, the pervasiveness of the TV medium suggests that many people outside the social sciences might want to know about some of these results even though they may have less specific interest in some of the technical references and statistical methods.

This research was carried out at the Yale University Family Television Research and Consultation Center in the Psychology Department at Yale. Specific funds for most of the research described herein came from a grant from the RANN Division (the Telecommunications Branch) of the National Science Foundation (DAR #76-20772)[1] to Yale with the coauthors as principal investigators. Specific consultation and administrative support came from NSF staff members, Rolland Johnson (now at the University of Iowa) and Charles Brownstein. The large number of observers, protocol judges, and raters we employed precludes our thanking each of them by name here although we have cited them in formal reports provided to NSF. Of particular importance in carrying out this study were our key research associates and assistants, Ms. Rhoda Brownstein, Dr. Roni Tower, Dr. Lonnie Sherrod, Dr. Robert Kruger, Ms. Sandy Gitlitz, Mr. Daniel Tuteur, Mr. Paul Christoph, Mr. John Caldeira, and Mr. Richard Gerrig. Valuable statistical consultation came from Dr. Dominick Cicchetti and Dr. George Huba. Ms. Virginia Hurd was our staunch administrative assistant throughout, and valuable clerical aid came from Ms. Cheryl Olsen, Ms. Muriel Jarmack, and Ms. Charlotte Shah.

Although our promises of anonymity preclude our thanking children and parents or school personnel by name, we wish to dedicate this book to the children and their families who participated in this study and to the many preschool and kindergarten administrators and teachers in the New Haven area who showed a responsible concern not only for the children in their charge but also for the importance of obtaining scientific data about developmental patterns and television-viewing. We have continued to be in touch with many of the families and schools and value these associations.

Jerome L. Singer and Dorothy G. Singer

---

[1]The interpretations of data, speculations, and inferences presented in this book are solely those of the authors and in no way reflect the specific policies or point of view of the National Science Foundation.

1 Television: Its Potential Role in the Cognitive and Emotional Development of the Child

INTRODUCTION

It is possible that the television set now established in 99% of homes in the United States may actually be changing human consciousness and the nature of our cognitive development? We put the proposition in its boldest form because we think behavioral scientists (along with many intellectuals in the humanities) have preferred to ignore the "idiot box" that sits in the living rooms, bedrooms, or kitchens of millions of homes, peered at for at least three hours daily by milions of children and adults. We are now into the second generation of regular TV-viewers in this country; the fans of "Howdy-Doody" and "Miss Frances," the "Mouseketeers," the kids who bought coonskin hats in the millions after watching "Davey Crockett" are now many of them parents and *their* children are growing up watching even more television, much of it in vivid color. Behavioral scientists have occasionally decried the amount of violence represented on the 19 in. screen and have in the past decade begun studying the effects of such material on overt behavior, especially in children. They have paid less attention, on the whole, to other issues concerning the impact of the medium—its cognitive implications, its role in forming constructive social attitudes, its potential for educational use, not just providing information but in enhancing the emergence of cognitive skills that the growing child can draw on independent of the TV medium for effective adaptation and learning.

Children are growing up today in an environment that includes an element of daily visual stimulation never before a part of human experience. Three- and four-year-olds get up at 6:30 a.m. and go over to a little box on which they watch cartoon figures bouncing around or pounding each other into pieces, soon magically revived; by 8:30 a.m., when bundled off to day care center or nursery school, they have already watched for at least an hour. At noon if they attended school only for a half-day, they are in time for the "Gong Show" in which miniature adults on the screen also dress in absurd costumes, leap about frenetically, or are dragged screaming from a stage in the midst of a caterwauling song. Often well into 9:00 or 10:00 p.m. they continue to watch the movements on the box, usually only vaguely grasping the plots or the meaning of words used or distinguishing between commercials and program content. But the moving figures hold their attention!

In other generations of human history when three- or four-year-olds awoke they perhaps followed their parents around, performed some household chores, and tagged after the adults out into the fields. *Or else they read or played.* Even with the advent of movies in this century, visits by very young children were occasional, took place with parents or other adults present to some degree, involved a large screen and a very special setting. The radio offered little to hold the attention of the very young child and, for the five- or six-year-old and up, called for an active effort to transform the auditory material into some private visual representation to sustain interest in the plot or characters.

Television is really different. It's there in the home all the time, it's small in size, its figures move and talk and sing, and the segments flash by with a rapidity different from the ordinary sequences of real life interactions. A recent book, *The Plug-In Drug,* by Marie Winn (1977), a professional writer, has provocatively examined the potentially addictive qualities of TV-viewing and has implied that many of our current ills from juvenile violence, the drop in national reading scores or SAT levels, through the increase in drug abuse are attributable to the medium. Ms. Winn may not be technically correct in some of her discussions of cognitive issues or in her hypothesis that the presumed heavier right-brain arousal of television may be weakening the verbal skills associated with left-brain activities. Still we think she is on the right track in emphasizing the fact that television can encourage a certain kind of cognitive passivity which leads to a "show me or entertain me" orientation by school children or college students and also in her emphasis on the fact that the time spent watching TV means less time spent reading or writing or actively exploring one's environment. We would emphasize even more than she does that the spontaneous play of children involving a mixture of games of mastery, games with rules, exploration and make-believe, or symbolic play are all critical phases of how a child learns about itself and its environment, practices verbal skills, tries out various emotions and cognitive discriminations or behaviors, and prepares itself for later social roles through sociodramatic pretending. Children sitting in front of TV sets are obviously playing or reading less than they might have done before the medium was available on so wide a scale.

We have begun with a challenge about some powerful implications of the television-viewing habit for the nature of consciousness. We would like to examine first of all some of the major developmental tasks that confront the growing child and then to suggest that play (and we are here emphasizing symbolic games, pretending, and make-believe) represents a major method by which children can develop the skills required for those tasks. We can look at television, which in a sense represents a form of vicarious play or fantasy, and examine some of the special cognitive properties of that medium. We next confront the question of how television-viewing and play are competitive for the child's time and whether there may be ways in which the two forms of experience may complement each other as part of the child's development. What are some of the dangers and limitations in development posed by even moderate TV-viewing (three hours a day for the child)? Ought we to abolish TV entirely as Winn wishfully suggests, or can we find ways of using the medium to good effect? What research still needs to be done to help us to move beyond "top-of-the-head" assertions by "authorities" toward a more systematic comprehension of the way television influences normal cognitive or social development?

THE TASK-DEMANDS OF GROWING-UP: THE SPECIAL ROLE OF IMAGINATIVE PLAY

In looking at the complexity of the developmental process, we think it may be helpful to think of cognitive and emotional growth somewhat in the way an industrial psychologist would look at a personnel selection process. In effect we need a job analysis first. What does it take to grow up into normal adolescence in a given culture or subgroup of a particular society or, in general, in the human species? Clearly a child by a certain age has to master certain motor skills, turning over first, creeping, crawling, pulling itself upright, and then standing alone before walking. Some of these performances depend on maturation of musculature and physiology more generally but others are greatly abetted by environmental circumstances. Or, at least, the emergence of the behavior is accelerated by adult aid and encouragement.

For our purposes we focus primarily on the task demands of developing the cognitive and affective systems of the child. For example, the child must be prepared with expectations and motor or cognitive "plans" (Miller, Galanter, & Pribram, 1960) to deal with each new setting or demand. In order to do this it must find a means of transforming externally derived information into a miniaturized private representational system, rapidly encoded and decoded as situations demand. We have increasing reason to believe that language encoding and the imagery storage processes are separately organized and processed by the brain (Paivio, 1971; Witelson, 1976), but that both systems ultimately may interact to produce optimal storage (Rohwer, 1970). In imitating language the child gradually miniaturizes sounds, words, and eventually phrases into a form suitable for efficient storage and retrieval in the long-term system. The same process presumably occurs with the more global material of visual, auditory, or other sensory-modality information, and to the extent that the child rehearses images and verbal labels together, the chances of highly efficient voluntary retrieval of this material is greatly enhanced.

Piaget (1962), in his emphasis on *assimilation,* and Tomkins (1970), in the theory of *miniaturization* through repetition, are proposing that effective internal representation does depend on some kind of continuing private rehearsal process. We have elsewhere elaborated on these suggestions to propose that make-believe play and pretending in early childhood develop naturally as part of this very process of the child's gaining control over an internal or symbolic representation system (Singer, 1973). Pretending and the profound dimension of "as if" in human experience are intrinsic to the establishment of an efficient set of anticipatory guiding images, verbal labels, and plans with easily spun-out subroutines. Pretending itself depends on the level of the child's cognitive maturation and also the complexity or "realism" of the structures with which the child is dealing, as Fein (1975) has indicated in her experimental analysis of 18-month- to 2-year-olds simulating drinking from an empty cup or feeding a plastic "horsey" with invisible milk.

Although almost all children show some degree of make-believe or fantasy play, the persistence and elaboration of such play in the 3- to 6-year-old period appears to depend on considerable support and encouragement from adults as well as on opportunities for practice in privacy (Singer, 1973; Singer & Singer, 1976a). Obviously children whose play is more limited to games with rules or to mastery experiences such as climbing, ball-playing, or forms of motor exploration also master new schema and set up coding systems. But there is increasing reason to believe that those children whose play repertory in the preschool period includes a good deal of make-believe and fantasy play have a distinct edge in certain important cognitive areas (Smilansky, 1968). A study by Lewis (1973), for example, found that kindergarteners who played more elaborate and extensive sociodramatic or fantasy games showed better performance in picture interpretation tasks, in the amount of language employed, and in organization of language during picture interpretations. In free association tasks high fantasy-play children produced more responses, provided more associations remote from self or the home environment, and showed more use of categorization and associative linkage than of random naming. Lewis found her clearest differences in cognitive organization between the children of high IQ-high sociodramatic play and those with correspondingly high IQ and low levels of fantasy play thus ruling out sheer intelligence as a factor in the differences. Similar results have been reported recently by Dansky (1976) and in a series of studies summarized by Singer (1977).

Our own current research on 3- and 4-year-olds as well as several earlier studies using observation of free play have consistently found correlations between levels of make-believe and the use of more extended vocabulary or the introduction of more complex syntactic structures such as predicate nominatives into spontaneous language. A report by the late Corrine Hutt in England (1979) also suggests that working-class children whose spontaneous language is characterized by little variation and complexity show an increase in measures such as mean length of utterance and richness of vocabulary when encouraged to engage in make-believe games. The studies directed by Saltz (1976) on urban disadvantaged children trained in thematic play are also corroborative here.

We are suggesting, then, that growing up requires an increasing complexity of vocabulary, an ability to categorize materials, to retrieve words or images readily, and to generate sets of more remote associations or to recall details of verbally presented situations accurately (Tucker, 1975). Imaginative play provides an arena for rehearsing material and assimilating it to a greater variety of preestablished schema. By the very process of scaling the trucks or large environmental features down in the form of toys or small objects standing for large ones (as in blocks for buildings or pencils for airplanes), the child provides itself with manageable schema for effective later retrieval.

Let us briefly talk of the task demands for the growing child in the affective area. There is an increasing reason to believe that human beings grow up with a relatively differentiated but circumscribed affect system closely tied to facial representation and to the complexity of and rate of assimilability of information processing demands (Izard, 1977; Tomkins, 1962, 1963). An important feature of pretend play is that it again provides opportunities for expression and control of affect and the representation in miniaturized form of conflictual or frightening scenes or encounters. The child engaged in pretend play of adventurous or hostile encounters gains some sense of competence and power (Sutton-Smith, 1976) or empathy (Gould, 1972; Saltz & Johnson, 1974) and may in effect be establishing better organized schema or plans and subroutines for observing others' emotions and expressing or controlling its own. In our own research we have regularly observed that children engaged in make-believe play are also "happier" children. That is, when observers rate them for the positive affects of interest and curiosity or joy and the smiling response we find positive consistent correlations between imaginativeness of play, positive affect, concentration, elation, and coopera- tion with peers (Singer & Singer, 1976a).

Important task demands of socialization and moral growth also confront the child. Differentiating aggression or violence from adaptive assertiveness, impulsivity from means-end action, egocentricism from sharing, dependent demanding from sharing or helping, infantile sexuality from interpersonal intimacy—all these are demands we all must confront in the growth process. Make-believe play as child psychotherapists have long stressed is an important arena in which children can express and differentiate issues of this kind. Again, in a sense the play situation permits the child to examine an array of probabilities or possibilities with impunity and to store these miniaturized new schema more effectively.

Gould (1972), on the basis of her observations of free play in preschoolers, concluded that children who played more imaginatively also took roles other than self in play and thus developed an empathy for the victims of aggression. They were thus less likely to be directly aggressive toward others. There is a body of evidence that suggests that by elementary school age children who show imaginativeness in spontaneous play or in projective test performance are less likely to be overtly aggressive or impulsive and are better able to tolerate delays or are more socially cooperative (Singer & Singer, 1976b). In our current research as well as in earlier studies (Nahme-Huang, Singer, Singer, & Wheaton, 1977; Tower, Singer, Singer, & Biggs, 1979) we have generally found that imaginative play is also associated with peer group sharing or cooperation and with somewhat less demandingness or dependency on adults. Rubin, Maioni, and Hornung (1976) also report data suggesting a greater level of social maturity identified with sociodramatic play.

In summary, then, imaginative play can be viewed as a major resource by which children can cope immediately with the cognitive, affective, and social demands of growing up. It is more than a reactive behavior, however, for it provides a practice ground for organizing new schema and for transforming and storing material for more effective later expression in plans, action, or verbalization. Our own research and the increasing body of studies in this area suggest that play is an active process and one that depends to some degree on reinforcement, modeling, and general encouragement by parental figures (Dennis, 1976; Gershowitz, 1974; Shmukler, 1978; Singer, 1977).

INFLUENCES ON IMAGINATIVE DEVELOPMENT

A critical question that remains before us is to identify even more precisely those factors that are particularly conducive to encouraging imaginative play in early childhood so that such play can be effective in helping the child develop further its cognitive, affective, and social skills. Gershowitz (1974) demonstrated that well-trained or empathic adults who offered direction initially to a child and then pulled back were more likely to foster rich imaginative play in the youngsters. Shmukler (1978) has been carrying out an elaborate study of mother-child interaction patterns in relation to make-believe play and imagination with middle-class white parents in South Africa. In a sophisticated Boolean analysis of relevant variables she finds evidence that a variable reflecting a mother who tells stories to a child, is accepting of the child's uniqueness, and who shows leadership in stimulating play, but then withdraws, are the best predicators of imaginativeness.

A recent example of maternal input and its impact on a child's developing imagination can be cited. In an article on new developments in philosophy, Branch (1977) describes the childhood of Sol Kripke, an outstanding young American logician. Kripke's mother used to recite Gilbert and Sullivan passages to him when he was a preschooler. Subsequently intrigued by the word play of that delightful material the boy developed a whole world of gremlins, and abolute monarchy whose king was both the tallest and the shortest character in the realm. He used to delight his younger sisters with running episodes of this fantasy. The progression toward analytic philosophy and the complex word-play and mathematics of Kripke's modern examination of "truth" seems less surprising with such beginnings.

THE SPECIAL QUALITIES OF THE TELEVISION MEDIUM

Let us return now to examine the role of television in our job analysis of the child's cognitive and affective development. If play is as important as we have suggested it may be, then where does watching television fit into the child's repertory? It might be argued that television represents an important, easily accessible alternative to parental storytelling and subsequent spontaneous play. Indeed for many poor children whose parents are overworked, inaccessible, or lack cultural orientation to engage in story telling or reading to children it is possible that television affords a remarkable opportunity to come in contact with magic, fantasy, a richer vocabulary, and much information about other countries or about history and culture not ordinarily available to them. If one accepts some form of the psychoanalytic catharsis theory in which vicarious experience in the form of fairy tales or myths involving symbolic representation of crises of early childhood, for example, incest, parent-directed violence, or sibling hatred, can alleviate conflicts over sexuality and aggression (Bettleheim, 1975), then television may be serving as good or better a function for the broader society than bedtime stories ever could.

The fact is we do no yet know enough to assert the positive or negative evidence for the proposition that television may be providing a major form of alternative consciousness or that it may be serving much the same role as play in child development. The research described in this book, tracking 3- and 4-year-olds over a year or more and looking at relations between how much and what they watch on TV and their spontaneous play activities during the nursery school day is just a beginning in this direction. It is certainly clear from recording their make-believe play or from identifying their imaginary companions that a large percentage of their fantasy figures are drawn from TV characters, especially Batman, Superman, Bionic Man, Wonder Woman, and Bionic Woman. The pull of the powerful figures is a strong one. Even from "Sesame Street" our children are far more likely to adopt the Cookie Monster as a make-believe character than some of the more benign muppets on the show.

It can be argued, however, that television may be counterproductive to the development of imagination as a basic resource for the growing child. Of course it preempts time from spontaneous play as it obviously does for reading in the school age child (Hornick, 1978). Although 3- and 4-year-olds do indeed view the set with far less attention than older children and often drift into spontaneous play as our own studies indicate, play while the set is on is desultory and more fragmented. Television as a stimulus situation has special properties that require very careful examination (Singer, 1980).

1. Attention Demand. It is almost impossible to ignore a TV set if you are in the same room even if the sound is turned off and only the picture visible. The human brain has evolved to respond to movements in the environment, no doubt a basically adaptive mechanism. The activity in the little box across the room is continuous but not rhythmic—new faces or settings appear from moment to moment and evoke an orienting response from us. The rapidity of changes has been studied by the staff of the Children's Television Workshop in developing the "Sesame Street" format and it was possible to show (by use of a competing stimulus) that quick blackouts, lively movement, and pixillation hold the eyes of preschoolers on the screen with remarkable success (Lesser, 1974). In our own research in which we compared 3- and 4-year-olds reactions to the slow-paced "Mister Rogers" with the lively, quick-cut "Sesame Street" it was obvious that the latter show kept the children concentrating on the screen more consistently (Tower, Singer, Singer, & Biggs, 1979).

We need considerable research to determine whether the attention-attracting qualities of TV do present a psychological problem, indeed an addictive potential as Winn (1977) has suggested. Certainly it is much harder to read or to do homework in the same room with a working TV set. Those of us from the radio generation of the 1930s can attest to the great psychological differences between radio-listening and TV-viewing. The former was less likely to interfere with reading or playing; one could periodically blot out some of its impact. The TV set constantly draws us back to it.

2. Brief Sequences. Commercial television in this country has evolved a style of extremely brief sequences of events. An interaction between two people or a depiction of a news event or fictional plot sequences rarely runs beyond a couple minutes without a sharp change of scene or characters.

Staying with the face of an individual and slowly "arcing" closer, often an artistic touch in film, is almost never done on commercial TV because the fear that the audience attention will be lost. Commercials, themselves rarely more than 30 seconds long, burst on the screen tumbling after each other in breathless profusion after only a few minutes of a news broadcast or story line.

We have very little understanding of the psychological impact of this experience on the developing cognitive structures of the preschooler. Is life really like this? Can one really comprehend material presented at so rapid a pace? What effect does such frequent change produce upon the viewer? Certainly there are reasons to believe that the rapidity of sequences can have an arousing quality and may produce hyperactivity in the young child (Halpern, 1975) or serve to facilitate aggressive behaviors (Tannenbaum & Zillmann, 1975; Watt & Krull, 1977). In some of our research we find that only very bright 3- or 4-year-old girls are able to retain some of the main features of a "Sesame Street" show just a few minutes after watching it (Tower, Singer, Singer, & Biggs, 1979).

3. Interference Effects. The complete changes of material that follow so closely on each other in television must certainly have some special impact on our memory systems. We know that material to be stored even for later recognition must stay within a short-term memory system for a critical few seconds. If material is to be actively retrieved with any efficiency (not just passively recognized), it usually requires more time in short-term memory or a combination of exposure to the sensory modality with a verbal-labeling process and perhaps some few rehearsals in our own private "instant replay" system. The piling up of material with such rapdity in TV may lead to strong interference effects.

The issue for the child is whether this rapid succession of novel material may not only interfere with immediate recall or comprehension but also impede the development of the private rehearsal system. For the child to become involved in the assimilation process may demand some vocalization of words or sounds, some motor play, sometimes literally jumping around imitating a behavior sequence represented on the screen. With the demand character of the visual movement and the interference form new material it is conceivable that children do not have a chance to use brief play episodes to transform or miniaturize the content. They may simply not get into the habit of using this mechanism when confronted with the TV set.

If you think about it a great deal of the pleasure of life comes not only in the immediacy of an experience, a fine tasting wine or bread, sexual release, a beautiful bit of melodic phrasing on a piano or guitar. The instance passes rapidly but our memory of it lingers. We savour the great experiences of living and reexperience joy that way. Television moves on too quickly to allow such private activity unless we forcibly withdraw our eyes from the set or have already developed our imaginative capacities so that we can tune out a moving stimulus in order to daydream a little (Rosenberg, 1977; Singer, Greenberg, & Antrobus, 1971). Indeed the TV medium recognizes this problem by providing instant replays of sports events and even in the baseball parks themselves those great fielding plays we might remember for years are quickly shown again on giant screens near the scoreboard. It remains to be seen whether reliance on such external representations may be weakening the child's development of play sequences and private imagery as a basis for enjoyment of experiences and rehearsal or assimilation of novel material.

4. Complexity of Television Presentations.   It may be that the complex vocabulary and rapidity and variety of presentations on TV are actually sharpening the preschoolers' quickness to grasp material. Children may learn early to adjust to complexity and benefit from it. Aren't city kids, used to bustle and fast-talking people, supposed to be more verbal and quick to grasp communications than their country cousins? In a sense the television medium may have urbanized the nation along fast-talking Madison Avenue lines. Again we need some research to examine whether preschoolers are sharpening vocabulary and speed of comprehension through exposure to TV.

The study by Friedlander, Wetstone, and Scott (1974) suggest that children prefer much more slowly paced sequences of information presentation and can comprehend a good deal of material if not burdened with too hectic a pace. Our studies of recall of material from "Mister Rogers' Neighborhood," a slow-moving, child-oriented program, suggests that the less-intelligent child can recall more because of Mister Rogers' soft speech and careful repetition (Tower, Singer, Singer, & Biggs, 1979). We also noticed that although children's eyes wander from the set during that show and the youngsters even go off to play they can retain as much or more of what they have seen as children who stayed glued to "Sesame Street."

5. The Visual Orientation.   An obvious reason for the power of television is that it does a great deal of the work for us. Not only are we as humans more sensitive to visual displays just as beagles are more responsive to olfactory ones, but we also have the harder task when listening to radio drama of imagining the faces or movements of the characters or conjuring up some kind of mental representation of the exotic setting of a particular adventure. If we are reading we have to perform even more complex transformations from words to auditory or visual imagery. Even the preliterate 4- or 5-year-old who thumbs through a picture book has to fill in movements or extend through some private transformation the static images represented there. TV does the whole thing for us at one fell swoop and all it takes is the flip of a switch.

Visually presented material does largely appear to be processed more extensively by the right side of our brain in a global, parallel fashion. Printed material or complex verbal or mathematical sequences seem to engage the left side of the brain more. There is some reason to believe (Witelson, 1976) that boys are more differentiated in right-left brain function than girls in early childhood. Indeed the verbal advantages girls show (as evident in the language analyses emerging in this study as well as in many other studies) and the fact that boys reveal greater susceptibility to verbal difficulties such as stuttering or dyslexia, may reflect some limitations of this early specialization of brain function. Is it possible that the television-viewing that emphasizes concrete representation and spatial imagery may be playing further into this early limitation in boys' cognitive development? In the research we describe, boys are watching somewhat more than girls and even more as they go from 3 to 4. On weekends, according to our data, boys are especially likely to be plunked in front of the TV set, perhaps to keep them quiet, whereas girls are more likely to be off shopping with mother, helping with chores, or involved in some kind of play. Clearly we need some more extensive research on the kinds of processing involved in watching TV and some indications of whether or not there are differences in exercise of one or both hemispheres in relation to whether one is reading or watching television. Whereas it is unlikely that TV is turning our left brain to mush as Winn (1977) occasionally seems to suggest, it is possible that the ease of viewing is enhancing a strong preference for or reliance on global visual representations that makes children and later young adults more impatient with the effort required to process purely auditory verbal material such as teacher's lectures or to deal with reading material that require a series of transformations for effective encoding.

6. *Emphasis on Action and Violence: Emotional Range.* We have already mentioned how the rapid sequence format of TV may have an emotionally arousing effect. It is also the case that TV producers and writers believe they cannot hold an audience's interest or attention without vigorous movements or acts of violence being represented on the screen. The literature on the potential aggression-eliciting or modeling effects of violence are reviewed later in this book. What we should like to stress is that by its very format American television presents a set of models for vigorous motion that can spill over even in play toward direct aggression. Nursery school teachers complain of Kung Fu chops delivered to unsuspecting playmates, of games of construction involving imaginary cities or factories being disrupted by passing children who topple block structures with shouts of "Earthquake!" or "Towering Inferno!" Imaginative play has always included incidents of adventure and violence within a circumscribed framework, but many observers believe today that the frequent TV representations of realistic violence on so many shows may be conducive to imitative behaviors rather than to play transformations (Brodzinksy, Messer, & Tew, 1979).

Another trend of television in its attempt recently at providing equal sex representation has led to the presentation of super-female figures like Bionic Woman or Wonder Woman. Our data, as we see later, indicate that these characters are being adopted by preschool girls as their identification figures or imaginary companions alongside Superman and Batman. Boys, by the way, do not stray into identification with female superheroes.

We do not discuss some other important aspects of television that require attention as they have been extensively considered elsewhere. These include the excessive materialism and commercial socialization experience provided by U.S. TV, the continuing racial stereotyping (U.S. Commission on Civil Rights, 1977), the failure to develop extensive children's programming that can emphasize sharing, cooperation, and altruism. Our concern here is not to attack television but to understand it and eventually to learn how to use it effectively for optimal cognitive and affective development.

THE POWER AND LIMITATIONS OF TELEVISION

Having looked at some of the special stimulus characteristics of the TV medium, we can draw some tentative conclusions about what TV can offer the growing child and also some of the problems it poses for development. There are many poor children in our nation who might in the nineteenth century have grown up illiterate and vastly ignorant of the world outside their neighborhoods. Television is clearly opening vistas of a broader society and introducing a variety of vocabulary and language to which they would not ordinarily be exposed. Remember that the data on inverse relationships of language use and TV frequency we cited are from middle-class samples. At least at the level of a *recognition* vocabulary, TV must be doing more for the educationally disadvantaged than any educational system ever available before. If our society is not prepared to spend the money for smaller schoolroom classes, and for intensive high-quality formal education for its urban or rural poor, then television may be partially filling the gap. It is doing so, we believe, at a cost—it is substituting visual and oral experience for the ultimately more efficient and self-liberating skill of reading.

Television is also providing in its way a new culture background—a host of archetypes, identification and stereotype figures around which children can organize their imaginative experience. Again this is especially important for masses of children who because of cultural and educational limitations might have grown up semiliterate and minimally exposed to some of the great symbols of world literature and art. TV-viewers now know something of Greek mythology; Isis, long buried in Egyptian scholarship reemerges as a heroine on Saturday mornings; Robin Hood, Sherlock Holmes, and Sinbad the Sailor are known to children who might never have looked at a book before. True, our 3-year-olds are identifying with superheroes like Batman or Superman, but these are after all only slight transformations of the Hercules and Krishnas with whom millions of children and adults for thousands of years have peopled their imaginations. The danger is not so much that "pop culture" (following Gresham's economic law) will drive out 'high culture" but that the stimulus properties of the TV set may subvert almost completely the enjoyment and hence the practice of reading skills and independent imaginative play.

If TV does provide a "window on the world" (Liebert, Neale, & Davidson, 1973), we may well ask, "what world?" There is a broader world out there beyond our immediate experience peopled by senators, Rhodesians, Chinese ping-pong players, full of erupting volcanoes, oil spills, and forest fires. The work of Gerbner (1977) and his associates suggests that through both fiction and news television presents so terrifying a picture of the world that even moderately frequent viewers grossly overestimate the dangers of their daily life. The visual impact of a tragic occurrence has a vividness that stays in memory, whereas the reading of similar content in a newspaper might make it possible to quality the signficance of the event and to present it in fuller perspective.

The risk here for young children is not only an exaggerated fear, already documented in several reports, but also, again, the substitution of an external vicarious experience for one the child can control and assimilate. If television stimulates make-believe play then the child can engage in rehearsal processes, miniaturization, and can gain a sense of efficacy that permits a very different mode of storage of the material than is possible only from the gross viewing experience. At least that is a hypothesis worth testing. But the danger is that television-viewing may simply *preempt* play and, indeed, *the habit of play*, and remove a resource that could be of great value to the child.

RESEARCH OBJECTIVES

We have discussed some of the possible links between television, imagination, and aggression in rather general terms in this chapter. In moving from a general commentary to a specific study one must provide a set of procedures which can operationalize terms like TV-viewing of preschoolers, aggression, or imaginative play. In order to do so we have drawn on earlier research efforts. Thus, imaginative play is evaluated as it occurs during so-called unstructured time in nursery schools and is scored according to definitions developed in previous studies (Singer, 1973; Singer & Singer, 1976b; Tower, Singer, Singer, & Biggs, 1979). We have sought to explore not only this specific form of play but have looked at it in relation to other ongoing behavior of the children, for example, their emotional responses, their cooperation with other children, their overt aggressive reactions to children or property, their use of language. In effect the research procedure provides us with a chance to observe the interrelations of a series of affective, motoric, and cognitive responses of children over a year's time and to contribute to the general literature on the growth of play and language usage.

In moving to understand the possible impact of television we have opted to obtain periodic samplings of the children viewing patterns at home over a year's time. Daily records of children's viewing over two consecutive weeks were maintained by parents on four occasions during the year from February 1977 to February 1978. This provided us with perhaps the most extensive indication of preschoolers' viewing across time thus far available in the research literature. Clearly we could not test within this format many of the hypotheses about television's role in cognition that we have proposed in this chapter. If, however, heavy TV-viewing or the viewing of particular programs grossly interferes with imaginative play or with language development this should stand out fairly clearly from our data. Links, if any, between TV, aggression, and imagination can be examined across time. Our data also permit us to examine developmental changes in the preschool years in viewing frequency or content and how such changes might relate to behavior outside the home. We can also examine consistencies in TV-viewing for children, program preferences, sex differences in viewing, and possible home-life links to the importance of the TV set in the child's life.

Because practically no research like this has yet been conducted it was not possible to assert a series of precise alternative hypotheses. Nevertheless it is clear that if many parents or educators or TV industry representatives are correct we ought to find no relationships between school play and home TV-viewing patterns. Indeed, support for the null hypothesis would be an important outcome, all the more so because of the emotionality of groups like the PTA or writers like Marie Winn or Jerry Mander who emphasize the evils of the medium. Or we might find that TV is linked to greater imaginativeness; frequent viewing could be a stimulant for play despite the analysis we have provided in this chapter.

Our developmental field study approach also allows us to look at individual differences in play and TV-viewing patterns. Considering how dependent children are on contextual variations and how labile they are emotionally, it is interesting to see if consistent individual differences in play styles or other behaviors are discernible in the third and fourth year of life. Do such individual differences play a part in the possible links between TV and overt behavior as we have implied earlier? Can an established repertory of imaginative play skills "immunize" a child against direct imitation of violence on television? Are their consistencies in aggressive behavior already discernible in preschoolers of the type reported for older groups by Olweüs (1979)? Do such consistencies reflect heavy TV-viewing, viewing of aggressive shows, or are the TV-viewing patterns merely reflections of preferential attitudes by children already established in an aggressive behavioral style?

As we present our results in succeeding chapters we reexamine where possible relevant research and theory with respect to these questions and others. We have in the present chapter outlined some of our assumptions and expectations. As the reader will see, some of these initial views are not testable, some may be clearly unsupported by the empirical data, whereas others are at least in part confirmed. The critical issue, we believe, is that TV cannot simply be ignored. We need systematic evidence one way or another and the following chapters reflect some of the fruits of efforts to obtain such evidence.

2

The Developmental Study: Participants, Variables, and Procedures

The developmental phase of our research had two major objectives:

(1) We wished to observe systematically over a year's time the ongoing spontaneous play of 3- and 4-year-olds. From such observations we hope to ascertain interrelations between background characteristics such as age, sex, IQ, social class or imaginative predisposition, and the patterns of imagination, positive or negative emotionality, overt aggression, social interaction, cooperation, and extent or complexity of language usage expressed by the children in their free play. No previous study has tracked so many children over a year's time, recording with reasonable objectivity specific behavior, and examining consistencies within children of particular imaginative or other play styles or the statistical clustering of measures of play, affect, and language usage during what is in effect a third or a fourth of the child's present life span.

(2) Because television-viewing is a regular feature of the child's daily experience, we sought to relate frequency, program content, and other characteristics of home-viewing over the year to the various patterns of spontaneous play. We were also interested in some of the normative aspects of TV-viewing in 3- and 4-year-olds: How much do they watch, what programs, with whom, and with what consistency during a year? In choosing to study 3- and 4-year olds, we believed we were reaching a group who were relative initiates into the world of TV watching. By tracking them over the year we thought we might learn something of how they first related to the funny box in the home and how experience over a year's time might change their play behavior or viewing style.

SPECIFIC HYPOTHESES

Because there is as yet insufficient organized data on the spontaneous play patterns of preschoolers it was not possible to specify a series of precise hypotheses. As suggested in the previous chapter, however, we believed that although television might provide substantive material for the content of children's play, extensive watching might preempt the child's opportunities for practicing imaginative play or more complex or spontaneous language use. The *stuff* of fantasy, the character names or play situations, might be heavily influenced by TV, but the *structure, complexity,* or *richness* of imaginative play might be either unrelated to viewing frequency or perhaps even negatively associated with it.

With respect to language usage, one might argue that television provides a regular and varied talking stimulus for children, indeed presenting them with a richer diet of verbiage and explicit and implicit meanings than they might obtain from their own parents, older siblings, or playmates. Conversely, if watching the set is essentially a passive exercise then learning from TV should at best implement only the recognition store of the child and have little impact on functional, spontaneous expressive language use. Although our research design did not permit us to test the children's recognition memory, we could observe the extent of spontaneous language used during play and the syntactic complexity of such usage.

Previous research on play as reviewed in Chapter 1 suggests that imaginative play is closely linked to experiences or expressions of the positive emotions of joy and interest-surprise, persistence at a task, greater social interaction, and willingness to share or cooperate with peers, and, finally, to more complex language usage. We hypothesized that specific measures of the above behavior or language categories would intercorrelate and form a single statistical factor. We were less certain of the consistency of patterning of such a factor across different age groups (3s and 4s) or across the time periods of the study (February 1977, April 1977, October 1977, February 1978), however. It was conceivable that the interrelationships of these variables might reflect some developmental changes during the year.

Whereas some research with older children has suggested that more private aspects of imagination such as the reports of imaginary playmates or fantasy behavior in the home setting were correlated with spontaneous imaginative play at school, we had available little evidence for 3- and 4-year-olds of such consistency. We were, therefore, interested in examining possible associations between reports of fantasy obtained from children and parents based on home behavior with what we could observe directly during school play. Here, too, possible inverse relationships between frequency of home TV-viewing and measures of fantasy predisposition were anticipated.

Although our initial interest was in imaginative play and its possible links to television, it was inevitable that we would also have to examine the relationship of TV-viewing to the emergence of overt aggressive behavior in children. The increasing body of research tying spontaneous fighting or destructive acts in children to their amount of television exposure and especially to the observation of violent program content (as in so-called action-adventure or detective-police shows) has been well summarized by Comstock, Chaffee, Katzman, McCombs, and Roberts (1978), Bandura (1973), and Lefkowitz, Eron, Walder, and Huesmann (1977) [see also Chapter 6]. Whereas 3- and 4-year-olds, especially girls, do not show very much fighting or property destruction during play, we had an unusual opportunity to identify over the year's time those children who stood out from the group in their scores on aggression. We could then examine whether such aggressive boys and girls did indeed reflect the influence of TV by showing a greater frequency of watching action shows. In view of data derived from Tannenbaum and Zillman's (1975) study of the general arousal value of very lively programming and its effects on aggression, we expected that heavy viewers or those watching the hyperactive game shows that involve frenetic behavior would be especially prone to aggressive behavior in school.

There is considerable evidence that adults and children who have a well-developed imaginative life are less disposed toward frequent acts of impulsive antisocial behavior or aggression (Singer & Brown, 1977; Singer & Singer, 1976b). We proposed that children who showed a good deal of fantasy in home or school play might be less aggressive or that the fantasy capacity of the child might serve to moderate some of the links between TV-viewing and aggression.

In trying to clarify the possible causal tie between TV-viewing and overt aggression, a number of additional steps are necessary. One must rule out the possibility that a correlation between aggression and TV simply reflects the influence on both of a third variable such as IQ or social class. Thus, it might well be that less-intelligent individuals are more prone to violence and also to watching a lot of TV or, specifically, action shows. A series of steps to examine alternative explanations for any linkage between TV and aggression are presented in Chapter 6. A special feature of this study was the intensive examination of the family styles (based on home interviews with mothers) of children who represent the extreme scorers on frequency of TV-viewing and on the aggression variable (Chapter 7).

Other features of our approach need not be spelled out in detail here but will emerge as we present results. Sex differences in many of the variables have already been extensively documented in the behavior of preschoolers. We do, however, present data on play pattern, language use, and imagination differences between the sexes as well as information on differential TV-viewing and character identification patterns.

GENERAL RESEARCH STRATEGY

In formulating a research plan we decided to intervene as little as possible with the naturally occurring play of the children at school. Consequently our procedure called for unobtrusive observations of the children during free-play periods at four different periods over a year's time. Two independent observations of each child occurred a week or so apart within the four "probes," each of these about three months apart. Thus there were a total of eight separate observations. For each observation of the child we relied on two carefully trained assistants who watched and wrote down everything the child did or said for 10 minutes. These observers worked independently, kept separate running records, and were required not to confer with each other or to share information. The observers then rated their protocols independently on 14 behavioral variables such as imaginativeness of play or cooperation with peers. Ideally, we should have videotaped behavior and speech or counted specific behavior from written protocols but financial and personnel limitations precluded such an effort because we had more than 1000 observations of our children. During each of the four "probes" parents also kept daily logs for two consecutive weeks of their children's TV-viewing patterns.

The choice of behavioral variables scored by 1-5 ratings provided a simple and reliable method. We could demonstrate that after a few weeks of training, observers could reach statistically satisfactory levels of agreement in their scoring of sample protocols. Checking the reliabilities of observer pairs in the field during the actual probe periods yielded agreements on all variables that were significant at $p < .001$ for values of Cicchetti's (1976) variation of the *kappa* statistic, a stringent test of rater correspondence (see appendix in Singer and Singer [1978] for detailed report by R. Kruger on reliability procedures).

The 14 variables employed had been tried out in earlier studies with nursery school and older children (Singer & Singer, 1976a; Tower, Singer, Singer, & Biggs, 1979; Nahme-Huang, Singer, Singer, & Wheaton, 1977). They break down into several clusters conceptually. "Imaginativeness of play," "persistence" or "concentration," "cooperation with peers," and "cooperation with adults" may represent desirable or socially constructive behavior. "Aggression" as defined in our research involves attacks on others or harm to property. "Interaction with peers" or with adults simply reflects interpersonal contacts and might not necessarily represent constructive or "prosocial" behavior, as does "cooperation," although in actual observations the two turn out to be closely related. Because there is evidence that particular TV shows can influence preschoolers toward more cooperative behavior or more positive affect it seemed desirable to score spontaneous evidence of constructive behavior (Singer, 1978).

A group of variables—"positive affect" and the mood labels of "fear," "anger," "fatigue," "sadness," "liveliness," "elation" reflect the emotional component of the child's ongoing behavior as reflected in facial expressions, body gestures, and movement patterns. There is increasing research evidence of an innate differential emotional system (Izard, 1977; Lewis & Rosenblum, 1978), and our interest was in examining the natural clustering of these affective states along with behavior patterns, language variables, predispositional and background factors, for example, IQ, socioeconomic status, imaginary companions in home play, and with TV-viewing patterns. The earlier development and rationale for use of the behavior and mood variables has been outlined by Singer (1973) and various collaborators and students.

The language variables included in the study were drawn from counts of the specific words employed by the subjects. General productivity measures such as "number of words" used in the 10-minute sample, "number of separate utterances" (sentences, phrases or single words, or sounds separated by periods of silence or activity) made by a child during this period, the "average length of an utterance" (MLU) were first scored. Then specific percentages of the words uttered which represented parts of speech employed were included, for example, percentage of "nouns," "verbs," "adjectives," as well as indicators of more mature language, such as "predicate adjectives," "future verbs," "predicate nominatives." A previous study (Singer, Caldeira, & Singer, 1977) had suggested that ongoing imaginative play was linked to greater verbal productivity and earlier studies had also linked speech development to fantasy play (Singer & Singer, 1976b). The use of the language scoring could provide further evidence on the links between language and imagination and could also provide clues as to whether moderate or heavy TV-watching fostered or impeded language productivity or complexity.

In view of evidence suggesting the occurrence of social class or ethnic group differences in amounts of TV-viewing and the paucity of evidence on class links to play (Griffing, 1974), it was important to include estimates of these variables in our data. IQ estimates (measured by picture vocabulary) seemed essential to rule out the possibility that any major behavior differences that might emerge would simply be reflecting basic intellectual-capacity variations. Our measures of the imaginative predisposition of the child sought to ascertain whether self-reports of imagery and fantasy play by children (imagination interview), parents' reports of children's play with imaginary playmates, and the production of human movement associations to inkblots (Barron M responses) would link together the home play and more general "inner imagination" of the child with the school manifestations of fantasy and other play activities. Extensive earlier research had linked Rorschach Inkblot human movement associations to imagination, control of aggression, and socially constructive behavior patterns (Singer & Brown, 1977). Earlier work in this field had also suggested that children's reports of imaginary companions or of fantasy play at home did predict spontaneous imaginative play in school (Singer, 1973). It also seemed likely that parents' reports on children's imaginary companions might predict spontaneous play or positive affect (Manosevitz, Prentice, & Wilson, 1973).

In summary we proposed to examine four classes of variables: (1) the general background of the child in terms of social class, ethnicity, IQ, and imaginative predisposition; (2) the various categories of spontaneous play behavior; (3) the language produced during play; and, finally, (4) the patterns and content of home television-viewing. As we see later, except for the background factors, we can examine the last three classes of variables developmentally and also use them as dependent or independent variables for particular analyses.

PROCEDURE

Participants

Directors of nursery schools in the New Haven area were individually contacted and visited by principal investigators and staff to discuss in some detail the actual requirements of the study and the characteristics of the nursery school or day care center. This step was taken to insure that the research would involve a minimal disruption of ongoing activities and could be carried out in a reasonably unobtrusive fashion. In some cases meetings were held with boards of directors or parent groups involved in administering the schools. Following tentative agreements from the leadership of the nursery schools, meetings were then held with parent groups in each of the nursery schools describing the project in sufficiently general terms to avoid any clues as to experimental design or specific objectives. Implications of the voluntary nature of parent participation were made clear and parent questions were answered as fully as possible without revealing specific study hypotheses. As planned, parents were offered reimbursement of $75.00 toward the school tuition for participation in the program, maintenance of television logs, and attendance at training sessions over a year's time.

A detailed informed-consent protocol was provided to each family for signature by the parents. This form followed guidelines developed by the Yale Faculty of Arts and Sciences Human Experimentation Committee. In addition to the response to the consent forms, parents were asked to provide information on the child, some information on family occupational and educational levels, birth order, sex of children and family size.

Parent response to the project was on the whole encouraging. In some cases children did not attend school regularly or there were family plans to move very shortly after onset of the project. These families could not therefore be included in the project. Within the eight nursery schools somewhat more than 50% of qualified families did participate; on the basis of random assignments an additional group were asked to serve as controls who kept logs but did not attend parent-training sessions. The total sample after some early dropouts included 141 children.

The participating nursery schools and day care centers represented a range of such institutions available in the New Haven area within reasonable access to Yale University because it was desired to minimize travel time for the observers who had to make frequent trips to the nursery schools. Although these schools and day care centers are heterogeneous, some privately owned, some cooperatives, some institutionally related, each was included in the project because in the judgment of the principal investigators, the structure of the nursery schools permitted reasonably unobtrusive observation of the children; the pattern of school activities permitted a sufficient degree of spontaneous free-play behavior; the staff was understanding and cooperative, and so on. Because some of the children turned 5 as the study progressed, and entered kindergarten, the original eight nursery schools and day care centers ultimately expanded to a total of 49 schools including private and public kindergartens.

It was hoped initially that there would be a somewhat greater mixture of social classes and races in the participating families. Participation by black families was somewhat lower than had been hoped for. An examination of IQ and background variable scores of the 25 children from ethnic minorities (black, Hispanic, or Asiatic) in the present sample on the various independent and dependent variables of the study failed to reveal any major systematic differences from the remaining present sample and in the subsequent report of statistical analyses below they are included within the total group figures. Correlational analyses do indicate that ethnicity is related to some of the play and TV-viewing patterns.

Whereas there were some small but nonsignificant differences in IQ estimates (Peabody Picture Vocabulary Test) between children in some of the nursery schools involved in the project, random assignment of children to the parent intervention or control groups ruled out any systematic impact of these differences on the intervention phase of the research. Indeed there was no overweighting of particular nursery schools in any of the intervention groups. Although the nursery groups varied somewhat in quality of care as perceived by investigators and observers, these factors were again not relevant to the systematic parameters of the present study. Table 2.1 presents the basic information on age, sex, and socioeconomic status level (based on estimates of Hollingshead and Redlich's (1958) five-level gradation of socioeconomic classes). By far the predominant group of subjects fell into Class III. Estimates of SES levels were based on parental education and

TABLE 2.1
Sample Characteristics

	$\bar{X}$	SD
Age (months)	48.00	7.40
SES Index (1–5)	2.61	0.56
Peabody PVT (IQ)	116.70	14.30
Barron Inkblots (M)		
(maximum score = 26)	2.04	2.25
Imagination Interview		
(maximum score = 4)	1.52	1.06

Males = 79; Females = 62

occupation with additional information from residence neighborhood when this could be accurately estimated.

PRETESTING

The following instruments were used in carrying out pretesting with children in the study prior to the unobtrusive observation phase of the first probe:

1. Peabody Picture Vocabulary Test (PPVT)—IQ estimate.
2. Barron Movement Threshold Inkblot Series—estimate of Imaginative Predisposition. Our major score here was the number of human movements (people doing things) reported as associations by the children to the 26 inkblots. Other inkblot scores were also examined but these M responses proved to be the most significant. Previous research with older children had suggested that for somewhat older children perception of human movements is linked to other indications of imagination (Singer, 1973).
3. Interview on Imaginative Play (IIP)—direct questioning of child concerning imaginative play tendencies, imaginary companions, etc. There were four questions and a maximum score of 4 would suggest a highly imaginative child (Singer, 1973).
4. Television Viewing Patterns—direct questioning of child on favorite television shows and characters on TV as well as pattern of viewing. These data served primarily as a check on parents log-keeping.

Tables 2.1 and 2.2 present the basic data on the sample with respect to the pretesting of the children.

As can be seen from Table 2.2, there are no significant differences between the three intervention groups and controls with respect to IQ, class, or age or

TABLE 2.2
Initial Means For Intervention Groups And Controls[a]

Training	Imagination Training	Cognitive Training	TV Training	Control
	Mean	Mean	Mean	Mean
Age (in months)	47.8	47.84	46.88	49.33
Social class (I-V)	2.74	2.50	2.53	2.58
IQ	117.82	117.67	116.34	115.16
Barron Inkblots				
Movement Responses	1.88	2.03	1.77	2.41
Imagination Interview	1.29	1.41	1.47	1.87

[a]See Chapter 8 for discussion of training procedures.

with respect to the imaginative predisposition measures except for the somewhat greater imaginative predisposition of control group children.

Inspection of Table 2.1 indicates that the sample in this study is of somewhat above-average intelligence based on the IQ estimates from the PPVT. It is likely, however, that this is an overestimate of the children's general intelligence because it is based on a vocabulary measure and does not of course include the kind of intensive intelligence estimate including performance measures possible from an individual scale such as the Wechsler Preschool and Primary Scale of Intelligence (WPPSI). The imaginative predisposition scores obtained by our subjects are comparable to those found in our previous studies with similar age groups.

In addition to the above measures a parent questionnaire was developed concerning the child's report of imaginary playmates. We had already in the imagination interview queried children about their home play and fantasy life. This parent questionnaire was an additional attempt to collect data concerning the child's fantasy life as revealed in the normal course of home play. The findings for imaginary playmates are discussed in Chapter 5.

OBSERVATIONAL VARIABLES

The first set of baseline observations of the spontaneous play of the children occurred in February 1977. Children were observed on two separate days, on each occasion by two observers who independently recorded everything the child did for a 10-minute period (including verbatim speech). These observers subsequently independently rated the child on the series of 14 variables. Rater reliability scores were based on these independent estimates.

The following brief descriptions of each of the behavioral variables scored by our raters from the written protocols and supplemented if necessary by their own direct observation of the children.

1. Imaginativeness of Play. Here a child was scored high if he or she showed a good deal of "make-believe," introduction of settings, characters, or sound effects not immediately present in the physical environment. Transformation of a box into a car or pencil into an airplane would count as part of such a rating.

2. Positive Affect. Here the rating was based on evidence that the child showed a high level of positive emotionality. This included indications of smiling, laughing, intense interest or curiosity that are considered positive emotions.

3. Persistence. The degree to which a child showed the tendency to stick with a given activity or to persevere in a specific line of play was scored here.

4. Overt Aggression. Here the rating was based on evidence from the observations and written protocols that a child showed actual aggressive behavior, for example, striking or pushing another chld, seizing another's toy, knocking over blocks, or tearing up a poster.

5. Interaction with Peers. This variable is rated from the actual extent to which a child communicates with, touches, or makes some other form of direct contact with other children. Such contact can be hostile, positive, or neutral in intent or consequences.

6. Interaction with Adults. Essentially this rating simply refers to direct contacts with teachers, helpers, or (a rare occurrence) with the observers.

7. Cooperation with Peers. Here the rating is based on actual acts of cooperation and mutually shared activities, for example, a child who holds up a board while another piles blocks under it, a child who cooperates on a seesaw with another child, or who helps another to clean up a set of toys or blocks. This rating was an especially important one to identify pro-social or constructive interactions.

8. Cooperation with Adults. The rating here focuses specifically on acts of cooperation or sharing with adults. In practice these turn out to be rare during free play and often reflect a more dependent child.

The next group of variables reflect evidence of specific moods or emotions shown by the child. Facial expressions were employed to make judgments as well as gestures, gross body movements, and posture patterns. Because a child's moods are labile a child could obtain a high score for angry and for elated in the same 10-minute observation.

9. Anger. Here the rating was based on facial signs of annoyance, verbal expressions of hostility, or vague threatening gestures, footstamping.

10. Fear. This rating reflects the fact that a child was intimidated, excessively anxious in looking around at potential threats, clinging to a teacher for support or expressing in language as well as nonverbally evidence of terror.

11. Sadness. Key features in rating this variable were the indications of weeping, sniffling, verbal expressions of sadness, red-eyed appearance, bowed shoulders.

12. Liveliness (Motor Activity). This variable reflected a high level of physical activity, rapid movement, fast rate of speech. No emphasis was placed on a focus of the activity.

13. Fatigued-Sluggish. Here the rating reflected signs of sleepiness, slowed down motor activity, but without concomitant verbal or other signs of sadness or fearfulness. Some children actually curled up or began thumb-sucking and eyes drooped.

14. Elation-Joy. Here the rating specifically reflects frequent smiling, laughing, expressions of glee or enthusiasm. This score differs from positive affect, mentioned earlier, only because it does not include the affect of interest and curiosity or signs of intense exploration which are incorporated with smiling in the positive affect score.

A second set of variables derived from the protocols of 10-minute observations of the children a few days apart within the same probe period involved the actual speech of the children during these periods. A manual for scoring specific language represented in the protocols was prepared with detailed definitions of language forms, for example, number of words, number of utterances within a protocol, mean length of utterances, nouns, verbs, predicate nominatives, use of onomatopoetic terms ("bang! bang!"), direct references to television characters or programs, and so on. Language was scored by research assistants and supervised by a specialist in children's language development, but this was done only after independent scorings by these raters. The trained language specialist found no significant degree of disagreement on the enumeration of language variables in a series of protocols.

The behavioral variables and the language scores by no means exhaust all possible situations to be rated from direct observations with children during unstructured time in day care center or nursery. Nevertheless, they represent a fairly extensive subgroup of possibilities that might be influenced over the year or more of observation by the extent of television viewing or program content emphasized and also which might be influenced by the particular pattern of parent interventions. A more intensive examination of the specific *themes* and content of behavior and play is presented in Chapter 4.

TRAINING OF OBSERVERS

In order to collect behavioral samples of subjects we trained assistants in observational techniques. The observers were staff members and individuals selected from among students who answered ads in a local newspaper. Observers were generally psychology majors, both graduate and undergraduate, or members of the New Haven or Bridgeport communities who had some background in developmental psychology or who had been former elementary or nursery school teachers. Training took place over a period of three weeks before the pretesting and observations began. Training sessions were held four times during the study, preceding each observational period.

Observers were each provided with 16 typed protocols which were behavior samples collected in an earlier study. A set of instructions concerning ratings was included with each set of protocols. Observers were blind to the hypotheses of the study, and were given only such information about procedures that could in no way influence direction of results. The trainers were the two codirectors of the project and a research assistant who had trained observers on a previous study and who was familiar with our techniques.

The group met once a week for two hours over the three week period. At these sessions, each observer called out the rating he or she had given a child on each of the 14 variables described earlier. Each variable was discussed in detail and we attempted to give further examples than those offered in the instruction booklet. Observers had ample opportunity to discuss reasons for their ratings, and we pointed out our reasons for our rating scores. We attempted to reach a high rate of agreement on the five-point scale for each variable at each session.

The training sessions before the last two observational periods included films in order that observers might record the behavior of a particular child at play in the film. This was an attempt to simulate the actual nursery school situation. Observers rated the designated child and then we compared ratings and held discussions in order to obtain optimal agreement.

Observers were given further instructions concerning procedure. For example, assignments were made so that two observers would be a team. They were handed lists of subjects and given instructions concerning procedure to be followed in the schools such as introducing themselves to director and teacher. A letter had been sent to each school beforehand informing the director about the teams, dates, and times for observations. Observers were expected to familiarize themselves with the school; mixing with the children in an informal way before they were to begin observations. Detailed instructions concerning the actual recording of the behavioral samples were also provided. On returning from the field the observers separately rated protocols. A supervisor checked protocols for completeness and to make sure all ratings had been carried out.

OBSERVATIONAL PROCEDURES

Observers were told to record in an appropriate place on the record sheet the child's appearance, mannerisms, physical build, time they began and ended each recording, date, sex, and code number of each child. Observations were carried out only in free-play periods both indoors and out. Observers used a clipboard and stopwatch and tried to be unobtrusive as they recorded the child's actions and language. Language was recorded verbatim. Observers were instructed not to interpret behavior but to record accurately what took place. After the behavior was written down, each observer would then rate the child on the 14 variables on a five-point scale. Observers rated the children independently of each other. As noted earlier, reliability evaluations were uniformly high and suggested good agreement between raters (see Singer & Singer, 1978).

Members of the staff and selected observers were also trained in testing procedures for the administration of the Peabody Picture Vocabulary Test. The Barron Inkblot Test, the predisposition to imagination questionnaire, and the television interview. The research assistant in charge of the observers and one of the directors of the project checked all scoring on these instruments. Testing took place before the observations began, and although there were some overlap most children were tested before the observations. Observations took approximately three weeks to complete within each probe period.

CHILDREN'S TELEVISION-VIEWING LOGS

The following is a brief summary of the procedure employed in developing the logs, arranging for their distribution to parents, insuring that parents understood the instructions for maintaining the logs, and increasing the veridicality of parents' ratings. From time to time during each of the four two-week logging periods, spot check phone calls were made by staff and questions were asked of parents to insure that they continued to understand the procedures and to describe how they were going about the log-keeping.

Estimates of children's favorite programs and other viewing patterns were obtained directly from the children by means of an interview and also were obtained from parents in the form of a brief questionnaire that they filled out at the close of training sessions during the period of the first TV probe. These reports could then be compared with statistical analyses from the logs themselves.

Some practical issues that arose in log-keeping of this kind should be noted. The logs were prepared as indicated by reviewing the local *TV Guide* and related magazines or newspaper listings for the New Haven area. The first actual TV logs from parents could not be obtained until February 1977, although the preparation of the log forms had gone on some months earlier.

The actual listings that appeared on the logs reflected programming that had been included in the new fall season. When the CBS network drastically changed its programming in the beginning of 1977 in response to the great increase in ratings for ABC network shows, it was not possible to revise our logs in time to reflect these changes. Therefore, it was explained to parents that they would have to do much more actual writing in of program titles rather than simply checking off programs on the daily forms.

1. Instructions. The parents received detailed recording instructions enclosed with the TV log packets. They were asked to circle the program watched on the logs. The parents were instructed to note how intensely the child watched a program on a scale of 1 to 5. A rate of "1" means that the child scarcely watched the program or paid any attention to it, whereas "5" meant that the child watched with great interest and absorption (see appended directions). In addition parents were asked to note whether the child watched the program alone, with parents (P), siblings (S), other adults (O), or other children (C) and were instructed to include any combination of people, that is, other adults and other children. Included were directions to indicate if the program watched was at home (H) or away from home (A).

2. Log Returns. In the TV packet two self-addressed stamped envelopes were enclosed for the parents to mail the completed logs back to the television center. Parents who failed to return the logs on time received a written reminder followed by a phone call. Except for one or two instances where there was illness involved or a move from the community, all logs were received within two weeks after the termination of the logging period.

3. Transcribing. The TV logs were transcribed onto a weekly summary sheet. Every show the child watched was noted along with the intensity and with whom it was watched (see summary sheet in the appendix).

4. Preparation for Statistical Analysis. (a). Time watched: Each day's viewing was totaled and noted at the bottom of the sheet. A probe period total was achieved by summing all 14 days. The two week sample was treated as one unit. All statistics are based on *weekly* averages of a two-week sample in each of four probe periods, February 1977, April, 1977, October 1977, and February 1978. Therefore when analyzed, if a child watched five hours on the first Monday of the logging period and three hours on the following Monday, a total of eight hours was entered for that day. Means and standard deviations were found for the two-week sample, males versus females, 3s versus 4-year-olds. Further analysis includes comparisons of a weekday versus weekend viewing. In referring to our logs, we characterize viewing by average number of hours of viewing by a subgroup, for example, 4-year-old boys for a week in February 1977, etc.

(b) Intensity: Here we scored absorption in a program. Because attention was limited and programs were generally a half-hour we had parents score intensity by a *given* program but took into account its actual running time. For example, if a child watched an hour and one-half program with an intensity of "4" according to parent's rating the intensity would be multiplied by three. The mean intensity for the sample was achieved by summing all the prorated intensities and dividing by the total number of half hours. As with the viewing time the mean intensity is based on a two-week period. Thus a child could conceivably watch very little TV but by concentrating hard on what shows it watched obtain a high score on this variable for a given probe period. Indeed, to anticipate, we found that concentration on TV-programming measured this way, tended to correlate with the average persistence the child showed during school free play.

(c) "Who watched with": Data on whether the child watched alone or with specific others was based on a half-hour time period. Combinations of with whom children watched the shows were entered for analysis. How many hours a child watched TV alone, or with parents, and any combination of people were summed for the two-week period and entered for analysis.

(d) Programs viewed: The programs available for viewing by this group and actually reported on the logs by parents were classified into nine categories and coded:

1. Cartoons, e.g., "Bugs Bunny," "Flintstones."
2. Children's shows (commercial TV): "Captain Kangaroo," "Shazam."
3. Educational TV or Public Television child-oriented shows: "Sesame Street," "Zoom," "Mister Rogers."
4. Family comedy: "Happy Days," "I Love Lucy."
5. Variety/Game shows, e.g., "The Gong Show," "Donny and Marie."
6. Adult-Family shows, e.g., "The Waltons," "Little House on the Prairie."
7. Action/Adventure or detective, potentially violent, or suspenseful: "Six Million Dollar Man," "Starksy and Hutch," "Kojak," "Emergency."
8. Sports: boxing, hockey, auto racing, football.
9. Newscasts and documentaries.

The categories were divided into the top shows in each category by a quick view of the summary sheets. For example, in Category 1 the shows listed were: "Bugs Bunny," "Scooby Doo—Dynomutt," etc. If a child watched a show not listed in our program breakdown it was included under the general category for that type of program, for example, a special.

The individual programs were combined in categories to determine how many hours children watched a program under the various categories. The programs were also summed individually to determine how many hours a specific show such as "Sesame Street" was watched. The number of hours watched and number of children who watched that amount of time were also noted. For example, "Sesame Street" could be watched for as much as 15 hours over a two-week period. It was noted how many children indeed watched it 15 hours, 14, and so on.

Rank order tables by sex and age were developed for programs by both the total amount of time a program was watched and for the number of children who viewed that program at least once during the two-week period.

Reports of frequency of viewing by children between 2 and 6 can be estimated from the Nielsen ratings for given periods. In addition the popularity of particular programs as estimated by the Nielsen system can be compared with the data available in our study, keeping in mind that Public Television ratings (which cover programs like "Sesame Street" and "Mister Rogers' Neighborhood") were not included. Our subjects are from Class III SES levels and are therefore not fully representative statistically of the New Haven metropolitan area. Still the similarity to Nielsen scores is impressive. In general the average viewing of our subjects was slightly below that of the general population of chldren of this age in the New Haven area and also involved somewhat less viewing at late hours, as best as we can estimate by a comparison of those data.

Although our statistical analyses of program viewing presented in the subsequent chapter are based on our categorization of program content (in keeping with other researchers and industry practice), we have carried out factor analyses of the "natural" linking of individual programs. In general these results are in keeping with the a priori categorization, particularly in suggesting that although general frequency of TV-viewing is linked to the most popular of children's shows, cartoons, the other specific programs cluster together more or less as classified. Thus, shows like "Six Million Dollar Man," "Wonder Woman," and "Starsky and Hutch" do correlate more closely with each other than they do with other types of programming, for example, "Brady Bunch," "Waltons," "I Love Lucy," "Little House on the Prairie." For this reason we feel that classification of programs as cartoons, educational TV, action-adventure, and so on provides us with our most reliable categories for use in relation to the behavioral variables of the study.

In effect our major TV variables included general frequency of viewing (based on average weekly hours in a given probe period), average hours of weekly viewing of each of the categories of programming, and average viewing intensity. We also factor analyzed our data to consider whether using the average hours per category without including total viewing time or whether hours per category as a proportion of viewing time made any difference in our results. In both cases our patterns of intercorrelations and factors were sufficiently similar so that we are presenting herein data for total average weekly viewing hours and average weekly hours per content category as our TV variables.

3

A Year to Grow: Patterns of TV-Viewing, Behavior, and Language

INTRODUCTION

A year in a preschooler's life represents a substantial portion of the child's developmental pattern. Within this period rapid changes occur physically as well as mentally. Piaget, for example, devoted considerable time to delineating six stages of mental development, within the sensory-motor period—the first two years of a child's life (Singer & Revenson, 1978).

Subsequently, within each of the next three periods, preoperational, concrete operations, and formal operations, he continued to examine language, play, morality, and concept formation through this use of a detailed stage approach. He was constantly aware of the subtle change that occurred within a child's mind that enabled the child to move from global, egocentric thought to a more rational, logical human being. Thus if we examine one year in a preschooler's life and look at the effect of television on the child's life, any changes as a result of TV-viewing might have considerable impact compared to the effects of TV-viewing on an older child or adult within a comparable period.

Although Piaget carefully examined the origins of a child's intelligence, he used small samples (initially, his own three children). More recently, psychologists such as Joseph Church (1966), Howard Gardner (1979), Michael Lewis and Leonard Rosenblum (1978) have continued in this way, reporting their results based on small numbers of children. Language experts such as Lois Bloom (1974) and Catherine Garvey (1974) have also worked with small samples of subjects, and although their work is thorough and excellent, it is difficult to generalize from their findings to a large number of children. Our study is a promising effort to examine a large sample (141 children) over a year's time in terms of developmental changes.

In presenting the results, we focus on a series of specific questions that can arise about early childhood play, its relationship to language and television-viewing patterns. We take into account, of course, the fact that some of the children were 3 at the beginning of the study and others 4, so that we have data to look at in the year's growth of the 3-year-olds compared with the 4-year-olds. Similarly, we can compare the differences in play patterns across sexes as well. We are also be able to look at a number of questions that have been important in general in personality theory in psychology as well as issues relating to the nature of the television medium and its impact on 3- and 4-year-olds.

WHEN DO TV-VIEWING PATTERNS EMERGE IN CHILDREN?

An important initial assumption of this study needs to be repeated. It was our feeling in choosing children who were approximately 3- and 4-years-old at the outset of the study that these ages represented the beginnings of television-viewing. A major outcome of our study so far makes it clear that this assumption is simply incorrect in the light of current trends in television watching. Our 3s as well as well as our 4-year-olds proved to be very *experienced* viewers according to parental reports and quite obviously in terms of the total amount of viewing carried on. Although, of course, the predominant types of programming they watched were child-oriented shows, the fact remains that the range of programming viewed by these children, some of them barely beyond the toddler stage, included every type of programming available to the television audience before midnight.

Whereas it is true that "Mr. Rogers' Neighborhood" and "Sesame Street" were more extensively viewed by the younger children in our sample than most other shows, and that cartoons also predominated, the fact remains that *a very sizable proportion of the viewing time of our sample* over the year of observation was devoted to essentially *adult* programming. We deal with this issue further in the following, but it requires mention at the outset because it relates to critical issues currently before the public concerning hours of viewing accessible to children and whether regulation of programming or commercials at certain periods will be effective in reducing drastically children's exposure to a predominantly adult type of program or commercial format.

This issue is heightened further by the fact that viewing patterns were after all recorded by parents who might have been expected to want to put their "best foot forward" to some extent. Actually, our checks on this suggest that they did not do this to any great degree. Even if parents "covered up" a bit, the amount of adult-programming viewing they have reported for their children must be taken especially seriously. If we add to this recognition, the fact that our sample is clearly middle class in socioeconomic status, and that viewing patterns of lower socioeconomic groups have been shown to be more extensive and more adult-oriented (for older children at least), the odds are that a broader and more representative national sample of preschool children would reveal even greater frequency of viewing and particularly more viewing during later hours of clearly adult-oriented programming.

HOW CONSISTENT ARE CHILDREN IN THEIR SPONTANEOUS PLAY BEHAVIOR?

An extremely important issue in our research with preschoolers involves the extent to which they show sufficient consistency in their day-to-day behavior. In the late 1960s and during much of the 1970s, a major controversy has raged in the field of personality psychology concerning the degree to which certain personality traits show consistency across varying situations or across time periods. The present study provides an opportunity to contribute evidence concerning consistencies in spontaneously occurring behavior across time for 3- and 4-year-old children. Such data are otherwise relatively unavailable in the literature because most studies of behavioral consistency have been carried out over relatively short time periods, or, in the case of longitudinal studies, have begun with older children and have involved much longer time gaps.

The reader should keep in mind the fact that with such young children the likelihood of behavioral consistency is not very great. The children are already in the midst of a great period of growth and evolution. They are also, because of their immaturity, especially susceptible to all kinds of extraneous influences. Because the observations take place in a nursery school setting, one cannot control whether the same children will be in the group from one day to the next, whether the child had ample sleep the night before or is feeling well on this particular day, whether a sudden disruptive child may appear in a group on this particular day, whether there may be influences from the teacher that might suddenly change the pattern of play from what it was like on the previous day or a few months before.

Given all of these possible influences, we cannot seriously expect extremely high consistency across a couple of days or systematically across a year's time in the children. Nevertheless, because of the fact that we have in effect eight data points, two apiece in each of the four probes, each independent of the other in the sense that they are taken on different days (and, as a matter of fact, often by different observers) it is worth examining whether we can demonstrate any degree of consistency better than chance in the behavior of these children along the dimensions employed in the research.

Table 3.1 presents results for the behavioral variables across the four observation periods from February 1977 through February 1978. The table indicates the number of correlations between each combination of observations, for example, observation 1 (February 1977), observation 2 (February 1977), observation 3 (April 1977), observation 4 (April 1977), etc. By correlating each of these eight observations in every combination with each other, we obtain a matrix that indicates to what extent the scores on the variables for the child at different times relate back to each other in a comparable way relative to the total group. The percentage of correlations in this matrix that are statistically reliable at $p \leq .05$ are listed in one column of the table.

The second column reports on the correlations obtained across the two major divisions of the study, the combined February and April 1977 probes, which were essentially prior to the possible effects of intervention, and the last two probes, October 1977 and February 1978, which might reflect intervention effects. For these correlations the two observations a few days apart during a given probe were averaged. The data from this table make it clear that there are, indeed, reasonably impressive patterns of consistency in the

TABLE 3.1
Self-Correlations Of Variables Across Each Pair Of Eight Observation Periods[a]

Behavioral Variable	Percent Correlations Significant at $p \leq .05$	Correlation Between Means of First Two and Last Two Observation Periods
Imagination	100%	.385***
Affect	50	.296***
Persistence	0	.046
Aggression	50	.297***
Interaction/Peers	100	.520**
Interaction/Adults	50	.242**
Cooperation/Peers	33	.160
Cooperation/Adults	17	.100
Fear-Tense	50	.254***
Anger-Annoyed	67	.349***
Sad-Downhearted	33	.110
Fatigue-Sluggish	33	.236**
Lively-Excited	67	.270**
Elated-Pleased	83	.285**

[a]Eight observations during four "probes" or observation periods, February 1977, April 1977, October 1977, February 1978.
*$p < .05$; **$p < .01$; ***$p < .001$

spontaneous behavior of the children. For imaginativeness of play, for example (a rating based on the degree to which the child introduces elements of pretend and make-believe and transcends the immediacy of time and place during free play periods) 100% of the correlations between the various time periods are significantly better than chance. The correlation between the first and second half of the year's ratings is .385, which is significant at $p < .001$. This is certainly an impressive result for such young children.

The findings for positive affect or emotionality, smiling and laughing, indicate that 50% of the intercorrelations across time periods are significant and there is a correlation between the first two and last two probes of .296 also significant at $p < .001$. Especially high is the correlation for simply the amount of time the child is involved in direct interaction with other children. Here, again, 100% of all of the combinations of time periods yield significant correlations and the overall correlation between the two half-years is .520, $p < .001$. Surprisingly, even for the amount of aggression rated for the child, 50% of intercorrelations are significant and the correlation between the first two and last two observation periods is .297, $p < .001$. This result is impressive because often aggression may be manifested in retaliation to accidental or unintentional provocation by another child. Nevertheless, these data suggest that to some degree we must have some children who are relatively consistently aggressive and that this pattern of behavior is already established by the ages of three and four.

Of the behavioral variables only persistence in a play sequence shows no statistically reliable consistency. This is somewhat surprising in view of other results obtained later in the study which indicate that children who are likely to watch TV with considerable absorption at home are also likely to show persistence during spontaneous play in school. Nevertheless, we obtain no satisfactory consistency across the time periods. The variables of cooperation with adults and with peers do not show great consistency, but here because the very definition requires the occurrence of an opportunity for sharing by the child it is likely that the variable is inherently more situationally determined at any given probe period. Of the mood variables, only the likelihood that the child is sad, downhearted, or crying is at chance level of consistency. Again, one might expect that such behavior would be particularly subject to a specific kind of provocation that might not occur again during any of the other observation periods.

If we consider next the language usage by the children, we find consistency only for two very general aspects of speech behavior, the total number of words used during a particular play period or the total number of separate utterances emitted during an observation period. These results suggest that although the child is presumably showing considerable growth over the year's time in the vocabulary and components of language, the overall tendency of the child to speak is already reasonably consistent by ages 3 or 4. That is to say, in a spontaneous play situation some children are consistently more likely to be talking out loud and communicating either about the game to themselves or talking directly to others in the course of the 10-minute observation period over the year's time. For number of words 83% of all of the possible correlations between observation periods were significant and a correlation between the means of the first two and the last two observation periods was .523, $p < .001$. For number of utterances, the results were also 83% and .466, $p < .001$.

Of all the other language variables only one showed significant consistency. This was total *television references*. Fifty percent of the observation period scores for this variable were significant and the correlation between the means of the first two and last two observation periods was .400, $p < .001$. This result suggests that we already may be seeing children who are especially influenced in a regular way by television so that they consistently use words relating to television characters or incidents in the course of their spontaneous play. Our data from a careful thematic analysis of the specific features of play in the protocols of extreme high and low television viewers suggest that frequent reference to TV characters in the course of play is indeed linked to high TV-viewing and also to the involvement in more "action-adventure" play (see Chapter 4).

We can next look at the consistency of television-viewing frequency and patterning in the children in the study. Keep in mind that this information is based on the actual reports recorded on log sheets by the parents. It might be argued that we are simply obtaining evidence that the parents themselves put down more or less the same thing for their child from probe period to probe period (and theoretically could have done this even without paying the slightest attention to what the child was watching—that is, just to maintain their own consistency). This supposition seems unlikely on several counts. First of all, we did double check as indicated earlier, and in addition there do turn out to be significant associations between children's television viewing patterns and their overt behavior, as we shall see later. We have already mentioned the fact that consistency in spontaneous play does seem to be associated with the intensity of TV-viewing—that is, the less distractible the child is in watching a TV show, the less distractible he may also prove to be in the course of his play behavior in the nursery school. Because of specials and programming changes, parents did have to write in the names of specific shows as well, and these changed from period to period.

The correlations between all of the combinations of total weekly TV-viewing hours for the four probe periods are significant 100% of the time with a correlation between the first two probes and the last two of .63, $p < .001$. The parent's report of viewing intensity of the child is significant 100% of the time for the combinations of the four probe periods and the correlation is .56, $p < .001$, for the first two versus the last two probes. Parental reports on other viewing patterns are also highly reliable in comparable fashion.

If we next look at the kind of TV shows the child is watching, we find again similar consistencies. Thus, the results indicate that 100% of the combinations of probes yield significant correlations for the viewing of cartoons with a correlation between the means of the first and last two probe periods of .769, $p < .001$. For the viewing of situation comedies, one gets a comparable result with 100% of correlations significant and with an r of .81, $p < .001$. For the tendency to watch adult-family shows, the data are equally strong with 100% of possible correlations significant and with an r of .72, $p < .001$. For the viewing of the action-detective (violent shows again there is 100% significant correlation and an r of .35, $p < .001$ between the first and last observation periods. Indeed, the weakest evidence of consistency is on the viewing of commercial children's shows such as "Captain Kangaroo" or other programming directed specifically at children and appearing on commercial networks. Consistency of watching the Public TV educational shows is relatively high with an r of .51, $p < .001$, between the first and last two observation periods.

In general, therefore, we seem to be finding, again, a rather considerable consistency in the frequency and in the pattern of children's viewing of television. Because we are dealing with 3- and 4-year-old children over a year's time, we cannot avoid the implication that rather well-established habits are already discernible in these children.

Data from a study by Hollenbeck and Slaby (1979), which appeared after we had completed this research, further clarifies this issue. They observed 72 infants who were 6 months of age and found that these children were already being exposed to TV on the average of one hour a day at home. Their mothers reported that the sets themselves were on about 6.5 hours daily. Our data therefore reflect a comparable habituation.

TELEVISION-VIEWING, PLAY BEHAVIOR, AND LANGUAGE PATTERNS

About one-third of a sample of 158 children (Lyle & Hoffman, 1976) watched 2.5 hours or more of television on weekdays and Saturday mornings in an earlier study. As children grow older they tend to watch more television. Over one-third of first graders watch four hours per day and sixth to tenth graders watch 5.5 hours per day. Television-viewing reaches a peak in early adolescence and tapers off after tenth grade (Lyle & Hoffman, 1972; von Feilitzen, 1976). Data from our study reveal that preschoolers are watching 23 hours per week on the average with a range of two hours to 72 (!) hours per week.

Children in our sample (over 75%) tend to watch TV chiefly during the hours of 4:00 p.m. to 8:00 p.m., although a number of them are watching the action-detective shows later in the evening. Programs most frequently watched during the 4:00-8:00 p.m. hours are educational television ("Sesame Street," "Mister Rogers'", "Zoom," "Electric Company") as well as such programs as "Star Trek," Cartoons ("Jetsons," "Popeye," "Mighty Mouse," Spiderman," "The Flintstones," and family situation shows such as "The Brady Bunch," "I Love Lucy," "Happy Days"). The news and game and variety shows are also represented depending on the day of the week. The rank order of programs for the four log periods is presented in Tables 3.2 and 3.3. *"Sesame Street"* remains the top favorite among the children in all four

TABLE 3.2
Rank Order Of Programs For The Four Log Periods—
Total 3-Year-Olds (Male And Female)

Program	Feb. 1977 1. N = 62	April 1977 2. N = 64	Oct. 1977 3. N = 53	Feb. 1978 4. N = 51	% Who Watched
1. Sesame Street	47	44	38	39	73%
2. Electric Co.	32	32	19	32	50
3. Mr. Rogers	35	26	19	25	46
3. Captain Kangaroo	29	31	21	23	46
5. Muppet Show	23	26	26	32	45
6. News	32	23	22	22	43
7. Brady Bunch	26	23	24	23	42
8. Game Shows	17	21	36	20	41
9. Flintstones	27	25	17	24	40
10. Happy Days	22	20	13	23	34
11. Bugs Bunny	32	21	11	12	33
12. Zoom	20	15	19	16	30
13. Laff-a-Lympics	24	13	16	11	28
14. Donny and Marie	14	16	12	17	26
15. $6 Million Man	13	16	18	8	24
16. Mickey Mouse	17	11	12	11	22
17. Movies	20	7	11	10	21
17. Wonderama	17	15	10	7	21
17. Star Trek	20	13	7	9	21
17. Little Rascals	20	22	4	3	21
21. Disney	18	8	10	10	20
21. I Love Lucy	14	11	11	11	20
21. Nancy Drew/Hardy	12	13	11	9	20
24. Odd Couple	15	13	8	8	19
25. Bionic Woman	9	13	11	8	18
26. Soap Operas	12	9	6	13	17
27. Talk Shows	14	4	5	13	16
27. Banana Splits	14	5	6	12	16
29. Krofft's Supershow	13	8	8	4	14
29. Emergency	10	8	5	10	14

TABLE 3.3
Rank Order Of Programs For The Four Log Periods—Total 4-Year-Olds (Male And Female)

Program	Feb. 1977 1. N = 54	April 1977 2. N = 56	Oct. 1977 3. N = 48	Feb. 1978 4. N = 49	% Who Watched
1. Sesame Street	39	30	29	29	61%
2. Muppet Show	26	26	20	31	50
3. Electric Co.	34	26	19	20	48
4. Flintstones	28	19	24	27	47
5. Brady Bunch	22	19	22	30	45
6. Bugs Bunny	29	23	14	15	39
7. Mr. Rogers	28	18	17	16	38
7. Captain Kangaroo	21	25	19	13	38
9. News	24	16	14	23	37
10. Mickey Mouse	23	9	19	19	34
11. Happy Days	23	17	12	15	32
12. Laff-a-Lympics	21	14	13	15	30
12. Game Shows	20	13	14	16	30
14. Zoom	18	14	19	9	29
15. Banana Splits	24	20	9	14	28
16. Wonderama	25	15	9	7	27
17. I Love Lucy	14	10	9	20	26
18. Donny and Marie	13	16	9	10	23
18. Movies	16	4	11	16	23
20. Disney	23	10	8	4	22
20. Nancy Drew/Hardy Boys	10	8	14	14	22
22. Krofft's Supershow	15	9	5	10	19
22. $6 Million Man	7	11	13	9	19
24. Little Rascals	14	18	3	3	18
24. Odd Couple	14	13	6	6	18
26. Star Trek	16	4	8	7	17
27. Talk Shows	8	5	5	12	15
27. Emergency	12	8	2	9	15
29. Soap Operas	9	4	5	6	12
29. Bionic Woman	8	7	4	5	12

log periods. In general, educational television leads the list of shows, with minor fluctuations among the top four for each probe period. What is surprising, is that *game shows* are watched by over one-third of our sample, and this remains consistent during the year. Our hunch is that parents are watching these shows with their children and consider these as relatively benign programming. We question the ability of these youngsters to understand the content, and we believe that the frenetic activity on many of these shows contributes to the aggressive behavior we have found and discuss in a later chapter.

We may ask why children have particular preferences for shows. Studies conducted in the 1950s indicated that children watched television primarily for escape (Bailyn, 1959; Maccoby, 1954; Schramm, Lyle, & Parker, 1961). Maccoby outlined three patterns of escape: (1) children forget their problems while they view television; (2) children identify with a character and can be sexual, aggressive, disobedient, and not punished; and (3) children engage in wish fulfillment, that is, they can identify with the hero and vicariously satisfy themselves. Cecilia von Feilitzen (1976) in a survey of 3- to 15-year-olds in Sweden, has proposed that there are five main needs in children satisfied by watching TV: (1) entertaining or emotional functions; (2) informative or cognitive functions; (3) social functions; (4) nonsocial or escapist functions: and (5) mode of consumption functions (the sight and sound attractions).

Our method of data collection precludes our drawing firm conclusions concerning the specific motives on "uses and gratifications" hypotheses for children's viewing. It is clear that the most heavily viewed programming involves primarily cartoons or (as in the case of "Sesame Street") much pixillation, rapid movements, and magical effects with puppets or Muppets. We can speculate that the rapidity of movement on the screen in cartoons has the kind of attractive power to children we discussed in chapter 1, mindless, perhaps, but compelling. We need a good deal more research to determine whether some of the special attractiveness of cartoons or muppets also reflects ease of understanding or organizing material.

The possibility that the viewing attraction of TV for such young children involves some special quality of the format rather than the meaning or identification potential of the content gains support when we look closer at the actual programs watched. "The Brady Bunch" is clearly popular and includes a family group easy for children to grasp or relate to. But can 4-year-olds or 3s keep up with the plot?

Thirty-seven percent of our children watched the news! How much did they comprehend of that material? More than a quarter of our 4-year-olds watched "I Love Lucy." It seems unlikely that they could follow the intricacies of the plot or keep up with the rapid pace of speech. More likely they were attracted chiefly to the bouncy character of Lucy herself and to the rather frenetic actions that typify that show.

CHANGES ACROSS THE YEAR: BEHAVIORAL VARIABLES

We can next ask what particular types of spontaneous play behavior or features of language or patterns of TV-viewing show growth across the year's time for these 3- and 4-year-olds. Naturally, one should expect growth in many areas of behavior just as there are obviously tremendous changes in physical growth and motor coordination for children during the years between 3 and 4 and 5. There may, however, be differential growth rates for certain patterns of play behavior or language and for the orientation to television which have never been looked at systematically with samples of this size before.

Tables 3.4, 3.5, and 3.6 indicate the averages for the three classes of variables—behavior, language usage, and TV-viewing for boys and girls and for initial age, 3 or 4, of our subjects. Keep in mind that the intervention, that is to say, the training of parents, has taken place in the period from April through September and therefore any possible changes influenced by parental training of children may be coming into play here. We look more closely at specific effects of intervention later.

Inspection of these tables and also statistical analysis of age and probe period effects on scores in these variables indicate that there is relatively modest evidence of growth on the behavioral ratings. It is, of course, possible that because ratings were carried out by different observers and they themselves had no sense of continuity of a given child, they might have been making their ratings relative to the current pool of children. Therefore these ratings may be relative rather than absolute. Detailed descriptions of the play behavior and of the imaginative performance of the children and a more molecular analysis of specific play patterns that are rated as imaginative reveal some evidence of growth patterns (see Chapter 4).

Despite this qualification in our scoring, the 4-year-olds, boys and girls, show considerably more make-believe and imaginative play than do the 3-year-olds. There is a general trend toward increase over the year, but with much variability. Especially puzzling is the drop in imaginative play for 4-year-old girls as they become 5, a finding that is also consistent with a surprising drop in their language usage during the fourth probe. At this point it is not possible to determine whether we are witnessing perhaps a change in play style which the girls are evincing.

A variable like persistence clearly shows an increase for the boys even with some variation if we divide the four probe periods into first and second halves. This result, although also evident in the 3-year-old girls, again does not show up in the 4-year-old girls because of the puzzling drop in persistence during the February 1978 probe. The finding of an increase in persistence is also reported in the data of parents on the intensity with which the children watch television. Thus the degree of concentration which the children show at home while sitting in front of the TV set does also seem to increase somewhat roughly like the amount of concentration they show while spontaneously playing in the nursery school.

We would not necessarily expect any particular changes in the emotional variables with age. We do find some trend toward increased cooperativeness across age periods especially for the younger girls.

Some sex differences may be mentioned at this point. In general, the boys seem to play more imaginatively than the girls, although these results are not

TABLE 3.4
Patterns of Behavior Across Observation Periods

Variable	Boys—3-Years-Old				Variable	Boys—4-Years-Old			
	Feb. 77 Mean	Apr. 77 Mean	Oct. 77 Mean	Feb. 78 Mean		Feb. 77 Mean	Apr. 77 Mean	Oct. 77 Mean	Feb. 78 Mean
Imagination	2.14	2.20	2.36	2.20	Imagination	2.62	2.42	2.61	2.67
Positive Affect	2.81	3.03	3.11	3.00	Positive Affect	3.21	3.24	3.05	2.81
Persistence	2.81	2.80	3.09	2.77	Persistence	3.12	3.05	3.04	3.37
Aggression	1.51	1.51	1.73	1.66	Aggression	1.51	1.33	1.38	1.65
Interaction with Peers	2.89	3.44	3.08	3.33	Interaction with Peers	3.28	3.65	3.29	3.57
Interaction with Adults	2.97	3.44	2.90	3.22	Interaction with Adults	3.10	3.46	2.91	3.02
Cooperation with Peers	2.90	2.97	2.84	2.98	Cooperation with Peers	3.27	3.33	3.01	3.09
Cooperation with Adults	2.88	3.04	2.82	2.55	Cooperation with Adults	2.99	3.29	2.69	3.17
Fearful/Tense	1.26	1.15	1.22	1.17	Fearful/Tense	1.19	1.05	1.19	1.10
Angry/Annoyed	1.40	1.55	1.85	1.78	Angry/Annoyed	1.43	1.28	1.64	1.78
Sad/Downhearted	1.26	1.19	1.24	1.23	Sad/Downhearted	1.18	1.09	1.36	1.28
Fatigue/Sluggish	1.44	1.16	1.32	1.23	Fatigue/Sluggish	1.15	1.08	1.29	1.18
Lively/Excited	2.60	2.91	2.99	3.16	Lively/Excited	2.96	3.21	2.97	3.09
Elated/Pleased	2.48	2.78	2.79	2.64	Elated/Pleased	3.01	3.30	2.82	2.65

(continued)

TABLE 3.4 (continued)

Variable	Girls—3-Years-Old				Girls—4-Years-Old			
	Feb. 77 Mean	Apr. 77 Mean	Oct. 77 Mean	Feb. 78 Mean	Feb. 77 Mean	Apr. 77 Mean	Oct. 77 Mean	Feb. 78 Mean
Imagination	1.90	2.05	2.10	2.02	2.23	2.05	2.40	1.98
Positive Affect	2.70	3.05	2.85	2.98	2.86	3.14	2.85	2.73
Persistence	2.93	2.88	2.87	3.02	3.15	2.92	3.19	2.79
Aggression	1.16	1.23	1.19	1.28	1.11	1.20	1.16	1.21
Interaction with Peers	2.88	3.37	2.99	3.22	3.18	3.38	3.37	3.18
Interaction with Adults	3.22	3.36	3.07	3.59	3.11	3.31	2.94	3.08
Cooperation with Peers	2.86	3.03	3.06	3.33	3.03	3.38	3.23	3.30
Cooperation with Adults	3.14	3.11	2.93	3.15	2.85	3.17	2.91	3.39
Fear	1.18	1.15	1.16	1.28	1.29	1.03	1.21	1.25
Anger	1.25	1.48	1.40	1.48	1.35	1.36	1.56	1.41
Sad	1.18	1.17	1.19	1.16	1.45	1.17	1.21	1.38
Fatigue	1.39	1.20	1.55	1.18	1.40	1.34	1.44	1.59
Lively	2.34	2.85	2.34	2.30	2.55	2.75	2.39	2.16
Elated	2.45	3.07	2.48	2.65	2.64	2.81	2.48	2.41

TABLE 3.5
Patterns of Language Across Observation Periods

Variable	Boys—3-Years-Old				Boys—4-Years-Old			
	Feb. 77 Mean	Apr. 77 Mean	Oct. 77 Mean	Feb. 78 Mean	Feb. 77 Mean	Apr. 77 Mean	Oct. 77 Mean	Feb. 78 Mean
No. of Words	63.4	110.3	132.5	124.1	108.9	165.6	154.9	190.9
No. of Utterances	17.0	27.3	30.5	29.6	26.1	37.5	33.2	41.8
Mean Length Utterances	3.59	3.95	4.03	4.08	4.18	4.19	4.35	4.54
Declarative Utterances (%)	47.1	54.4	48.5	54.7	56.5	52.4	58.6	60.5
Imperative Sentences (%)	26.1	26.6	31.7	25.6	23.0	25.7	21.4	24.3
Questions (%)	26.7	19.0	14.1	16.6	20.4	21.9	17.1	15.2
Exclamatory Utterances(%)	19.7	14.7	26.4	29.4	19.1	16.5	18.0	21.4
Proper Nouns (%)	3.9	3.6	2.2	2.9	2.4	2.7	2.8	2.6
Common Nouns	10.5	12.6	9.1	9.8	11.1	10.4	8.9	9.9
Total Nouns (%)	14.4	16.1	11.3	12.6	13.5	13.1	11.7	12.5
Personal Pronouns (%)	11.2	12.5	11.6	12.1	13.5	14.4	11.1	12.5
Impersonal Pronouns (%)	9.6	7.8	6.2	6.6	7.9	6.2	6.9	7.6
Possessive Pronouns (%)	2.6	2.6	2.2	2.0	1.8	1.4	1.9	1.9
Total Pronouns (%)	23.4	22.9	20.1	20.8	23.2	22.0	19.9	21.9

(continued)

TABLE 3.5 *(continued)*

Variable	Boys—3-Years-Old				Boys—4-Years-Old			
	Feb. 77 Mean	Apr. 77 Mean	Oct. 77 Mean	Feb. 78 Mean	Feb. 77 Mean	Apr. 77 Mean	Oct. 77 Mean	Feb. 78 Mean
Descriptive Adjectives (%)	2.5	3.6	3.9	4.0	4.3	3.7	4.4	3.7
Possessive Adjectives (%)	.2	.1	.1	.3	.2	.1	.3	.2
Total Adjectives (%)	3.7	5.0	4.8	4.3	5.5	5.0	6.1	5.2
Adverbs (%)	9.1	9.7	13.2	10.0	8.0	9.5	8.8	10.1
Present Verbs (%)	18.7	20.1	16.0	17.1	17.5	18.6	15.2	17.1
Past Verbs (%)	2.1	1.3	2.2	2.7	2.3	2.3	1.9	2.6
Future Verbs (%)	1.2	1.6	1.2	1.1	1.8	1.4	1.3	1.7
Conditional Verbs (%)	.6	.6	.1	.3	.7	.7	.4	.4
Total Verbs (%)	22.7	23.0	19.5	21.2	22.1	22.4	20.0	21.8
Onomatopoeia (%)	3.6	2.9	1.3	4.4	2.6	4.0	3.1	2.5
TV References (%)	.6	.3	.1	.6	1.5	.5	.7	.3
Predicate Nominatives (%)	.8	2.4	1.9	1.9	.9	1.3	1.7	1.7

Variable	Girls—3-Years-Old				Variable	Girls—4-Years-Old			
	Feb. 77 Mean	Apr. 77 Mean	Oct. 77 Mean	Feb. 78 Mean		Feb. 77 Mean	Apr. 77 Mean	Oct. 77 Mean	Feb. 78 Mean
No. of Words	76.5	108.2	114.4	137.9	No. of Words	139.1	139.2	143.5	112.0
No. of Utterances	19.7	26.8	26.8	32.2	No. of Utterances	30.9	31.3	29.2	24.5
Mean Length Utterances	3.79	3.88	4.46	4.20	Mean Length Utterances	4.59	4.42	4.47	4.11
Declarative Sentences (%)	58.6	49.2	53.9	58.8	Declarative Sentences (%)	57.6	57.3	57.1	52.2
Imperative Sentences (%)	19.3	36.6	27.6	23.0	Imperative Sentences (%)	25.3	27.1	16.9	21.5
Questions (%)	22.1	14.2	18.5	18.2	Questions (%)	17.1	15.7	19.3	22.7
Exclamatory Utterances (%)	16.8	15.5	22.8	16.1	Exclamatory Utterances (%)	14.0	9.0	8.6	13.5
Proper Nouns (%)	3.2	3.9	2.6	1.2	Proper Nouns (%)	2.4	3.1	1.9	1.8
Common Nouns (%)	13.3	9.4	9.9	10.6	Common Nouns (%)	10.0	11.3	12.0	10.3
Total Nouns (%)	16.5	13.3	12.5	11.7	Total Nouns (%)	12.4	14.4	13.8	12.0
Personal Pronouns (%)	13.1	13.5	13.0	13.1	Personal Pronouns (%)	13.3	13.1	13.0	12.2

(continued)

TABLE 3.5 (continued)

Variable	Girls—3-Years-Old				Girls—4-Years-Old			
	Feb. 77 Mean	Apr. 77 Mean	Oct. 77 Mean	Feb. 78 Mean	Feb. 77 Mean	Apr. 77 Mean	Oct. 77 Mean	Feb. 78 Mean
Impersonal Pronouns (%)	10.0	8.0	7.4	8.2	6.9	7.8	7.0	9.5
Possessive Pronouns (%)	5.9	2.3	2.3	2.1	6.5	1.6	1.5	1.7
Total Pronouns (%)	29.1	23.8	22.7	23.5	26.6	22.5	21.5	23.4
Descriptive Adjectives (%)	2.8	2.1	4.1	3.5	3.2	4.1	3.6	2.9
Possessive Adjectives (%)	.0	.1	.1	.2	.1	.1	.1	.2
Total Adjectives (%)	3.7	3.4	8.9	6.2	4.2	5.8	4.9	4.8

	Girls—3-Years-Old					Girls—4-Years-Old			
Variable	Feb. 77 Mean	Apr. 77 Mean	Oct. 77 Mean	Feb. 78 Mean	Variable	Feb. 77 Mean	Apr. 77 Mean	Oct. 77 Mean	Feb. 78 Mean
Adverbs (%)	7.2	10.5	9.0	10.0	Adverbs (%)	11.3	8.9	10.0	8.7
Present Verbs (%)	20.6	19.3	18.1	16.6	Present Verbs (%)	17.7	19.6	16.0	16.7
Past Verbs (%)	1.5	2.4	1.8	2.9	Past Verbs (%)	2.6	2.3	1.9	2.5
Future Verbs (%)	1.1	1.1	1.3	1.7	Future Verbs (%)	1.1	1.1	1.7	1.1
Conditional Verbs (%)	.5	3.6	.5	.3	Conditional Verbs (%)	.4	1.9	.5	.2
Total Verbs (%)	23.4	23.7	21.7	21.6	Total Verbs (%)	21.7	23.2	20.0	20.5
Onomatopoeia (%)	1.2	1.6	1.6	1.5	Onomatopoeia (%)	1.6	.9	1.3	.9
TV References (%)	.2	.4	.0	.1	TV References (%)	.2	.2	.1	.0
Predicate Nominatives (%)	.6	1.4	1.6	1.7	Predicate Nominatives (%)	.5	1.4	1.9	1.4

TABLE 3.6
Patterns Of Television-Viewing Across Observation Periods

TV Category	Boys—3-Years-Old				TV Category	Boys—4-Years-Old			
	Feb. 1977 Mean Hrs. Weekly	Apr. 1977 Mean Hrs. Weekly	Oct. 1977 Mean Hrs. Weekly	Feb. 1978 Mean Hrs. Weekly		Feb. 1977 Mean Hrs. Weekly	Apr. 1977 Mean Hrs. Weekly	Oct. 1977 Mean Hrs. Weekly	Feb. 1978 Mean Hrs. Weekly
Cartoons	5.06	3.29	4.66	6.97	Cartoons	12.48	6.02	10.62	11.60
Commercial TV Childrens' Shows	6.74	6.40	6.86	5.32	Commercial TV Childrens' Shows	10.27	5.35	4.62	4.71
Educ. Childrens' Shows	9.01	4.04	4.97	6.07	Educ. Childrens' Shows	7.29	2.27	2.62	3.09
Sit. Comedies	3.53	2.22	2.83	3.52	Sit. Comedies	5.69	3.55	4.52	4.85
Variety/Game	2.19	1.16	1.48	2.25	Variety/Game	3.32	1.49	1.91	3.45
Adult Dramatic Shows	3.14	1.69	1.94	1.70	Adult Dramatic Shows	3.74	1.42	1.93	2.07
Action/Adventure	2.99	1.72	1.77	1.73	Action/Adventure	2.84	1.11	1.53	1.83
Sports	.69	.13	.69	.47	Sports	.74	.14	.69	.43
News	3.23	1.47	.83	1.55	News	1.27	.86	.71	1.71
Total Weekly Viewing	36.56	20.78	22.33	28.90	Total Weekly Viewing	47.40	21.48	28.06	33.14

Girls—3-Years-Old

TV Category	Feb. 1977 Mean Hrs. Weekly	Apr. 1977 Mean Hrs. Weekly	Oct. 1977 Mean Hrs. Weekly	Feb. 1978 Mean Hrs. Weekly
Cartoons	7.54	4.54	6.41	6.93
Commercial TV Childrens' Shows	6.31	5.64	4.05	4.95
Educ. Childrens' Shows	7.25	4.14	6.45	8.41
Sit. Comedies	7.42	4.12	4.55	4.76
Variety/Game	4.29	2.06	2.76	3.48
Adult Dramatic Shows	3.79	1.77	2.10	1.52
Action/Adventure	2.89	1.48	1.38	1.21i
Sports	.17	.23	.41	.38
News	1.81	1.39	1.64	1.21
Total Weekly Viewing	41.05	24.90	29.00	31.52

Girls—4-Years-Old

TV Category	Feb. 1977 Mean Hrs. Weekly	Apr. 1977 Mean Hrs. Weekly	Oct. 1977 Mean Hrs. Weekly	Feb. 1978 Mean Hrs. Weekly
Cartoons	6.23	3.41	1.97	4.25
Commercial TV Childrens' Shows	7.58	6.16	2.53	3.55
Educ. Childrens' Shows	7.94	3.48	4.00	4.83
Sit. Comedies	3.06	2.84	1.32	3.55
Variety/Game	2.23	1.36	.84	2.53
Adult Dramatic Shows	.94	.64	.45	1.25
Action/Adventure	1.48	.86	.95	.80
Sports	.25	.11	.11	.08
News	1.85	.80	.34	1.78
Total Weekly Viewing	31.20	18.35	12.33	21.75

very dramatic. Nevertheless, they are statistically significant over the four probe periods for the variable of sex ($p < .015$). There is, as has often been noted, a more sizable difference in aggression manifested by boys and girls with, again, a highly significant result ($p < .01$) across the four probes with the boys showing more aggression than the girls.

CHANGES AND CORRELATES OF LANGUAGE USAGE

With respect to language development, it is clear that 3-year-olds are less advanced than 4-year-olds and that girls initially in our study showed considerably more language ability than boys. The evidence indicates that boys increase significantly more than girls do during this period in number of utterances and in number of words used during the probe period. Inspection of Fig. 3.1 or Table 3.7 indicates, for example, that if we look at the number of words used during 10 minutes of spontaneous play, 4-year-old boys are significantly higher than 3-year-old boys who use only about 60 words during a 10-minute period compared to more than 100 by the 4-year-olds. Four-year-old girls are obviously far above the boys, using close to 130 words during the period whereas 3-year-old girls are speaking approximately on the average of 18 more words during a 10-minute period than the boys. What follows, then, during the year is a dramatic acceleration in language for the 3-year-olds of both sexes with an even more striking increase for boys than for girls. By the fourth probe, the initially 3-year-old boys use actually somewhat more words than the initially 3-year-old girls. Indeed, the acceleration is marked and the contrast between the initially 4-year-old boys and 4-year-old girls is so great because of the drop in this fourth probe that we see the 4-year-old boys speaking approximately 190 words in a 10-minute period while playing, whereas the 4-year-old girls are speaking only 112.

We can conclude from our data that the spontaneous sheer output of words during free play increases as much as 50% for our total sample, with boys

TABLE 3.7
Number of Words Spoken During Play In Each Observation Period For Males and Females By Age And Probe Period

	Age At Outset	Probe 1	Probe 2	Probe 3	Probe 4
Males	3	62.1	107.3	134.9	124.1
	4	112.3	175.7	154.9	190.9
Females	3	77.2	101.2	103.8	112.0
	4	132.2	140.2	143.5	137.9

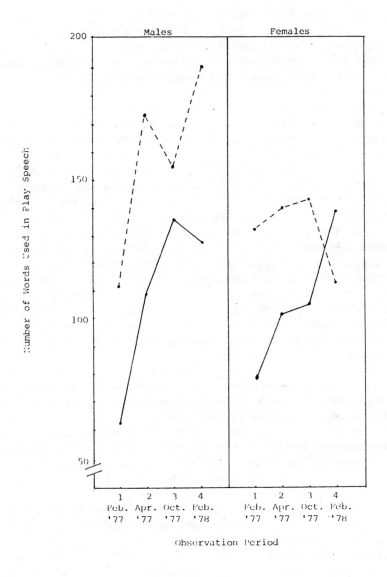

FIG. 3.1. Age by sex by observation periods trends for number of words used in play speech.

nearly doubling their verbal output over the year. Were it not for the drop in language shown in our fourth probe for the 4-year-old girls a sizable growth might be in evidence across the sexes. The number of separate utterances shows a 30% increase and the average number of words within an utterance, although remaining close to four words, shows an increase especially for the boys.

Examining the language changes more closely suggests that the major pattern of change is reflected in: (1) a drop in questions; (2) a drop in personal pronouns or in possessive pronouns ("I, my, mine"); (3) sizable increases in the usage of descriptive adjectives; (4) increases in past tense verbs along with a drop in present tense verbs; (5) increases in onomatopoeia (usually sound effects); and (6) some increase in qualification sentences, analogies, metaphors, for example, "This is like that" or "Pretend this is a train." Although our analysis of parts of speech is of limited value it seems likely that we are observing primarily an increase in sheer verbal output and expressiveness. Most language still involves declarative and imperative sentences or questions but there is an apparent reduction in the egocentric frame of reference and a broadening of temporal perspective as past tense becomes somewhat more evident in language use. Although future verbs do not show much growth overall we do find that such an even broader time perspective emerges in those children who are oriented more toward imaginative play. Future verb use is generally one of the only language classes besides output that shows links to the behavioral variables.

We found a few modest correlations between television viewing and language. Positive correlations emerge between weekly television-viewing and imperative sentences and exclamations; negative correlations between weekly television-viewing and questions, future verbs, and adjectives. We may interpret this to mean that our heavy TV-viewers were using commands more than our light TV-viewers, and, thus a more assertive or aggressive style. Our heavy TV-viewers were perhaps not as inquisitive about their environment, nor as facile in describing things as our light TV-viewers. Thus descriptive language may be reduced as a consequence of heavy TV-viewing. There were slight, positive correlations found between weekly telelvision-viewing and mean length of utterances, suggesting that television may tend to facilitate language somewhat, but it may encourage a more aggressive use of language. Again, causality cannot be determined precisely from this data.

Language is also related to the other imagination variables, our imagination interview, the Barron Inkblot score for human movement, and whether or not the child has an imaginary companion. These children high in imagination tended to use more words, greater number of utterances, and more declarative sentences. Could this result simply reflect the fact that brighter children are more verbal and by saying more increase the chances that they will be scored as more imaginative? It is difficult to separate play from language, but when IQ is partialled out the relationship between language and imagination persists. When number of words is partialled out, correlations between imagination variables and other behavior variables such as persistence or cooperation with peers remain stable. One of our main theoretical problems is to determine whether or not symbolic or imaginative play can indeed be occurring when the child manifests no overt language. It seems that language and play are interacting continuously, and we cannot yet determine which takes precedence.

A substudy carried out on a sample of our language protocols by a linguistics specialist, Dr. Shlomo Ariel (now at the University of Tel Aviv) indicated that one could identify play patterns that suggested imaginativeness without the use of language. He then examined frequency of language usage and utterance lengths of the children's communications when they were not actively involved in make-believe games, for example, asking the teacher for a drink, drawing, or cutting and pasting, etc. He found that number of words and lengths of utterance during imaginative play were correlated with language in other situations but nonverbal imaginative play did not correlate with more general language usage.

Number of words, number of utterances, mean length of utterance, and declarative sentences seem to be mature forms of speech because they correlate positively with age and IQ. Pronouns, verbs, imperative sentences, questions, and exclamations correlate negatively with IQ and age. These forms of language seem to be more closely related to the egocentric nature of the younger child who clearly is seeking help or information, exclaiming about each event, and is more concrete and action-oriented than the older child.

In general our language data suggests a much greater spurt for the boys during the year's time. The indication is that for girls having started initially well ahead of the boys in language expressiveness by 5 years of age may be entering into a new phase of socialization. Perhaps older girls are now ready for a more organized kind of experience. It may also be that certain socialization pressures on girls are also beginning to emerge. In general, this pattern seems to go along, as we see in the following, with a change in television-viewing by the older girls.

CHANGES IN TV-VIEWING

Table 3.7 indicates the pattern of television-viewing for the subjects divided by age and sex groups for total viewing and also for type of program watched. The data presents a dramatic contrast between the sexes. Boys at 4 are generally heavier watchers than boys at 3. Although both groups declined from an initially somewhat higher level in February 1977 (perhaps due to experimental influences) the initially 4-year-olds by the end of the fourth probe are watching somewhat more on the average than the initially 3-year-olds.

The girls, conversely, show a rather different pattern. Initially, 3-year-old girls are even heavier viewers than boys of the same age, but there is a decrease in viewing trend so that 4-year-old girls are watching far less than 4-year-old boys and by the last two probes, their rate of viewing is by far the lowest of all of the groups. Again, we find this puzzling change in behavior patterns of the 4-year-old girls who are now 5.

We have some indication that by the age of 5, girls are, indeed, beginning to be socialized more and drawn into relationships with their mother. For example, 4-year-old girls show an especially large drop over the year in Saturday morning TV-viewing, whereas 4-year-old boys are showing a relative increase in amount of time spent viewing at that hour. Inquiry from parents suggests that mothers are taking girls along on shopping excursions, leaving boys behind to watch TV. In general, we may be again picking up part of a change in the orientation of the girls toward a more clearly identifiable maternal identification around age 5. For some reason this seems to be reflected also in the change of language usage and in the spontaneity of nursery school play. We discuss some further, more speculative implications of these changes in our concluding chapter.

In looking at television effects across the four probes we cannot avoid consideration of seasonal variation. It is very clear that the lowest TV-viewing for our sample came during the April probe when the children were much more likely to be outside playing. Unfortunately, the study design did not permit sampling of a sufficient range of seasons to balance off this dramatic effect. Still another accidental factor must be taken into account. Although in general we see an overall drop in television from the initially high levels (perhaps as a consequence of some experimental influence on the parents), the blizzard of February 1978 shut down schools and kept children indoors to a greater extent than even was the case in the previous February. Keeping that in mind, the relative drop in viewing during this final probe compared with the initially high level at the beginning of our study may suggest that some possible experimental effect is indeed operating.

Table 3.6 also presents the data on type of programming watched by the children during the year. It is evident that for boys, if anything, there is an increase in the percentage of boys watching cartoons within each age group over the year and across age groups. With respect to commercial TV children's shows the results do not reflect any great increase as a function of age. For girls there is also a more modest increase in cartoon viewing and no really special effects with respect to commercial channel children's shows. Boys show an initially very high level of watching programs like "Sesame Street" and "Mister Rogers" at both 3- and 4-year-old levels. There is a trend toward a decrease in the watching of these shows by the older boys, however. For girls there is a high rate of watching such shows for the 3-year-olds, but a fairly steady drop for the girls, although the girls in general tend to watch Public Television more than the boys. Although the children do not spend a large number of hours watching the action-detective shows during the week, it is clear that a majority of them do watch such shows and that there are no really sizable changes for the boys in the pattern of such viewing. Girls do show a distinct decline in the watching of these more violent TV shows from age 3 to age 4 or from age 4 to age 5. With respect to viewing trends, again the 4-year-old girls show a decline in the amount of time spent watching TV with parents or other adults compared to the 3-year-olds, whereas the change for boys does not reflect such a pattern clearly. Boys do show an increase of watching with siblings whereas girls show a decline in this respect.

In general, the developmental trends with respect to television-viewing are somewhat masked by major seasonal variations with indications that children are more likely outside playing during April and October and show the least viewing at those times. Nevertheless, our subjects, who at the end of the year have reached the ages of 4 or 5, are averaging four hours a day of viewing and this is approximately what the average is for older children according to earlier statistical reports. *It seems clear that the television habit as suggested earlier has been well established for these children. A surprising amount of their waking day is spent in TV-viewing.*

SOME IMPLICATIONS OF THE DEVELOPMENTAL TRENDS

Our data on the whole suggest perhaps that the ages of 3 and 4 chiefly reflect a consolidation of preoperational patterns and quantitative growth rather than any significant qualitative or "stage" changes in our children. Verbal output generally increases during spontaneous play with some changes in descriptive language use, increased time perspective with respect to the past, somewhat less emphasis on pure self-reference "I or mine," but on the whole no dramatic alterations in overall point of view. Imaginative play and cooperative play with peers show modest increases. Although there are considerable individual differences in growth patterns, much of what we observed over the year suggests a consolidation and deepening of differentiated schema, more awareness of or reference to the past, but little shift toward a future perspective. The differences widely reported in language usage for the sexes are evident with some suggestion that our most mature girls may be moving toward a change in pattern with less-overt language usage in play, less pretend play, and a decline in TV-viewing. Essentially our data suggest a relative plateau in what may be an overall "spiral" phase of development (Werner, 1948).

The reader should keep in mind that we have observed children in the course of spontaneous behavior during "free play" or unstructured activity. Thus we could not test for changes in *capacity*. Nevertheless it is apparent that the naturally occurring behavior of the cohorts of 3- and 4-year-olds we observed did not reflect really major shifts in focus on structure. We could see that there were more words spoken in general as the children grew older and a trend toward shifts in self-references or time perspective. On the whole similarities in language, play behavior, and in TV-viewing were more evident than differences in the years between 3 and 4 or 4 and 5.

4 Dimensions of Spontaneous Play

INTRODUCTION

Carrie runs around the nursery school shouting, "I'm Peter Pan." She waves her arms as if they were wings and it is clear to an observer that she is pretending to be flying. Florence sits in a make-shift "house," a piling up of blocks and cardboard crates, and simulates cooking Peter Pan's dinner. In actuality, no utensils other than some clay moulds are in evidence. Florence is pretending that she is Wendy. Both children had wached Peter Pan on television the night before and are now engaged in recreating within their own limited range of mental schema the plot of this classic story.

Observing these children and other preschoolers in their natural play settings enabled us to devise a set of definitions of categories of behavior which could be extracted from the flow of ongoing activity shown by the child and used for further quantitative analysis. Given information manifested in the foregoing examples of spontaneous play, we are struck by how much each child has transformed its environment through the introduction of novelty from its own memory and through the willing suspension of response to what is "actually there" in the physical environment. Through varying degrees of imitation and efforts at assimilation—"Not copying with a view to accommodation" [Piaget, 1962, p. 30]—children are developing their symbolic capacities. They are remembering scenes they have witnessed and reconstructing them. Because they approach each situation with only a limited range of cognitive schema they must inevitably truncate and distort what they have witnessed (at least from an adult standpoint). Nevertheless, in the very effort at replaying the material they are, as suggested in the foregoing, transforming their immediate environment and presumably practicing new kinds of cognitive structures.

For theoretical reasons we have asked in this study: How consistent is imaginative play for a given child across a year's time? Is the imaginative play in the home environment reflected in reports by the children or the parents of fantasy play comparable to the imaginativeness as it emerges in nursery school activities? How does the occurrence of make-believe play relate to evidence of a positive or negative emotional orientation in the child or to social behaviors such as aggression or cooperation? Are there systematic relationships between imaginative play and patterns of television-viewing.

Whereas television-viewing might stimulate imaginative play by providing interesting content as suggested in our little vignette above, it is also possible that extensive viewing might preempt the child's opportunity for home practice of make-believe play. Therefore we could anticipate either no relation of TV-viewing to imaginativeness or possibly even a *negative* correlation between the two patterns of behavior.

Still another issue we have raised involves the notion that children who have developed imaginativeness as a resource may have a medium for translating some of the aggressive material that they view on television into a *play* format rather than imitating this *directly* in aggressive attacks on other children. Earlier research has suggested that the availabilty of imagination in children's behavior repertory can be useful for cognitive development, in separating fantasy from reality, and in stimulating verbal skills (Singer, 1978; Singer, 1973; Singer & Singer, 1976b). It was therefore conceivable that imagination as measured either by overt spontaneous play or by reports of home fantasy activity might serve as a moderating factor in relation to some of the potentially noxious influences of television-viewing.

We were also interested more generally in social interaction patterns that the child would manifest, the extent to which there would be evidence of aggression or unpleasant emotions, or the extent to which we could identify what have been called "pro-social" behaviors such as cooperation with adults and peers. We also wished to look at the different emotional patterns that the child showed over the year's time and to link these if possible to other aspects of play and to the television-viewing situation. An increasing body of research suggests that human beings share a limited but relatively differentiated set of specific emotions which are themselves closely related to the information processing tasks which confront the person (Izard, 1977; Singer, 1973; Tomkins, 1962, 1963). This study is one of the first to look at patterning of emotions during children's spontaneous play and see whether these emotions relate in any systematic way either to other dimensions of play and imagination or to the pattern of home television-viewing.

IMAGINATIVENESS OF PLAY IN THE
NURSERY SCHOOL SETTING:
BEHAVIORAL CORRELATES

The finding that a 3- or 4-year-old child who engages in make-believe play in a given observation period will continue to show comparable levels of such play over a year's time proves to be one of the major outcomes of our study. These data suggest that the occurrence of make-believe play in the nursery school depends not only on the social context or specific stimulation by teachers or peers. It would appear that a tendency toward pretending and fantasy play is already well established in quite a number of the children by the third year of life. As indicated in our chapter on developmental patterns, imaginativeness of play as scored during the first half year's ratings correlated .385 ($p < .001$) with itself in the second half-year's ratings. When one considers all of the interruptions, intrusions, and situational factors that might come into play to interfere with our identification of consistency in the child, these results are rather impressive.

The tendency to play imaginatively is also closely linked with ratings by the observers of more positive emotions and with indications that the child is experiencing joy. The average correlation between imaginative play and positive affect over the year's time in boys is .66 ($p < .001$) and for girls it is .52 ($p < .001$). Imaginative play is also positively associated with the mood ratings of liveliness and elation. Thus, the child who shows various make-believe transformations during play also emerges across the year's time as one who is engaged in a good deal of smiling or laughing and who is motorically active.

A special implication of make-believe games for behavior is that their inherent logic and the necessities of the plot lines lead to longer sequences of play or persistence and concentration. In other words, once the child has committed itself to a make-believe game the necessity for a kind of beginning, middle, and end leads to the spinning out of longer sequences of activity then is often characteristic of very young children who tend to respond (from an adult's point of view) with impulsivity and dependence on momentary external stimulation. It is of interest therefore that imaginativeness of play correlates with our measure of persistence at .39 ($p < .001$) for boys and .42 ($p < .001$) for girls.

Imaginativeness of play also turns out to be positively linked to social interaction and in particular to sharing and cooperative behavior. It is negatively associated with evidence of fearfulness and sadness or fatigue as scored by observers of the children. Finally, children who play more imaginatively are also more inclined to use more words, to make more utterances in general during the observation period, and to show a greater length for a given utterance on the average. Imaginative children also use more complex grammatical constructions such as adverbs, adjectives, predicate nominatives, and future verbs.

It might be argued that the correlation of imaginative play and positive emotion is simply a function of the fact that children who speak a great deal will elicit more positive ratings from observers. It is also true that it was usually necessary for the child.to speak in order to evaluate whether make-believe elements were included in a game. Thus it could be argued that the relationship of imagination to other variables may be in part a function of general verbal expressiveness by the child. As it happens, when we exmained the correlation between imaginative and positive affect, partialling out the correlation between each of these variables and the number of words spoken during an observation period, the correlation of .67 between them across the year drops only to .53 ($p < .001$). Thus, the effect of eliminating the impact of verbal productivity does not make much difference in the occurrence of a positive correlation between imagination and positive affect.

Another issue that might be raised is the extent to which IQ may be a controlling variable and that imaginativeness and verbal expressiveness may both be reflections of the general intellectual level of the child. The correlation between imaginativeness and number of words spoken during a 10-minute play period averaged across the entire year for boys was .64 ($p < .01$). When the effect of IQ was partialled out we still obtained a highly significant correlation of .63. In the case of girls the correlation between imaginativeness of play and the number of words used was .64 ($p < .01$); with IQ partialled out the correlation was still an impressive .59 ($p < .01$).

Of interest also is the fact that imaginativenss of play was also associated with somewhat more complex language usage such as the use of forms like the predicate nominative, the beginning of metaphoric language usage, and also the use of future verbs as parts of speech in the child's language. It might be argued again that in order to rate imaginativeness of play we must count to some extent on the occurrence of certain parts of speech to help us understand what the children are doing. The fact remains that in our data we found evidence that imaginativeness of play during one probe period can predict the likely occurrence of future verbs in the next probe period. Thus, it is not possible to assert that the scoring of imaginative play at any given probe is simply a scoring artifact, that is, that language is necessary to score imagination. What seems more likely is that we were observing a complex feedback process. Thus the child in the effort to express imagination and to communicate the details of a pretend game must use language with other children. In its expressiveness of language the child is in effect practicing new word combinations and increasing its propensity for vocabulary differentiation. We are thus almost certainly dealing with a transactional process rather than an artifact of scoring. Figure 4.1 presents results of correlational analysis across the four probe periods of the study presenting the relationship between observed imagination in nursery schools and the number of words children actually used during these 10-minute play periods.

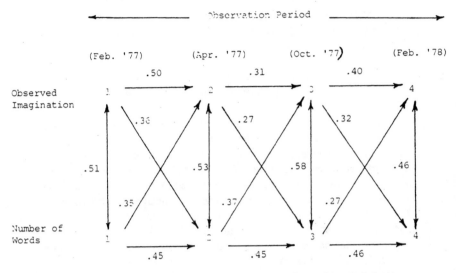

FIG. 4.1. Diagram of sequential, simultaneous, and cross-lag correlations across the four observation periods for observed imagination and number of words used in play speech.

The diagonals of this diagram (Fig. 4.1) indicate the correlation between observed imagination at Probe 1 and number of words used at Probe 2 or the number of words used at Probe 1 and the score for imaginativeness of play at Probe 2. We would expect that if the number of words was invariably the "causal" factor, the diagonal from Words 1 to Imagination 2 should consistently be higher for all three comparisons than the correlation of Imagination 1 to Words 2, etc. Actually the data are mixed in this respect. The correlation of Words 1 and Words 2 with Imagination 2 and Imagination 3 tend to be higher but not appreciably so than the correlation between Imagination 1 and Imagination 2 with Words 2 and Words 3. For the fourth probe, Imagination 3, correlates much higher with Words 4 than the reverse. These data would suggest a much more likely possibility that we are dealing with what Pervin (1977) would term a transaction effect in development, a mutually reinforcing relationship betwen variables.

In general, our data are supportive of previous assertions made in the literature based on generally much smaller sample sizes and observations of children over a much shorter time period. It seems clear that children who play at make-believe games are reasonably consistent in such activities, and that such a tendency in play is linked in general to more positive behavioral manifestations such as cooperativeness, to indications of considerable enjoyment, and to extensive language usage. Parental concerns that children engaging in pretending games are "losing touch with reality" or inclined to be shy and seclusive are utterly unwarranted by our data. Rather, we see clear evidence that make-believe games are tied into a variety of constructive and potentially adaptive cognitive and social patterns during the year's time.

IMAGINATIVENESS OF PLAY IN SCHOOL AND HOME TV-VIEWING PATTERNS

What of the relationship between television-viewing patterns and imaginative play? Here our results are much less conclusive. In general imaginativeness of play as evidence *in the nursery school setting* is not related very much to the pattern of frequency of television-viewing at home. There is a small positive correlation between the degree to which the child concentrates intently while watching TV program at home and the imaginativeness shown in nursery school but this relationship holds only for boys. Dividing our subjects into those who are above and below the median in imaginativeness of play, we find if anything that the boys who play more imaginatively tend to be somewhat more frequent TV-viewers.

Multiple regression analyses that examined the pattern of relationships between variables that predicted given patterns of behavior suggested that children who watched the commercial channel TV shows oriented to children a such as "Captain Kangaroo" or who watched adult-family drama (non-violent) were more likely to prove imaginative in spontaneous play whereas those children who were more likely to watch the variety or game shows with their "hyped-up" quality turned out less likely to be imaginative in spontaneous play.

In general the best way we can say is that children who play imaginatively in the nursery school are somewhat more likely to be watching what might be termed more "benign" programming, family dramas like "The Waltons," situation comedies like "Happy Days," "I Love Lucy," or "The Odd Couple," and commercial TV shows such as "Captain Kangaroo," and they do not appear to be especially watchers of the more active shows such as "The Gong Show" or the action-detective shows. These results are not very strong ones, however, and our hypothesized inverse link between imaginativeness and television-viewing patterns or aggression cannot be supported from our data on school play.[1] We shall see, however, that this hypothesis gains some support when we look at imaginativeness as scored by other methods representing the child's predisposition to imagination on the Barron Inkblots or the presumed fantasy-life of the child reflected in home behavior as reported on by parental accounts of imaginary companions.

---

[1]In two subsequent studies, one with approximately 200 preschool children from a somewhat lower socioeconomic status and another with more than 150 3rd, 4th and 5th grade children we have found statistically significant inverse correlations between the viewing of the aggressive action shows and imaginativeness.

THE DIMENSIONS OF PLAY AND
TELEVISION-VIEWING:
A FACTOR ANALYTIC STUDY

A more comprehensive picture of the relationship of ongoing play behavior in the child to background variables and television-viewing emerged when we explored the underlying dimensions of the variables by looking at the matrix of correlations for the means acorss the year's observations for the behavioral variables, the language variables, television-viewing variables, and eight background-personality variables on the 87 children from our total sample for whom we had complete data. We carried out these analyses with the larger sample using various methods for entering scores for those observations missing (generally because of illness). We here present our most complete data, however; no differences of consequences emerge for the various factor analyses.

An initial factor analysis with iterations was carried out and the resulting factors were then subjected to a varimax orthogonal rotation. This analysis yielded three factors which accounted for approximately 36% of the total variance in the matrix; only factors with *eigenvalues* above 7.0 were examined.

The first factor, accounting for 48% of the cumulative variance, exhibited its highest loadings for imaginative play, positive affect, cooperativeness with peers, and interaction and also for the language variables of number of words employed and number of separate utterances. (See Tables 4.1 and 4.2 for examples of the factor structure.)

This factor clearly suggests a pattern of variables that would reflect the general activity, social gregariousness, and a kind of enthusiastic playfulness on the part of the preschoolers. The factor tends to be somewhat more male-oriented than female—that is, the pattern described is somewhat more common among males than females. A child who scored high on the ratings and language usage scores that load on this factor would be characterized as showing a good deal of imagination, a good deal of positive affect and joy during play, as well as cooperativeness, general interaction with other children, an ability to persist in an activity over a period of time, and a good deal of verbal expressiveness. The child would also be relatively unlikely to be showing much fear, sadness, or sluggishness during the course of play.

These data bear close comparison with the dimension of "playfulness" identified in studies with kindergarten children and also with high school groups by Lieberman (1977). This investigator found that she could identify five playfulness traits, which included physical spontaneity, social spontaneity, cognitive spontaneity (comparable to our imaginative play dimension), and indications of manifest joy and a sense of humor.

In effect, the identification of this dimension suggests that a major way in which children differ when we look at them in terms of their ongoing

TABLE 4.1
Principal Components Factor Analyses Of Behavior, Language, And TV-Viewing Comparing Probes 1 And 4 And Presenting The Cumulative Year-Long Factor Results

	Loadings on Each Varimax Rotated Factor								
Variable (Only Substantial Loadings Listed)	Factor 1: "Playfulness"			Factor 2: "TV & Aggression"			Factor 3: "Inner Imagination & Self-Control" Versus Aggression-Dysphoria		
	Feb. 1977	Feb. 1978	Year-Long Total	Feb. 1977	Feb. 1978	Year-Long Total	Feb. 1977	Feb. 1978	Year-Long Total
Imaginativeness	.62	.68	.78				.24		
Positive	.87	.61	.78					.25	.43
Persistence	.52	.29	.31		-.21			.27	
Aggression				.20	.23	.38		-.50	-.67
Peer Interaction	.78	.81	.83						
Peer Cooperation	.74	.33	.62						.35
Fearfulness	-.51	-.46	-.41						-.31
Anger	-.20	-.23		.23	.28	.24	.24		-.54
Sadness	-.49	-.32	-.40					-.29	-.36
Fatigue/ Sluggishness	-.65	-.48	-.60			-.20			
Liveliness (motoric)	.69	.68	.75			.20			
No. of Words Used	.54	.77	.77				.58		
No. of Utterances	.56	.73	.78				.52		-.30

Mean Length of Utterance		.51		.47			.45		.34
Predicate Nominatives									-.32
Imperative Sentences		.34	.30						
Future Verbs									-.28
Television References	.21						-.53		.40
Sex	.35						-.21	.38	.23
IQ	.27	-.33	-.27	-.30	-.27	-.26	.32		.22
Age			.34	.48	.42	.49	.21		
SES			.21	.21	.46	.33			
Ethnic Group									
Imagination Interviews							.39	.42	.41
Barron Inkblot Movement (M)							.33	.29	.32
Imaginary Companion Index							.40	.52	.48
Hrs. of Weekly TV				.96	.94	.93			
TV-viewing intensity		.22	.21		-.23	-.22			
Cartoons				.61	.56	.61			
Educational TV						-.16			
Variety/Game Shows				.84	.67	.79			
Adult Family Shows				.68	.55	.69			
Action/Adventure Shows				.72	.58	.74			
% Common Variance	46.8	47.2	48.0	33.0	33.3	35.1	20.1	19.5	16.8

TABLE 4.2
Factor Pattern Resulting From Maximum Likelihood Factor Analysis With Direct Quartimin
Oblique Rotation

Variable (Only Substantial Loadings Listed)	Sorted Rotated Factor Loadings		
	Factor 1: "Playfulness"	Factor 2: "TV & Aggression"	Factor 3: "Inner Imagination & Self-Control
Liveliness (motoric)	.843		
Peer Interaction	.806		
Positive Affect	.758		
Imaginativeness	.750		
No. of Utterances	.685		.309
No. of Words	.684		.354
Fatigue/Sluggishness	−.572		
Peer Cooperation	.508		.464
Weekly TV		1.031	
Cartoons		.783	
Variety/Game Shows		.745	
Adult Family Shows		.712	
Action/Adventure		.634	
Aggression	.318	.305	−.657
Anger	.324		−.522
Concentration/Persistence			.513
Sadness	−.254		−.456
Barron Inkblots (M)			.283
Sex	−.363		−.305
Imagination Interview			.354
Ethnic Group			
Mean Length of Utterance	.292		.438
Predicate Nominatives			
Imperative Sentences			
Age			.296
Educational TV			.329
Fearfulness	−.254		−.436
Imaginary Companions			.320
IQ	.293	−.294	
TV Intensity			
% Common Variance	16.3	12.6	10.0

spontaneous play in the nursery school situation is in the extent to which they show a kind of general joy and excitement as well as imaginativeness and verbal expressivity. An almost identical finding was reported by Shmukler (1978) in a study in South Africa carried out at the same time and employing our behavioral ratings.

The second factor that emerges from our analysis of the means of the children across the entire year accounts for 35% of the cumulative variance. This factor reflects high loadings on observed physical aggression, the occurrence of anger during play, and the various measures representing television-viewing including frequency of weekly TV-viewing and especially the viewing of the more action-oriented and frenetic and violent programs. Background variables such as IQ, socioeconomic status, and ethnicity also load highly on Factor 2.

This factor clearly represents a dimension that reflects home-viewing of television and spontaneous behavior in school of an aggressive or angry type. A child who scored high on this factor would be watching a lot of TV and especially the more adult-oriented active or violent shows, and also might be somewhat less intelligent, somewhat more likely to come from a lower socioeconomic background (within our relatively restricted middle-class sample), and might more likely stem from an ethnic minority group. There is no special loading for sex on this factor indicating that (even though boys are in general far more aggressive in nursery school than girls are) the overall dimension reflects equally in both sexes. Clearly this dimension links television-viewing with aggression and we discuss further analyses and implications of this linkage in a subsequent chapter.

The third factor that emerges accounts for 17% of the cumulative variance. The variables exhibiting high loadings on this dimension reflect cooperative behavior with peers, persistence or the ability to concentrate, mature language usage, the indices of imaginative predisposition, presumably reflecting home imaginative play, and the viewing of educational television programming such as "Mister Rogers' Neighborhood" and "Sesame Street." There was a tendency for high scores on the scales composing this factor to be somewhat more typical of girls than boys. Clearly the factor describes a more mature, privately creative or imaginative, and intellectually curious pattern of behavior in a preschooler.

A child who scored high in the variables that load on this factor would be likely to show a good deal of sharing and helping behavior with other children in the course of play, would be likely to be relatively persistent and play in longer sequences, would show little signs of negative emotions such as fear or anger, would be most unlikely to be aggressive during play period, and would show better language use. Indications of slight positive loadings for IQ and age suggest that this child might be brighter and that the factor in general would be more linked to the older child and especially the older girl. What also emerges very clearly on the factor are that the measures of imagination as obtained through interviews with the child, information from the parents about imaginary companions, and the child's imaginative response to inkblots (associations emphasizing human movement) load sizably on this factor. Thus we seem to be dealing with a pattern of constructive social behavior that seems linked to greater maturity and perhaps also to further development of "inner imaginativeness." We use the term "inner imaginativeness" for the variables such as the imagination interview, the Barron Human Movement Inkblots and the imaginary companion index that all reflect more private experiences of the child, fantasy playmates, "pictures in the head," or inkblot reactions rather than the gross motor activity that goes into observed imaginative play as observed in school and which loaded more strongly on Factor 1. Of course, it is entirely possible that the parents' descriptions of the children's imaginary companions reflect in part make-believe as observed during play at home; the children's own self-report in this respect also reflects such home make-believe play. It is also possible that such play is already becoming more internalized and less evident in the gross motor activity of variables observable in the nursery school. It is worth noting that the identical differentiation between observed imaginativeness of play and our dimension of inner imagination using the same variables that we employed was obtained in the factor analysis carried out by Shmukler (1978) with a sample of middle-class white children in South Africa.

One of our concerns was the extent to which the same pattern of factors could be identified across the year's time. In other words, how stable and how consistent are the factor structures of play which have emerged? The same factor analyses from the correlation matrices obtained on these variables in each of the four probes during the year are prepared. We also made use of different methods of factor analysis with the same set of data.

Looking at the identical variables on the sample of 87 subjects from the first and last probes of the year (February 1977 and February 1978) led to a principle factor analysis with iterations followed by a varimax rotation. The resulting factor structures at each probe period were virtually identical to those yielded by analyses of the means averaged across the four probes (see Table 4.1). The factor structure thus seems to be stable across the year-long period of observation. The average of the subjects' means obtained for the eight separate observations (two per probe period) across the entire year gives us the most robust result because it contains more observations and therefore less error variance and it is this one we present here.

A maximum likelihood factor analysis with quartimin oblique rotations was also performed on the 33 mean variables on the 87 subjects using our final total scores. The resulting factor pattern (see Table 4.2) is virtually identical to the orthogonal one revealed in the preceding analyses. The method of oblique rotation allows us in addition to consider some finer details of the factor structure that has emerged. The correlations of the specific factors with each of the variables in the study (Table 4.3) are in general congruent with the factor pattern, reinforcing our sense of the stability of the factor structure of the data. It is apparent that certain variables such as observed imaginativeness of play relate especially to Factors 1 and 3 in the same direction.

The relationships between the factors are considered next by the correlations and covariances across the three oblique factors. Factor 1, which seems to be the most general factor, accounts in general for the largest percentage of the variance. It correlates positively although modestly with both Factors 2(r_{12} = .16) and 3(r_{13} = .14). Factors 2 and 3, however are negatively related (r_{23} = –.23). Cooperativeness with peers and imaginativeness as reflected in the third factor are inversely related to the aggressiveness and the high television-viewing of Factor 2. Thus we seem to be seeing evidence supporting

TABLE 4.3
Factor Structure Resulting From Maximum Likelihood Factor Analysis With Direct
Quartimin Oblique Rotation

| | Correlations of Factors with Variables | | |
Variable	Factor 1: "Playfulness"	Factor 2: "TV & Aggression"	Factor 3: "Inner Imagination & Self-Control"
Sex	−.32		.26
IQ	.28	−.30	.31
Age			.30
SES		.46	
Race		.21	
Imagination Interview			.35
Barron Inkblot M Responses			.28
Imaginary Companion Index			.32
Imaginative Play	.78		.23
Positive Affect	.77		.36
Concentration/Persistence	.19		.52
Aggression	.27	.51	−.68
Peer Interactions	.82		.28
Peer Cooperatin	.56		.56
Fearfulness	−.33		−.45
Anger	.28	.37	−.52
Sadness	−.31		−.50
Fatigue/Sluggishness	−.60	−.18	
Liveliness (Motoric)	.83	.25	
Number of Words	.69		.46
Number of Utterances	.72		.41
Mean Length of Utterance	.34		.50
TV References		.16	
Predicate Nominative	.18		−.26
Imperative Sentences		.21	
Future Verbs	.35		
Weekly TV	.18	.97	
TV, Intensity of Viewing			.24
Cartoons	.22	.76	
Educational TV			.30
Variety/Game Shows		.70	
Adult Family Shows		.67	
Action/Adventure		.66	−.21

one of the major hypotheses of our study at least in regard to cooperative behavior in play and measures of inner imagination. Children who scored high on the scales loading Factor 3 might be somewhat inclined to score low on Factor 2, but these same children still show a good deal of general playfulness as measured by Factor 1. Playfulness seems in a certain sense a more general dimension, at least within the scope of the kinds of measures we have employed.

We have so far presented the factor analyses including variables measured in very different ways. What patterns emerge if we limit our matrix of intercorrelations only to the behavioral variables? Table 4.4 indicates the results of an oblique analysis which yields three factors. The first is essentially our playfulness factor with highest loadings for positive affect, motor liveliness, peer interaction, imaginativeness, and peer cooperation. The second factor reflects major loadings for aggression and anger, a negative loading for cooperation with peers, and a positive loading for liveliness. The third factor describes what are most likely the characteristics of the particularly uncomfortable child, fearfulness and sadness. It is worth noting that liveliness loads on Factors 1 and 2 reflecting the fact that a motoric expressiveness may be characteristic of the imaginative, "happy" children as well as those who are uncooperative or respond with annoyance or aggression during play.

In summary, factor analytic evaluation suggests that we can identify three basic dimensions along which the spontaneous play of the child can be measured. There are consistent across the months of the year and also seem to hold up when different approaches to statistical anlaysis are employed. A canonical analysis of groups of selected variables reflecting play behavior and TV-viewing indicates the same basic structure as that which emerges from factor analysis, although we defer discussion of this procedure to the chapter on aggression. In effect, the three factors we have identified imply that if we try to categorize children on the basis of their spontaneous play and in relation to other known information about them, we can locate each child on a dimension that reflects more or less playfulness with a good deal of evidence

TABLE 4.4
Sorted Rotated Factor Loadings From Maximum Likelihood
Factor Analysis With Direct Quartimin Oblique Rotation
With Subset Of 11 Variables On 87 Subjects

Factor	1	2	3
Variable			
Positive Affect	1.01		
Liveliness (Motoric)	.84	.30	
Peer Interactions	.71		
Imaginative Play	.68		
Peer Cooperation	.52	−.30	
Aggression		.85	
Anger		.76	
Fearfulness			.94
Sadness			.61
Fatigue/Sluggishness	−.37	−.28	.26
Persistence	.34	−.28	
% Variance	31	12.6	12.4

of joy and imagination as well as persistence in play. We can also locate children on a dimension of variation in the extent to which they show aggression, flashes of anger, or (particularly as suggested by the canonical analysis) unwillingness to be cooperative with the adults, and that this dimension also relates strongly to the pattern of home television-viewing. A third way of measuring the ongoing play of children reflects variations in social maturity, characterized by willingness to share, evidence of general good feeling and persistence in play, somewhat more advanced language usage, and indications of imaginativeness in private play. At the second-order level we might suggest that most children can be categorized in general on an overall playfulness dimension but that there may be an inverse relationship between the dimensions of aggression and television-viewing and those of inner imagination and cooperative or socially mature play behavior. If we return now to a consideration of our initial questions in this chapter, what do we conclude?

First of all, it seems clear that we can indeed identify a dimension of make-believe play as rather consistent for the child over a year's time. The spontaneous imaginative play of the child seems to be part of a more general pattern of good-humored playfulness and social interaction. Contrary to expectations at the outset of the study, based on earlier research (Singer, 1973; Singer & Singer, 1976b), the observed imagination of the child in the nursery school seems somewhat independent of other measures of imagination which reflect either the child's performance on producing imaginative responses to inkblots, or the parents' reports of the child's imaginative companions and fantasy play at home. These three variables seem rather to reflect a more internalized imaginative development that may be a somewhat more mature aspect reflecting a longer term internalization process (Singer, 1973). Our data suggest that this more mature pattern of social interaction (with its negative relationship to overt aggression or dysphoric moods) is linked to the development of *inner imagination* rather than to *observed imaginative play,* at least in our 3- and 4-year-old children.

It seemed worthwhile to explore in greater detail some of the properties of this inner imagiantion dimension. For this reason we examined at greater length the role of imaginary playmates in the children as reported by their parents. Thus, in effect, we employed the parents' observation of the ongoing home play behavior of the child as an alternative measure of imaginativeness to that of the spontaneous observed behavior in the nursery school. We deal at length with this interesting variable of imaginary playmates in the next chapter.

Whereas, in general, imaginativeness does indeed seem related to more constructive behavior tendencies in the child, we have still a question as to whether imagination is systematically linked to television-viewing. With respect to observed imagination during play our evidence is not supportive of our original hypotheses on the whole. There are suggestions that children who watch more benign and less violent or hyperactive content programming are more likely to be more imaginative. These findings are not strong. Indeed, our more imaginative children tended to be somewhat more frequent TV viewers if we score imagination only on the basis of ongoing play in the nursery school.

If we attempt to see which combination of variables (background and TV) best predict the average imaginativeness of play shown across the year we do find some indications of interest for the hypothesis, however. The six variables that yield a multiple r of .45 in estimating imaginativeness of play with an $F (6,99) = 4.21$ ($p < .01$) include sex (male), age, imaginative play predisposition interview, situation comedy viewing, the proportion of action-adventure TV shows watched relative to total TV-viewing (negative loading), and IQ. In effect, then, the brighter older boys who score higher on our imagination interview, who watch a higher proportion of situation comedies but relatively fewer action-adventure shows are most likely to be our most imaginative children in observed play. Is it possible that these children are being socialized away from the more grossly active programming, as one notes later, and perhaps toward a more *androgynous* viewing pattern rather than towards the traditional male sex role?

A follow-up study a year afterwards by Ms. Rena Repetti of our staff involved interviews with forty children of our study. Her findings do indeed suggest that the children who show more imagination in the follow-up interview are also those whose parents describe *themselves* as less traditional in sex-role orientation. These children are also less stereotyped in their characterization of playthings and of adult occupations. They are also more likely at age 5 to be watching the Public Television programming rather than other shows.

When we consider the measure of inner imagination the results are somewhat more supportive of our hypothesized inverse link between imagination and television-viewing or imagination and aggression. The third factor clearly sets up a negative pattern of relationships between the imagination measures and the occurrence of overt aggression in spontaneous behavior for both boys and girls, although the trend is stronger for girls. The fact that there is at the second order level an inverse correlation between Factors 2 and 3 suggests again that a dimension that includes cooperation with other children, and various measures of inner imagination is inversely related to a group of measures that include aggression and television-viewing. In order for such a finding to emerge from our statistical analyses, there must indeed be a significant number of children who have more evidence of private imagination and whose play behavior is free of aggression and characterized by more sharing and helping of other children and who at the same time are less likely to be watching television and in particular the more aggressive content available in local programming. Thus there is some support for our hypothesized inverse relationship between imagination and TV-viewing and for the same inverse link of imagination and aggression. This pattern seems to be predominantly reflected by the more internalized aspects of imaginative-ness rather than to the expression of make-believe in overt play.

It is important to stress that our data were based on a larger number of children than have usually been observed in studies on ongoing play. We have also fitted more data points across times than have previously been reported for this number of subjects. Because of the care we have taken in training of observers we have reasonable confidence in the reliability of the actual scoring. Our data seem relatively strong. The correspondence of our results to those obtained with different measures by Lieberman (1977) for a slightly older age group is encouraging. If we note that the playfulness and inner imagination findings with relatively identical measures and observation methods were obtained by Shmukler (1978) with a very different national group (middle-class white South Africans) it begins to look like we may be dealing with relatively basic and stable dimensions of the ongoing play of preschool children.

AN ANALYSIS OF THEMES AND STRUCTURE OF PLAY

Most of our emphasis so far has been on play variables rated globally by observers from their own written protocols. We had accumulated by the end of the year protocols for eight separate observations on well over 100 children (two observations a week or so apart in four probe periods three months apart). These more than one thousand samples of spontaneous play constituted a rich source of data on the actual content as well as the structure of play in preschoolers. Limited economic resources precluded an analysis of the entire set of records, however. Instead we decided to examine for suggestive purposes a subsample so that we could look intensively at a large number of variables reflecting the specific games played, the roles assumed by children during make-believe, the indications of recurrent psychodynamic themes, for example, cleanliness, orality, sexuality, dependency, and so on, and the different types of play, games with rules, mastery play, as well as make-believe. We could also look more specifically at content for evidence of TV influences.

To delimit the sample in a fashion relevant to our concern with TV and imaginative play we selected 40 children who scored well above or well below the group means over the year on the dimensions of imaginativeness of play and frequency of TV-viewing. We thus had four rather clear groups: high imaginative-high TV-viewers; high imaginative-low TV-viewers, and low imaginative-low TV-viewers. Each group was composed of six boys and four girls (a reflection of the general trend in our data for boys to show somewhat higher scores on both TV-viewing and imaginative play). IQ scores did not differ significantly across the four groups. The groups were composed also of comparable numbers of 3- and 4-year-olds. The high TV groups averaged 50 hours of viewing per week, whereas the low-TV groups averaged 18 hours of weekly watching.

Recognizing that our small sample might preclude some elegance in our statistical analysis we opted for an exhaustive examination of play content as an initial venture in this area. We attempted to list all of the types of structural and content elements that might be of interest in which a child could do in 10 minutes of "free play." We prepared definitions for all the variables scored. These were broken down by the following a priori categories:

1. Location and environmental features of play, spaces and playthings.
2. Social structure of play.
3. Major themes, e.g., adventure, family, school, doctor.
4. Roles assumed, e.g., mother, father, baby, superhero, victim.
5. Type of play: sensory-motor, mastery, rules, symbolic.
6. Dynamic themes: orality, anality or cleanliness, separation, rejection, sibling rivalry, etc.
7. Television references in play.

In effect we are asking "where did the child play, what use of space was made, was play solitary or with others, what type of play was involved—for example, pure sensory-motor, mastery, rules, games or make-believe—to what extent was there evidence of transformations—for example, changing a stick into an airplane or one stick into an airplane and another into a boat etc.?" We looked at specific roles played by the children in the course of make-believe—for example, father, mother, superhero, cowboy, spaceman—at the specific themes in such play—for example, house, school, cops and robbers, space exploration—and at the relative emphases on orality, food and eating, toilet-habits or cleanliness, sibling rivalry, sexuality, and so on.

Ultimately we settled on 76 variables. A preliminary scoring of the protocols as a class exercise yielded indications that with three training sessions we could obtain an average of 80% agreement on scoring of 69 of the variables for 12 raters unfamiliar with these children but who had similar child observation experiences with a different sample. We ultimately rerated all protocols with two independent raters again obtaining comparable reliability. The reader may recall that we had two separate protocols of each of the eight independent observation periods because we also relied on two observers. To avoid confusion we chose only the protocol of those two that was most detailed and apparently more carefully written where possible. Because the protocols were so similar we relied on coin tossing for the many cases where such distinctions could not be employed.

Following scoring of the 320 protocols (eight per child across the year) we averaged the raters' scores on each variable and generated a correlation matrix treating the observations for pilot purposes as subjects and thus basing our data on 320 cases. We also carried out repeated measures analyses of variance to look at changes in variables over the year's time.

To summarize: We had raters unfamiliar with experimental hypotheses score eight protocols of play from each of 40 children. These protocols reflected eight separate days spread out during a calendar year. The scoring reflected detailed listing of specific types or patterns of play. We already knew the child to be high or low in rated imaginativeness of play and in frequency of TV-watching (although raters were unfamiliar with this information).

DIMENSIONS OF PLAY THEMES

An oblique factor analysis yielded seven factors emerging from the protocols. As can be seen from Table 4.5 these factors fall into fairly identifiable patterns. Factor 1 is characterized by extensive role-playing of adventurous characters, TV-superheroes, and playing the aggressor in games. Factor 2 is clearly a contrast to this first pattern because it involves make-believe play around dolls, dress-up, realistic home settings, and assumption of family roles along with employment of dynamic themes of orality or cleanliness and toilet behavior.

Factor 3 is a bipolar factor that contrasts gross physical activity during the observation period or use of exercise toys with an emphasis on play with art supplies or activities like drawing or moulding clay. Factor 4 reflects the primary pure make-believe focus of play and includes scores for clearly imaginative games, use of miniature toys, playing out occupational roles, or realistic adventures. It is also characterized by more reliance on transformation and on shifts from immediate reality to fantasy as well as on shifts in time perspective.

Factor 5 presents still another potential dimension of play—a reliance on rituals, for example, "Ring-around-the-rosy," language play, punning, dancing and singing, or playing with board games and puzzles. Factor 6 reflects a particular animal-oriented focus in play, cuddling stuffed animals, pretending to be an animal, or reference to or involvement with the animal pets available in the school. Finally, Factor 7 reflects an intriguing combination of playing the very structured games with rules with evidence that the child generally undertakes the role of a victim in games or makes references in conversation or play to separation fears or rejection and dangers from disasters or monsters.

In effect then these results suggest that for our sample of forty children it was likely that their behavior during free-play time fell along one or more of these seven dimensions, adventurous fantasy play, domestic fantasy play, gross physical activity versus art play, general emphasis on make-believe, involvement with ritual games or dancing and singing, pet play, and finally, rules games. At the second order level our factors were also intercorrelated.

TABLE 4.5
Factor Loadings for Play Themes and Behavior Across Year (N = 40)

Factor 1: Heroic, Adventurous Play Themes ("Traditional" Boys' Play)

Adventure themes (fantastic, superhero, spaceman...)	.68
TV-related fantastic characters (Bionic Man, etc.)	.71
Fantasy characters roles	.63
Hero roles	.62
Aggressor roles in pretend play	.61
TV characters roles (Fonz, Gilligan, etc.)	.77

Factor 2: Family Pretend Games (Playing "house") ("Traditional" Girls' Play)

Dolls	.37
Dress-up clothes	.38
Family games	.74
Mother roles	.69
Father roles	.37
Baby roles	.64
Orality, hunger, basic deprivation	.51
Cleanliness and toilet behavior	.37

Factor 3: Gross Physical vs. Artistic Play

Physical-motor play	.65
Art forms and drawing	-.61
Exercise toys (large motor)	.63
Art supplies used	-.55

Factor 4: General Make-believe Play Style

Make believe play	.74
Miniature toys used	.49
Occupations (doctor, nurse, fireman, postman)	.36
Adventure (more realistic)	.45
Transformations—degree of introduction of pretend	.80
Transformations—Divergent activity or novelty in general activity	.71
Reality vs fantasy	.60
Time perspective (short vs long and present vs future)	.39

Factor 5: Ritualized and Structured Play

Ritual play (repetitive)	.60
Language play (puns, rhymes)	.50
Dancing and singing	.47
Fames and puzzles	.44
Animal roles (large, fierce)	.50

Factor 6: Animal-oriented Games

Materials: stuffed animals	.45
Animal games (small, cuddly)	.58
Animal (small or pet)	.55

Factor 7: Rules Games and Fearful Themes

Games with rules	.63
Victim role in pretend games	.55
Separation fears, death, rejection	.48
Dangers (disasters, monsters)	.43

This somewhat speculative analysis (because it is based on an N of observations not subjects) does suggest that make-believe play is a somewhat more general dimension encompassing both domestically oriented pretending and the games of adventure or heroism as Factors 1, 2, and 4 are significantly intercorrelated. Factor 6, the pet or animal play, is also linked to Factor 4 slightly.

In effect these data suggest that although all children may play in each of the ways suggested by a factor, there are consistencies of play style that favor one or another of these dimensions over a year's time. Some children may generally be observed engaging chiefly in adventurous games, others playing house or family roles, others preferring to dance and sing, still others either to jump and exercise rather than to become involved in art or table-centered activity. Of Piaget's (1962) classifications we do find evidence of mastery or sensory-motor play primarily in Factor 3 and rules games in Factor 7 as well, of course, as the symbolic play of Factors 1, 2, and 4. It is intriguing that rules games still play a minor role for these children as Piaget's theory might suggest. Nevertheless the linkage of rules games with evidence of play themes or verbal references suggesting fear and separation anxiety poses the possibility that for the children of 3 or 4 who seem the most preoccupied with dynamic problems, structured rule play may be a useful recourse as a defense.

In general the data do not afford support for a more general compensatory theory of fantasy play. Rather we see adventurous play or domestic play as two major possibilities differentially chosen by some children but not necessarily grossly linked to evidence of special concerns. The orality or cleanliness emphasis in the family play is an inevitable consequence of such a home theme. Our data suggest diversity rather than a focus of all play around the key themes of psychosexuality emphasized in the earlier psychoanalytic literature.

OBSERVED IMAGINATIVENESS AND PLAY THEMES

Our sample of 40 children reflect two groups of 20 who are extremes on rated imaginativeness of play. Our more microscopic analysis affords, first of all, an opportunity to establish whether the more global scoring of the original observers accords with the more detailed examination of protocols by judges who have not actually seen the children involved. The data from a repeated measures ananlysis of variance yields a significant result for high-low observed imagination with subject's scores on Factor 2 ($F = 9.2, p < .005$), Factor 4 ($F = 45.5, p < .005$), Factor 5 ($F = 7.4, p < .01$) and Factor 6 ($F = 7.1, p < .05$). Children who had been rated by direct observation as consistently high in imaginativeness were also scored from protocols as more likely to be playing family pretend games, general make-believe games, ritual and language play games, and finally, animal games. Clearly we are finding evidence that the original observers' are in accord with a new group of judges. Only Factor 1 does not differentiate between high and low observed imagination. Presumably almost all children showed some degree of adventurous game themes in their play. Indeed because there is a heavy emphasis of TV characters in Factor 1, it seems possible to argue that the pervasive effect of TV-viewing has a leveling influence in providing a common set of play themes for both groups of children, those generally more given to make-believe play and those who show it very little.

Of interest is the evidence that the highly and consistently imaginative children are not restricted in play to solitary games or to a purely fantastic side of play.[2] The high imaginatives also show more social play and participate, if anything, even more than low imaginatives in the ritual games and singing or dancing that occurs in the spontaneous play of the preschoolers. Indeed according to the protocols children from the high imagination group are rated as significantly less likely to play alone ($F = 10.2, p < .005$). The imaginative children are also significantly higher on the variable of "initiates play" ($F = 10.8, p < .005$). This is also a suggestive result. In a subsequent study with 200 preschoolers, which is still under analysis, we introduced a variable defined as leadership. This correlated significantly and positively over the year with imaginativeness of play. Thus the child who is consistently high in make-believe play in the nursery school is by no means a solitary, withdrawn, or defensive child. Rather he or she is more likely to be social and to show leadership in stimulating play in others.

We had anticipated that our high imaginative play children might be more inclined to carve out delimited territory in the course of their activities and to play in more "bounded" space. This did not prove to be the case. They seemed at least at this early phase to be likely to move about the room as the low imaginative play children.

In addition to the themes of cleanliness and nurturance that characterized their make-believe family play the high imaginatives differed significantly from the low imaginative group in producing more emphasis on danger ($F = 6.9, p < .05$) and power ($F = 4.8, p < .05$). Although such themes are inherent in many adventure and fantasy situations, these data may lend support to the possibility that high imaginatives have a medium for reenacting in miniature many of the inevitable conflicts and concerns of the child.

Sex Differences in Play Themes

A glance at the factors of play which emerge quickly suggests that Factor 1 (adventure) must reflect a typical boys' play style whereas Factor 2 is more

---

[2]The authors are indebted to Mrs. Susan Bers for calling attention to this possibility.

likely a typical girls' play mode with its focus on playing house, family, and nurturant roles. Based on factor scores, however, gender relates chiefly to Factor 2. That is, girls prove to be playing family games significantly more than boys in almost all of the eight observation periods. By contrast the boys played significantly more adventure and superhero games than girls in only one period of the eight.

If we examine the patterns even more closely we seem to be able to pin down an important early social trend. Girls are moving closer to boys than ever before in their identification with heroic figures, adventurous achievement, and feigned aggression. This almost certainly reflects the broader impact of the woman's liberation movement and some differences in the way parents tolerate adventure themes in girls' play. Even more specifically we can identify a special effect of television: the introduction of female super-heroines, "Wonder Woman," "Bionic Woman," and "Charlie's Angels." Girls do seem to be identifying with such figures in make-believe although they also play at male superhero roles as well. We consider some further evidence on this point in our chapter on imaginary playmates.

Boys it is clear are still not moving in the direction of girls' games, however. They are far less likely to be observed participating in family-theme play. If we again keep in mind the extreme youth of these children we cannot fail but be impressed by how early a separation of sex roles is emerging. The few sex differences that emerge in behavior for boys and girls at birth (Maccoby, 1980) cannot account, we believe, for the sizable differences that appear within the first three or four years in play styles. Almost certainly girls are being encouraged actively through modeling and direct reinforcement by mothers (Fein, 1975) as soon as they begin to show signs of pretend capacities toward nurturant roles whereas boys are steered toward more traditional sex roles of adventure and aggression. Boys who play with dolls or who become involved with nurturant behavior (putting a pretend baby to sleep, cooking, or cleaning a house) may still be labeled as "sissy" by nervous parents or caregivers concerned about "homosexual" trends or by older siblings who have already accepted traditional sex differences. Until this national queasiness about allowing males the opportunity to accept and practice nurturant roles abates we cannot expect a full devleopment of genuine androgyny (Singer & Singer, 1977b).

Television and Play Themes

Our data make it clear that television has a major influence on the *content* of the imaginative play of our children. The most frequent references to characters and adventures which occur are drawn from TV shows, cartoons, and so-called fantasy-action shows such as "Six Million Dollar Man," "Wonder Woman," and so on. Because children are not yet reading and it is clear from parent interviews that the stories they are read or told by parents are not drawn from comic books, the emphasis on specific superheroes reflects directly the TV influence.

Despite the widespread viewing and commonality, we see some differences emerge as a function of the extent of TV-viewing. High TV-viewers irrespective of imaginative level are rated from play protocols as significantly higher on the variables "initiates attack" ($F = 5.3, p < .05$), "reacts to attack with aggression" ($F = 9.9, p < .01$), and "withdraws, weeps or cowers in response to aggression" ($F = 7.0, p < .05$). Clearly the heavier viewers seem to be more uncomfortable, aggressive, or impulsive in their play. These data point to a potential ominous influence of television, although we cannot refute with confidence the alternative possibility that the more aggressive or fearful children are simply attracted more to heavy TV-viewing, at least from this *particular* set of data drawn from the larger study (see Chapters 6 and 7 for more detailed examination of this issue).

The relationship of TV-viewing to play is more complex, however, if we take imaginative play differences into account. Using repeated measures analyses of variance over the eight observations we find that the children who are heavy TV-viewers but also high scorers in imaginativeness of play show significantly lower scores on Factor 3 (physical activity vs. artistic activity) ($F = 5.0, p < .05$). Clearly the combination of TV watching and some imaginative play propensity leads to less gross movement and more emphasis on focused art activities. This impression is strengthened further by the finding that the high TV-high imaginativeness of play children show higher scores on the items in Factor 5 (ritual play, dancing, and singing) than do high TV-viewers with low imaginativeness scores and the low TV-low imaginativeness children ($F = 4.6, p < .05$). It may be, then, that for the child with the capacity for imaginative play the effect of TV may not only be somewhat negative but also may foster some degree of more artistic or aesthetic orientations.

Our data throughout the total sample and from family interviews (see Chapter 7) suggest that certain family influences that foster imaginativeness may also steer the child to more watching of programming of a somewhat more socialized, age-specific nature. We generally notice that more imaginative children are somewhat more likely to be viewers of the Public Television shows, especially "Mister Rogers' Neighborhood" and "Sesame Street." The effects of the Mister Rogers' show on positive affect, imagination, and prosocial behaviors in preschoolers has been observed in several studies (Coates, Pusser, & Goodman, 1976; Friedrich, Stein, & Susman, 1975; Singer & Singer, 1976b; Stein, Friedrich, & Vondracek, 1972; Tower, Singer, Singer, & Biggs, 1979). We may be observing some effects therefore, in which parents' who subtly or actively foster the imaginative play propensities of their children may also be directing the children toward the viewing of more "benign," nonaggressive programming and of the Public Television shows that emphasize constructive activity for preschoolers. Ms. Roni Tower who collaborated with us on various phases of our research program has gone on to the collection of data on such parental influences on children's play. We had earlier observed the children who show more spontaneous imaginative play at nursery school are more likely to have mothers who rate *themselves* as higher on traits like "creative," "ambitious," "idealistic," or "energetic," whereas children who show little imaginative play have mothers who emphasize more "extroverted" or "social" self-concepts, for example, "attractive," "compassionate," "friendly," and so on (Singer & Singer, 1976b). Ms. Tower's extensive and statistically more sophisticated current research is indicating that children who show more imaginative play (using our definition and observation procedures) are more likely to have both *fathers* and mothers who rate themselves higher on items like "creative," even with IQ held constant across groups (Tower, in press).

Interviews with such parents from the present study suggest that part of the influence of parents on children may involve either restricting TV-viewing sharply or steering the children toward shows like "Mister Rogers' Neighborhood," "Sesame Street," or "The Brady Bunch" (as a situation comedy deemed acceptable to many concerned parents). Recall, too, that one multiple regression analysis for our total sample suggests that in predicting imaginativeness of play we find that situation comedy viewing has a positive and statistically significant role in the equation whereas viewing of action-adventure shows is negatively linked at a significant level on the equation (if we take both scores as a proportion of total TV-viewing).

We have moved somewhat far from our initial findings here mainly to point to the possibilities for much more needed research on both positive and harmful consequences of TV. We can at least say that in our small scale analysis of the play themes TV-viewing relates in a rather complex fashion to imaginative play or to play more generally. The heavier watchers of TV on the whole seem more likely to be overtly aggressive or to become victims of aggression or to show more negative affect according to our protocols. Those high TV-viewers who are also high in imaginative play seem also likely to be more generally artistically inclined or likely to play at dancing and singing than the other three groups in this subsample of our population.

Changes in Play over the Year

Finally our data allow us to look more closely then was possible for the larger sample at changes in play over the year. The protocols make it clear that there is a decrease over the year in gross physical activity or larger motor activity and a significant increase in the direction of more art play ($F = 5.0, p < .05$) and more ritual play or singing and dancing ($F = 4.6, p < .05$). Play also becomes more social ($F = 2.04, p < .05$), although this trend levels off by midyear and seems then at a new plateau. Finally, with respect to play themes we see an increase in references to sexuality ($F = 2.2, p < .05$), which closely parallels the increase and then leveling off of social play. By contrast, the themes of "danger, disaster, physical mutilation, etc." show a steady increase over the year (F = 2.8, $p < .01$).[3] This last finding may reflect: (1) an increasing awareness of children of the real dangers that confront them in life; (2) an increased ability to express such fears verbally; (3) an increased response of fearfulness occasioned by the comparable increase in TV-watching over the year, since Gerbner and Gross (1976) have shown that heavy TV-viewing is associated with overestimation of the worlds' dangers by children and adults; or (4) the fact that increased capacities for plot formation in play increase also the likely references to dangers which make for interesting story lines. Considerably more research is needed to help us understand which of these or other possibilities can explain such an increased representation of fear in the preschool years.

CONCLUSIONS

In conclusion, then, it is clear that fantasy games and make-believe can indeed be identified as a regular part of ongoing play of preschool children. Children show reasonable consistency in engaging in such games by the ages of 3 or 4 and indeed such imaginative play seems to be a part of a cluster of behavior that reflects enjoyment, interest, persistence, expressive language, and cooperation and sharing with other children or adults. Considering how much development in language and motor coordination is going on between ages 3 and 4 or 4 and 5, it is interesting to see that playfulness patterns are already emerging as consistent features of the personality styles of many children. Parents who are concerned when they see their 3- or 4-year-olds talking to themselves or "distorting reality" in the format of pretend games should realize that such activities appear to be part of an enjoyable playfulness and extensive language usage that may have important adaptive possibilities for their children.

We also have indications that children who have begun to "internalize" imaginative activities in the form of private images of people in action (the human movement resposnes on inkblots) or fantasy companions may also show more constructive and cooperative social interaction patterns during spontaneous play and may be less likely to be overtly aggressive or, possibly, less involved in watching as much TV on an undiscriminating basis. Imagination may indeed be a major alternative experiential and response system for the preschooler growing up in our television environment.

---

[3]We are indebted to Mrs. Susan Bers for calling our attention to these relationships.

5 Imaginary Playmates

INTRODUCTION

Josie, aged 3-1/2, had for about six months now insisted that an extra place be set at the table and extra dishes laid out for her invisible friend, Louisa. Although a little concerned, her parents and grandmother accepted this daily ritual. They noticed also that Josie would occasionally offer some food to Louisa and seem to be walking hand in hand with this invisible companion on her way to bed at night. Indeed, two pillows had to be left in bed; one for Louisa. One day after being caught outside in a heavy rainstorm, Josie came back to be changed; wrapped in a new sunsuit and beach towel, she sat down for her lunch. When her grandmother asked if Louisa was hungry, too, Josie said, "Don't you know? Louisa was drownded in the big puddle!"

"I guess we won't need to set a place for her then," said grandma.

"Oh no!", said Josie. "You have to put a place for my new friend, Frogman! He's not afraid of puddles!"

Parents as well as investigators of early childhood have often been intrigued by the evidence that many children do indeed seem to have imaginary playmates. Sometimes these companions are completely invisible, but are conversed with and allowed physical space much as if they were actually visible to the child. Often they are also actual stuffed animals, sticks or dolls that are given living properties beyond a specific play setting.

The phenomenon of such fantasy playmates is of theoretical interest on a number of counts. Many parents have expressed concern when they see evidence that their child is talking to thin air or is treating a stuffed animal or sometimes even a blanket as if it had human living properties. Does this represent a serious confusion of reality and fantasy that bodes ill for the child's future development? The possibility that such imaginary playmates may be early signs of psychopathology has been proposed in some of the first journal articles on the subject (Hurlock & Burstein, 1932; Svendson, 1934). Some of the kinds of concerns generally experienced about such playmates is reflected in the popular play and motion picture *Harvey*. In this story, a genial alcoholic man is regularly accompanied in his visits to various bars by an invisible 6-foot white rabbit named Harvey.

Piaget (1962) took a more benign view of the manifestation of imaginary playmates and regarded it as a part of a normal developmental process which in most children includes the important phase of symbolic play. Singer (1973) elaborated on this notion in relation to the nature of information-processing demands on the child and pointed to the potential adaptive function of imagery skills as part of the growth process. Imaginary playmates might be viewed from this perspective as a kind of trying out of different methods of dealing with information and of providing oneself with play opportunities. A large number of studies have been reviewed by Masih (1978) and these generally indicate that the phenomenon of the imaginary playmate is indeed more widespread than had been recognized. Sometimes such playmates have a clearly compensatory quality as in the case of the extensive use made by a group of blind children who recorded that they had "sighted" imaginary playmates (Singer & Streiner, 1966). Deaf children, however, did not show any greater reliance on such playmates than did a matched group of children who could hear (Singer & Lenahan, 1976).

Psychodynamic theories have tended on the whole to emphasize the conflict-related functions of the imaginary playmate or its defensive and compensatory role (Fraiberg, 1959; Green, 1922). Indeed, there is considerable discussion in the object-relations theories of psychoanalysis on the important role of "transitional objects," teddy bears, blankets or soft cloth, and other objects to which life is attributed including imaginary companions as part of the child's gradual differentiation of self from the physical and social environment. There is some evidence that the emergence of imaginary playmates may be a relatively adaptive or creative phenomenon in normal growth. Manosevitz, Prentice, and Wilson (1973) reported in general that children who had such playmates showed other constructive features in their day-to-day behavior and were reported by parents on the whole to be happier than children who seemed to show no signs of such fantasy playmates. Schaefer (1969) studied adults who were rated as being particularly creative on the basis of the literary or artistic products they produced. These creative persons reported themselves to be significantly more likely to have had imaginary playmates in early childhood on the basis of their recollection than did a comparable group of individuals who did not show such creativity. Turner (1972) and Singer (1973) have also pointed to relationships between reports of imaginary companions and tendencies toward general imaginativeness or creativity.

THE IMAGINARY PLAYMATE AS A MEASURE OF HOME FANTASY BEHAVIOR

As we have indicated in the results report in the previous chapter, we had essentially four types of data concerning the imaginative experience of our children. One of these was the report based on a questionnaire distributed to parents in midyear about the extent to which their children had imaginary playmates. This phase of our study to which one of our research assistants, John Caldeira (Caldeira, Singer, & Singer, 1978) made a significant contribution, was one means of getting at the extent to which the parents at home had opportunities of observing fantasy play in the child. It also provided us with some clues about the ways in which television material specifically might be worked into the imagination of the child by looking for indications that imaginary playmates reflected names or characters of television personalities or animated cartoons.

Two somewhat contradictory implications of the possible influence of television on the imaginative development of preschoolers may be proposed. On the one hand we might argue that television provides a considerable stimulus to the development of imagination. After all it offers a child a complex potpourri of story material, interesting characters, and remote settings, all of which may serve to stimulate symbolic play and provide content for various games much as fairy tales have traditionally done for the growing child (Bettelheim, 1975).

In Chapter 1 we have, on the other hand, raised the possibility that the tremendous power of television to hold the child's attention on the screen and the ease of watching alone may create a kind of passive orientation. Thus the child may simply prefer to watch television rather than explore its environment or to make the effort of producing imagery and fantasy characters as companions for its solitude. It remains possible that children who watch a lot of TV may not show much evidence of imaginary playmates. It also is conceivable that the imaginary playmates may be a sign that the child has developed a more extensive pattern of inner stimulation and this may play a counteracting role to the direct imitation of violent material observed either in the home or from television. Thus we might propose the possibility that imaginary playmates would be negatively related to the occurrence of aggression in the overt play of the child as observed in the nursery school. We also might expect that children who show a good deal of imaginary play might turn out to show more positive emotionality because they have the capacity for self-entertainment and we also anticipated that such children would demonstrate more persistence, peer cooperation, and, of course, spontaneous imaginative play in the nursery school setting.

It is also conceivable that having a make-believe friend to which you can converse increases your practice of the use of language. We might, therefore, predict that children who have imaginary playmates would show a more spontaneous expressive use of language during the observation periods at school.

OBTAINING EVIDENCE OF IMAGINATIVE PLAYMATES IN PRESCHOOLERS

There were two ways in which we obtained information about the occurrence of imaginary playmates in the children in our study. As part of the imaginative play interview each child was asked whether or not he had a "make-believe friend." This item was one of a group of items that provided the score for this measure. In earlier research there had been indications that this interview would be useful in estimating the extent to which the child would show imaginativeness in other situations such as spontaneous play or in the ability to tolerate delays as part of a game (Singer, 1961, 1973). Nevertheless the imaginary playmate item was only one part of the interview and with the children as young as preschoolers it seems perhaps an insufficient basis for reliance in connection with more complex statistical analyses. A study by Anderson (1977) has indicated that the imaginary playmate item does indeed correlate quite well with the other items on this interview, however.

For our purposes, it seemed in the present study more appropriate to obtain more detailed information from parents about the patterns of imaginary companions shown by the children. Accordingly, a questionnaire was prepared and mailed out midway in the study to parents. This questionnaire included items such as:

1. "Has your child ever had an imaginary companion? Yes—No—More Than One."
2. "Did this imaginary friend appear only once, more than once, or is it a steady companion? Only once—more than once—steady companion."
3. "Does your child talk to the imaginary companion? Yes—No."

Other questions asked about the sex of the imaginary companion, age of the imaginary companion, names assigned to the imaginary companion, the possible origin of such names, the age at which the child first developed imaginary companions, indications as to whether or not the child shared the imaginary companion with other playmates, siblings or family members, and so on. A list of sample characters from television were provided the parents with indications that they could check off whether any of these had emerged in the course of the children's home play as imaginary playmates.

We scored separately the items on existence of an imaginary companion and frequency of play with such a companion, but also created an imaginary companion index that was based on cumulative scores from the questions indicating presence or absence of the companion, frequency of play, and active interaction with the imaginary companion.

IMAGINARY PLAYMATE PATTERNS

A total of 111 parents returned imaginary playmate questionnaires for their children. To check on the possibility that we were getting some type of selective response pattern we compared the parents' report on this question-naire with the self-report obtained from the children as part of the imaginary play interview. No differences were found in the frequency of imaginary playmates in children of parents who did respond and in the frequencies reported of their imaginary playmates reported by the children of the small number of parents who failed to respond to our solicitation (χ^2 [1] = .06, $p < .50$). Children did in general report a higher frequency of imaginary playmates than did their parents. As a matter of fact, 65% of the children answered "Yes" to the question that they had some form of make-believe friends compared to 55% of such reports from the parents' questionnaire. This is not unreasonable because the children would know better than the parents whether or not they had an imaginary friend; some parents might indeed have failed to notice it or might have suppressed this information. Nevertheless, because we wished to have data that would represent the current situation, we decided to choose the parents' reports that had been obtained midway in the study rather than the childrens' reports that had been obtained at the beginning of the year.

When we identified those children who were described as showing a good deal of play with imaginary playmates and compared them with those whose parents reported little or no such play we found no differences between these groups in age or in IQ. There were no statistically significant sex differences in frequency of imaginary playmates although there was a tendency for girls to be described by their parents as having more make-believe friends. Boys were more likely to have animals as to make-believe playmates than were girls (χ^2 [1] = 6.02, $p < .02$). The girls in this study were significantly more likely than the boys to have a pretend companion of the opposite sex (χ^2 [1] = 5.50, $p < .02$). Of those girls who had imaginary playmates 42% described at least one male imaginary friend whereas only 13% of the boys were described by parents as having female imaginary playmates. We return to a discussion of this sizable sex difference in choice of playmates shortly.

It is of interest to note that about one-third of our children named their imaginary playmates after real people whom they knew, often actual friends. More than 90% of the children were described by the parents as actually talking aloud to the make-believe friends at one time or another.

It is of particular interest to note that children without siblings were clearly much more likely to have imaginary playmates (χ^2 [1] = 7.66, p < .01). This result seemed especially strong in the case of girls but held true for both sexes. These data suggest that imaginary playmates do have some adaptive and compensatory quality for the growing child. They may very well reflect an effort to "people" one's world when left to one's own devices but at the same time they engender opportunities for practicing imagery and conversation in the absence of external social stimulation.

It is worth noting that in general we have found a higher frequency of the occurrence of imaginary playmates than occurs in other reports where the percentages are closer to one-third of children (Jersild, Markey, & Jersild, 1933; Manosevitz, Prentice, & Wilson, 1973). This difference may in part reflect somewhat different ways of asking the question, some differences in the ages of the children, and also some differences in the definition of an imaginary playmate. Jersild, Markey, Jersild (1933) had reported that 79% of the children in a study they conducted had at least some clearly anthromorphized dolls or objects and our data do include reports by parents on transformations of stuffed animals into presumably living, human-like properties. We did not, however, count teddy bears or dolls where these were used to be carried around or treated in concrete fashion. Rather, there had to be a definitely humanizing quality and the treatment of the object as a friend or playmate. In this sense, Winnie-the-Pooh, Christopher Robin's elaborate enlivening of his little stuffed bear, would fall into the category of an imaginary playmate.

The sex differences we observed seem particularly interesting as they indicate important changes that are taking place in role relationships between boys and girls. The girls were more likely to transform their playmates into human rather than animal living beings and this would according to Ames and Learned (1964) place the girls higher on an "imagination gradient." Certainly, this seems in keeping with the generally greater verbal development of girls and is also in accord with the results described in other studies (Masih, 1978). Jersild (1968) has argued that these differences may simply reflect a cultural artifact because boys may be less willing to reveal private fantasies than girls. Certainly in free play in the nursery schools boys express more imagination than girls do (Singer, 1973), but in indications of home play we find more indications of imaginative behavior on the part of girls. Note that in the present study, the inner imagination variables, the inkblots, the imagination interview, and the imaginary companion index all loaded together on Factor 3, the factor that also showed fairly high loadings for girls.

The more frequent choice of opposite sex playmates by girls along with boys' emphasis on same sex imaginary companions is comparable to results reported by Manosevitz, Prentice, and Wilson (1973). There have been increasing reports on changing patterns of children's play (Singer & Singer, 1976b) all of which suggest that girls are moving in the boys' direction as far as games and playthings are concerned. Boys, conversely, have made very little movement toward adopting girls' games or toys.

One of the things we observed was that (in contrast with earlier studies of female aggression and television-viewing patterns such as the one carried out in the 1960s by Lefkowitz, Eron, Walder, & Huesmann, 1977) there are now female superheroes available for identification by girls. Indeed, some of our female subjects did include Bionic Woman or Wonder Woman among their fantasy friends. Girls also did include characters such as Superman or Batman. Boys, conversely, showed no such tendency and in general limited themselves chiefly to male superheroes when they chose characters from TV as imaginary playmates. It is likely this reflects a persisting dilemma in our society in which girls are being encouraged to broaden the scope of their own role relationships and identification patterns but a subtle but pervasive concern about homosexuality or demasculinization prevents boys from moving as freely toward adopting female fantasy playmates. As we note in looking at the issue of aggression, it is perhaps unfortunate that the heroic figures available for girls are primarily action-oriented and aggressive females. As we commented in chapter 4, it would be valuable if boys could be encouraged to move in the direction of greater tenderness and nurturance, the admirable traits that women have always shown.

In general, then, our data indicate that children do show considerable numbers of imaginary playmates. Indeed, it would be hard to argue that the occurrence of such make-believe friends suggests an inherent emotional disturbance or signs of serious conflict. Rather, make-believe friends seem to be common at least amongst the relatively middle-class children who made up the present sample. It is also clear that at least some proportion of make-believe friends are indeed drawn from television personalities although the majority of make-believe friends either reflect actual friends the children have or are combinations of figures overheard stories, television, or simply creative original products of the childrens' developing imaginative capacity.

IMAGINARY PLAYMATES AND OVERT BEHAVIOR, AGGRESSION, AND LANGUAGE AND TELEVISION-VIEWING

As suggested earlier, we were particularly interested in looking at the imaginary companion variable as an indication of a more general imaginative tendency in the child. We had in effect hypothesized that if imagination is evident in home play, at least in this form, it should manifest itself in the spontaneous play the child shows in nursery school and also should be linked to more positive emotionality, more persistent and elaborated sequences of play, less overt aggression, and more extensive language usage. We also were interested in determining whether there might be an inverse relationship between the occurrence of imaginary playmates and television-viewing frequency.

One way of looking at the data is to divide children into those with and without imaginary playmates and then look at their scores on the behavior variables for each of the four probes and for the cumulative means across the entire year on observed variables during play, language, and TV-viewing. Results from these analyses are not very conclusive. There are variations in consistency from probe to probe in the patterning. In general children whose parents reported them as having imaginary playmates at home also did show more imaginativeness in their spontaneous play in nursery school, more positive emotionality during such play, more cooperative behavior with adults, and somewhat more extended language usage. Parents' logs also indicated that the imaginary playmate group was watching less television.

Our data are much more clear-cut when drawn on the entire sample and rely on the quantitative scores available from the imaginary companion index and from the frequency of play with imaginary companion scores and include these in multiple regression analyses predicting the play variables, the language variables, and the TV-viewing. The advantage of multiple regression is that it takes into account the overall patterning of a group of variables as they predict a single criterion and in a sense comes closer to the way things work in real life. When we included the imaginary companion index along with age, IQ, socioeconomic status, ethnicity, imagination interview, and Barron Inkblots as predictor variables in looking at the children's scores on overt behavior and language, indications were that the imaginary playmate scores were consistently chosen early in stepwise multiple regression formulae and that in general they made sizable contributions to the best ordering of variables producing significant multiple Rs.

In general, for boys in a multiple regression equation that yielded a multiple correlation (R) of .609 among background variables, TV, and imaginativeness of play (the criterion), the best predictors included whether or not the children were watching cartoons, social class, age, and the imaginary companion variable. Indeed, the imaginary companions measure yielded a standardized coefficient of .25, significant at $p = .034$, and accounting for .046 of the unique variance. Attempting to predict the occurrence of positive affect during play the group of variables yielded a multiple R of .73, F = 7.75, $p < .001$. Variables contributing to this equation included the degree of intensity or the concentration children showed watching TV at home according to parent logs (standardized coefficient = .41; $p < .001$; unique variance = .133) and the imaginary companion index (standard coefficient =

.869, $p < .001$, unique variance = .225), as well as indications of negative relationships with the amount of television watched and a positive relationship with the watching of Public Television children's shows. The imaginary playmate variable was evidently the strongest single variable in the equation, however. This outcome is strongly supportive of the findings reported by Manosevitz et al. (1973) who also found that parents reported that children who had imaginary companions seemed to be happier and showed more positive attitudes. Our data of course are based in this case on direct observation of the emotions shown by the children during play. In the equation designed to predict the degree of persistence the child shows during play, age, and IQ are obviously highly relevant and show strong statistical results, but the imaginary companion index also entered strongly into the equation with a highly significant contribution and accounted for the highest percentage of unique variance (.225) in the equation that ultimately yields a multiple R of .56.

Of special importance is the equation generated in the effort to predict overt aggressive behavior in boys. Ultimately, only four variables entered into this equation. These data yielded a multiple R of .595, with an F of 10.12, and $p < .001$. Again, in this case, the intensity of play with imaginary companions reported by the parents for the child turned out to enter strongly in a negative way into this equation. This result suggests that boys who have imaginary playmates at home and who watch few action-adventure TV shows (see Chapter 6) are much less likely to turn out to be aggressive in overt behavior.

Of particular interest is the attempt to predict the degree of cooperation with peers, the sharing and helping which the child shows in overt behavior with other children. Here the imaginary companion variable turns out to be the major contributor to the extremely high overall multiple R which is produced, R = .97, F = 97.3, $p < .001$. Indeed the imaginary companion variable yields a standardized coefficient of 2.103, $p < .001$, and contributes a unique variance of .58 to the equation. It is worth noting, also, that watching of children's shows and adult programs including news, sports, cartoons, and action shows are negatively associated with the likelihood of cooperative behavior with peers in overt play according to this analysis. Similar results obtained for a number of the emotional variables with the variable of imaginary companions more likely to occur as predictor of positive emotions and negatively linked to somewhat more negative affective states such as fatigue and sluggishness. Particularly striking was the contribution of the imaginary companion measure to the prediction of fearfulness with indications that having an imaginary companion would be less likely to lead to the occurrence of signs of fearfulness or anxiety during a play situation.

Multiple regression results for girls showed some differences. Imaginary playmates did not predict spontaneous imaginative play in the girls although the girls' own imagination interview responses showed a trend in this direction. The imaginary playmate index also did not play a critical role in the prediction of positive affect for the girls. It is of interest, however, that watching of action shows was a negative contributor to whether or not girls would show positive emotions in spontaneous play. With respect to persistence during play, the imaginary companion index was an important contributor for girls. In the case of predicting overt aggressive behavior in girls, the imaginary companion index entered into the equation but in nonsignificant fashion. Watching of television seemed to be a more significant factor in the extent to which girls showed overt aggressive behavior.

It was in relation to cooperation with other children that the imaginary companion index made an especially strong contribution to the prediction equation for girls. As a matter of fact, the imaginary companion variable was clearly the most potent contributor to a group of variables that eventually led to a multiple R of .76, F = 4.26, $p < .001$. The imaginary companion index yielded a standardized coefficient of 1.78, $p < .001$ with .338 unique variance. It is interesting to note that the watching of action shows on television or of sports also entered strongly into this equation in a negative fashion, whereas the watching of educational television children's shows entered in positively in predicting cooperation with peers. Similar results are obtained in predicting cooperation with adults by the children. Again the imaginary playmate variable has a major contribution to make. With respect to the various emotions shown by the girls, it is clear that the imaginary companion variable is a strong contributor with a negative coefficient to the prediction of anger and fearfulness of the girls during play behavior. A similar very strong finding emerges for the occurrence of sadness by the girls during play.

Essentially similar results were obtained when we combined both sexes and carried out multiple regression analyses of the means across these groups.

In the attempt to predict the language the children used during play, best results were of course obtained for age and IQ. For boys the number of words spoken by the child and the mean length of utterances produced during play periods were at least partially explained by the imaginary playmate variable that accounted for .05 and .06 of the variance of each of those variables as part of the total equation ($p < .05$). In general the imaginary playmate variable did not contribute strongly to the prediction of language usage by the girls.

When the amount of television the child watched was used as the criterion to be predicted by behavioral and background variables, the imaginary playmate variable was a sizable negative contributor to the equation for boys and it accounted for .40 of the unique variance ($p < .001$) in the equation that ultimately yielded a multiple correlation of .84. In other words, boys who had no imaginary playmates were watching more TV. When the same analysis was performed for girls, no clear results emerged.

The ability of the imaginary playmate variable to predict imaginative play, persistence, cooperation with peers, and general happiness during spontaneous play seems to indicate that the extent to which a child has such fantasy companions at home may indeed reflect a more general indication of the child's imaginative capacity. The data are somewhat stronger for boys than for girls, perhaps because the girls show somewhat less variability; they tend to be more likely to have imaginary companions than do the boys.

Our results clearly do not support popular belief that imaginary companions are especially likely to occur among shy or maladjusted children. If anything, the evidence that a child has an imaginary playmate seems to be especially powerful predictor of the likelihood that a child will play happily in nursery school, will be cooperative with friends and adults, and may use somewhat more extensive language as well as being somewhat less likely to watch a good deal of television. Again the evidence of cooperative behavior with adults is comparable to the report of Manosevitz, Prentice, and Wilson (1973) in which children with imaginary playmates turned out to be actually more adept at talking with adults according to their parents' report. We did find that those children who had imaginary companions were more likely to be watching the educational or Public Television programs, such as "Mister Rogers' Neighborhood" and "Sesame Street."

Finally, let us take a look at some examples of the actual imaginary companions described in the responses by parents.

A young girl had a playmate called "Johnny" whom she actually called her "pretend friend." He was capable of changing his size and sometimes became so small that he could live under the dishwasher.

Another boy had an imaginary companion called "Giles" who was actually the name of a rather aggressive boy he encountered at school. He pretended that the family's new home was actually Gile's home and then made believe that Giles was sleeping in his own bed.

A young boy had an imaginary companion with no specific name but who was apparently an elf who engaged in scaring monsters away and sprinkling magic dust on a toy truck to make it appear quite huge. When the boy was especially frightened, he frequently called on his elfin friend to help him. When he was especially happy and had a new plaything or toy he made a special point of showing it to his imaginary elf.

Still another boy had as his imaginary playmate a perennial companion called "Sadie" who was a fox cub apparently derived from a library book that had been read to him. To this young lad, according to parents, Sadie is "warm, cuddly, brave, strong, kind, generous, intelligent, and has magical powers." The mother speculated that Sadie may be a substitute for a brother or a sister.

And then of course there is the young girl who had no less than five imaginary husbands. Her favorite was called "Flier" and was apparently attending high school or college. The others each had more conventional names. "Flier" was often described as engaging in mischievous acts while riding on a school bus. He had been described as being short with brown hair and wore an orange shirt. The parents had acknowledged him and had to talk with him at their daughter's request.

An unusual and intriguing example of an imaginary playmate was brought to our attention by the mother of grown children who heard of our work in this area after it had been presented at a professional meeting. She reported that she had twin daughters who shared an imaginary playmate between the ages of 3 and 5. The playmate was an ethereal creature named Fetiss. The girls treated her as if she were very real, however, and she accompanied them everywhere and shared their bed at night. Despite the shared fantasy the girls grew up to go somewhat separate ways in life, one as an artist and teacher, the other as a physician. The origin of this odd name had not struck the mother. She was pregnant with another child during the months of the development of the fantasy but could not recall anyone ever using the word "fetus" around the children during this period!

The imaginary playmate is indeed a fascinating phenomenon of the stage of life between ages 2 and 5. It seems in many ways a manifestation of a kind of effort of the child to deal with the situation when its own cognitive capacities, its increasingly complex stores or memories, and imagery capacity have moved beyond its own powers of movement, size, or freedom of locomotion. The development of a fantasy friend may be one of the first great creative acts of the growing child.

6 Television-Viewing and Aggression: Play Observations

How many parents might willingly introduce into their homes two neighborhood toughs who would daily demonstrate for their children physical fighting and violence as a way of resolving problems? It can be argued that, considering the remarkably high level of violent activity demonstrated on the television (Gerbner & Gross, 1976), regular exposure of children to this medium may be serving much the same effect as suggested in the fantasy question just raised. The possibility that widespread watching by children and youth is increasing the level of violence in American society continues to be the most controversial and emotionally arousing issue related to the television medium. Before turning to some of the findings of our current research report which bear on this subject, it may be useful to review briefly some of the major dimensions of the arguments and counterarguments concerning the link between television-viewing and acts of violence in children and adolescents.

THEORIES OF AGGRESSION AND THEIR RELATIONSHIP TO TELEVISION

Two major alternative positions have dominated the thinking of behavioral scientists concerning the nature of aggression and violence during the twentieth century. The most popular and widely believed theory has been espoused by many clinically oriented psychiatrists, psychologists, or mental health workers as well as in the popular writings of ethologists like Lorenz (1966). This position has also appeared to be most accepted by the general public. It is the theory that aggression as a fundamental human drive or motive is at least partially satisfied by vicarious experience or symbolic expression such as the viewing of aggressive films, plays, or athletic contests. Such instinct or drive theories of aggression are traceable to the influence of McDougall (1908) and Freud (1920/ 1955).

In the very influential studies of aggression as a consequence of frustration presented by the Yale group (Dollard, Doob, Miller, Mowrer, & Sears, 1939), implications of the drive theory of aggression were worked out in detail and in a form suitable for experimental research. One major implication of this work was that symbolic experiences of aggression could partially reduce an aroused drive. This notion, a scientific translation of Aristotle's early concept of *catharsis,* has served as a major argument for the position that people are naturally attracted to watching aggression and also that such viewing prevents excessive violence in the society by partially reducing some of the inevitable drives we all experience.

In effect, this position represents aggression either as an innate drive that builds up pressure for discharge and will emerge in the form of acts of violence (Lorenz, 1966) or as an inherent response potentiality that will be an inevitable consequence of the fact that most of us experience frequent frustrations (Dollard et al., 1939). Such a view can be used by writers, producers of television shows, or industry representatives to argue that people have always had a taste for watching violence, from the days of the Roman circuses through the public hangings and executions of the eighteenth and nineteeth centuries and the considerable violence represented in theatre and literature. Shakespeare's *Titus Andronicus* has more than a dozen acts of violence on stage and his greatest plays, *King Lear* and *Hamlet,* include the public tearing out of an old man's eyes and various poisonings and stabbings onstage. The Metropolitan Opera in New York City, which advertises itself as a center of civilization, regularly performs Richard Strauss' twentieth-century opera, *Salome.* At the end of this work the young princess kisses the mouth of the severed head of John the Baptist and sings passionately to this bloody object before she is crushed to death by the soldiers of King Herod at the curtain. By comparison with such violence in our classics the battles of cowboys or miniature figures of embattled cops and robbers on a 15- or 19-inch screen may conceivably be taken rather lightly or at least some may argue that they serve a cathartic role in reducing the aggressive tendencies of the viewers.

The second major position concerning the nature of aggression and its implications for popular media like television has developed only in the last 15 years with the emergence in psychology of what might be called social learning or cognitive-affective models of personality. Major theoretical and research positions have been generated by Buss (1971), Berkowitz (1969), and Bandura (1973). Buss has pointed out again and again that aggressive behavior is strongly supported by many aspects of society. It has a clear payoff value. This socially reinforcing factor alone can explain many of the violent actions humans undertake rather than assumed innate drives or instincts. Berkowitz has demonstrated in a variety of researches by himself and various collaborators and students that social conditions surrounding the observing of violence will determine what the reaction of an individual will be and that under most circumstances watching film violence may lead to an *increase* of aggressive behavior rather than to a decrease.

Bandura (1973) has carried out perhaps the most careful and detailed theoretical analysis of the nature of aggression from the standpoint of a theory of social learning. His extensive experimental work has indicated very clearly that children do imitate observed acts of aggression whether carried out by live adults or filmed models. Bandura has reviewed extensively all of the arguments favoring catharsis and has generated specific research to demonstrate that for young children there is a much greater likelihood that they will imitate observed violence rather than reduce their inclinations to such actions on the basis of vicarious experience. Even more recently, Baron (1977) has elaborated the view that violence is supported by social reinforcement and also by the cognitive awareness of the range of possible responses and of the specific instigations for aggression in a situation.

Clearly the social learning position would argue that exposure of children and adolescents to extensive demonstrations of violence is not a trivial question. Rather than reducing the likelihood that such children will engage in daily life acts of violence, the research of the social learning theorists argues that the likelihood of aggressive behavior will be facilitated by exposure to numerous examples of how human beings can hurt each other in various situations. They argue, further, that television not only demonstrates how to attack others but that it may reduce some of the sensitivities to pain which most of us share to some degree (Cline, Croft, & Courrier, 1973) as well as providing a basic moral support for violence because the good guy often ends the story by beating up or shooting the bad guy (Singer & Singer, 1977b).

A somewhat related position to the social learning point of view has emerged from research studies that have emphasized the general arousal properties of the nature of the television medium itself (Tannenbaum & Zillmann, 1975; Watt & Krull, 1977). These studies and theoretical analyses suggest that the very nature of the television medium with its rapid changes and efforts at producing high levels of emotional reactivity may simply lead to a more generally aroused organism and thus increase the chances of an aggressive response following exposure to TV. Individual clinicians have pointed to the possibility that a program like *"Sesame Street"* with its rapid cuts and material may not only hold the children's attention on the screen (as the technique is intended to do) but may also lead to increased hyperactivity and motoric predisposition to violence (Halpern, 1975; Singer, 1980).

Much of the support for the instinctive or frustration-aggression drive hypothesis continues to come from philosophers or literary critics who call attention to the wide and pervasive nature of human aggressive behavior, the recurrences throughout history of mass incidents of destruction, and also to the high degree of violence carried out within families between individuals tied together not only by law and birth but also by affection (Fiedler, 1966; Marcuse, 1966; Trilling, 1950). Freud's position was that the inevitable recurrence of the "death instinct," however defended against by the development of cultural structures from chess through cathedrals or Leagues of Nations, will confront us with the likelihood of an eruption of overt violence. This so-called tragic view of human existence is regarded by some as a most honest and realistic appraisal of our human situation (Trilling, 1950).

In contrast with this powerful philosophical view or with the enticing reports of Lorenz (1966) or Ardrey (1966) presumably based on wide observations of various animal species, the extensive experimental literature developed by behavioral scientists seems on the whole to argue for a social learning theory for the manifestation of aggression (Bandura, 1973; Baron, 1977; Scott, 1972). Laboratory studies with animals point again and again to the possibility that early social experience makes an important difference in the extent to which animals will later become aggressive even in their feeding behavior (Bandura, 1973; Scott, 1972). Literally dozens of experiments with human beings under reasonably controlled conditions point out again and again the extent to which aggressive behavior can be increased or modified by the nature of the social setting, the nature of the social instigation provided or by the available information in a situation (Bandura, 1973; Baron, 1977).

The best available evidence on the development of aggression in children derives from studies that indicate that family patterns are critical in the emergence of violence. Children who have been exposed to at least one and often two parents who themselves are physically aggressive to conditions of rejection or brutalization in the home turn out to be more likely to be aggressive or antisocial. The absence of opportunities for learning alternative forms of coping with frustration other than through the socially supported means of aggression combine with indices of parental aggression or rejection to be the most effective predictors that children will become aggressive in later life (Lefkowitz, Eron, Walder, & Huesmann, 1977; McCord, McCord, & Howard, 1969). Broader sociocultural evidence for particular patterns of violence such as those that can be clearly demonstrated in regions of the United States in which the ratio of homicides to suicides is much higher than elsewhere (Graham & Gurr, 1969) further support the implications of a social learning or cognitive analysis of the nature of aggression.

RESEARCH ON THE SPECIFIC EFFECTS OF TELEVISION IN RELATION TO AGGRESSION

Until the early 1970s an extensive review of available literature could only draw the conclusion that experimental studies in laboratory settings indicated that children might imitate aggressive models but no really convincing evidence supported the belief that extensive or violent television content viewing generated aggressive behavior (Singer, 1971). In the next six years with support from a number of government agencies and the incentive of the U.S. Surgeon-General's Committee on Television and Social Behavior a sizable number of studies emerged and provided a somewhat clearer picture. The extensive laboratory studies generated by Bandura (1971, 1973) made it clear that modeling of violent aggression can be demonstrated in young children. The work of Stein, Friedrich, and Vondracek (1972) demonstrated that children at play in nursery school settings will increase the level of aggression following daily viewings of a program like "Batman." Friedrich and Stein (1975) also were able to demonstrate in this and in an earlier study that children exposed to constructive materials on television would increase in pro-social behavior. Studies by Noble (1970, 1973, 1975) also point to aggressive outcomes in short-term controlled studies of children's play following exposure to aggressive film.

In general, the research evidence based on laboratory studies or short-term follow-ups (Murray, Comstock, & Rubinstein, 1972) make it clear that, at the very least, those children already predisposed to be aggressive who were exposed to television representations of violence are likely to increase their levels of aggressive behavior. Thus the evidence on the whole fails to support a catharsis theory and is inclined to support at least to some extent the facilitative role of television in producing aggressive behavior in children.

Whereas some studies (Feshbach & Singer, 1971; Milgram & Shotland, 1974) have yielded negative results as far as the antisocial implications of the medium there are indications from longer term studies that some correlation between overt aggressive behavior and television-viewing can be demonstrated. It has often been argued that laboratory research does not capture the essence of the actual television-viewing situation in which children partake. That is, most children watch TV at home, alone or with siblings or occasionally parents day after day over long periods of time. Indeed, if imitation of violence was as potent as is suggested by specific laboratory experiments one could argue that the sheer amount of violence presented on television alone ought to drive millions of people into the streets in daily rampages. Clearly this has not occurred and some social scientists and many more industry representatives are inclined therefore to minimize possible affects of the high degree of aggression portrayed in television fiction, documentaries or news.

Bandura (1973) has argued that the laboratory research primarily demonstrates an inherent potential of human beings. It supports a theoretical argument about the nature of imitative behavior. Other research may be useful in demonstrating the extent of the occurrence of the phenomenon and certain other conditions for its occurrence but the possibility of imitation is clearly present on the basis of the cumulative laboratory research evidence. Studies by Bailyn (1959; Chaffee, 1972; Schramm, Lyle, & Parker, 1961) have all followed up children over longer periods of time and related their television-viewing to measures of overt aggressive behavior. In general these studies do show positive correlations on the order of + .25. Such a result although not a powerful effect in predicting whether a *given* child who watches television is likely to be aggressive is nevertheless of theoretical importance in indicating that of all of the many possible causes for aggression there is at least some evidence that television-viewing does indeed play a significant if modest role.

By far, the most telling study to date has been that carried out by Lefkowitz, Eron, Walder, & Huesmann (1977). This research involved a 10-year follow-up of boys and girls originally studied in the third grade as part of a general study of the origins of aggressive behavior. These investigators found, first of all, consistent differences in aggressive behavior between boys and girls. The more aggressive boys also turned out to be more regular viewers of aggressive television. They also found that *"the greater was a boy's preference for violent television at age nine, the greater was his aggressiveness both at that time and ten years later.* The boy's preference for violent television correlated .21 ($p < .01$) with its concurrent peer-rated aggressiveness and .31 ($p < .001$) with his aggressiveness ten years later" (Lefkowitz et al., 1977, pp. 115–116). *In fact, what these authors have reported is that one of the single best predictors at age 9 of whether a boy will be aggressive on various ratings 10 years later is the amount of violent television programming he is watching.*

This study goes to extremely careful lengths to support the argument that the link between TV-viewing and aggression may indeed be a causal one rather than simply a reflection of two concomitant behavior patterns, the enjoyment of violence on TV and the inclination to be aggressive. The investigators' data indicate that it is possible to rule out controlling effects of intelligence, social class, or family background as a means of explaining the correlation between violence viewing and subsequent aggression. Thus the Lefkowitz et al. data turn out to be as yet the most telling evidence that watching violence by boys can have effects on increasing potential violence in later life.

The results for girls are if anything in the opposite direction, and their extensive analyses suggest the possibility that because of the greater support for aggression in boys by this society those girls who are initially aggressive subsequently may find an outlet in watching aggressive TV largely because they cannot express this behavior overtly. Another important point they make is that in the 1960s when the study was done, there were relatively few models of aggressive behavior in women on television. As we see later, in our own research this situation has drastically changed as a consequence of a somewhat questionable response to the movement for women's liberation. The heightened visibility of aggressive female models such as "The Bionic Woman, "Wonder Woman," "Police Woman," or "Charlie's Angels" have made available to girls a type of aggressive response for women that was not a part of the medium until the mid-1970s. The study by Lefkowitz et al. was carried out with children already in elementary school. More recently, Belson (1978) has looked at a group of boys in London who are between the ages of 12 and 17 and has followed their TV patterns and aggressive behavior over time. Belson's evidence suggests that watching of aggressive material on television particularly that associated with relatively realistic violent activities rather than slapstick comedy or cartoons is associated with aggressive behavior. It might be argued, however, that preschoolers might be likely to be influenced even by humorous or cartoon representations of violence because they are less capable of making some of the cognitive distinctions necessary between the context and realism of violence presented (Singer, 1978).

LINKS BETWEEN TELEVISION-VIEWING AND BEHAVIOR OF PRESCHOOLERS: IMPLICATIONS AND LIMITATIONS

The present study is the first to attempt to follow preschool children over an extended time period and to examine the tie between television-viewing and aggressive behavior. In this respect the study sought to look at relative beginners both in the areas of watching TV and in using aggression in behavior. Clearly if there is a major causal tie between frequency or type of television-viewing and the emergence of aggressive trends in children, we should be able to identify this as we track the children over a year which is so sizable a proportion of their total life span to date. In a sense we may have the opportunity to identify the very beginnings of preferences in viewing of television at the same time as we watch the first efforts at using violence by 3 and 4-year-olds.

The reader should keep in mind that when we talk of aggression in this study we are referring very specifically to the definition presented to our observers and raters. We have scored acts of aggression primarily within the scope of attacks on other children (or, in very rare cases, adults) or on the property of others, and we have been very careful to avoid defining as aggression instances of play acting in which a child pretends to shoot another child or hits two sticks together simulating a fight between imagined cowboys.

The present report is limited only to an examination of links between television and overt aggressive acts by the children. Indeed we should be careful in stressing that our definition does not literally count up the number of acts of aggression in a 10-minute period or over a year for a child. Rather, the child is rated as aggressive within a given 10-minute period and we then look at the correlation between aggression at Time 1 through Time 8, the independent observation periods in the study.

It is important to notice as a qualification of our results that we are not dealing with violent children. Indeed the word "violence" is inappropriate in this study because very few of the children ever attacked another with the kind of intensity that merits such a strong term. We are dealing with early manifestations of pushing, shoving, knocking over of others' toys, forcefully pulling at other's property, and minor acts of scratching or kicking. Even the most aggressive segment of our sample averages no more than a score between 2 and 3 on a five-point scale. In general, boys were consistently more aggressive than girls and only a very small percentage of the girls ever showed any aggression at all over the year's time. Nevertheless, it was possible to separate out those few girls who did show aggressive behavior and to obtain meaningful data by comparing them with the less aggressive girls.

It might also be argued that we are perhaps tipping the scales in our presentation toward a view of aggression as a potentially negative or antisocial response. Many parents might argue that aggression is a necessary response for survival in a society. It may reflect an early self-assertion that can be ultimately useful, an indicator of potential manliness in boys and of effective self-protection for girls. Although we cannot deny others the right to such values, we have tried in the present study to look carefully at the types of aggressive behavior manifested and are inclined to believe that these in general have not reflected effective behavior for these small children but rather have put them in some jeopardy of extensive repercussions either from other children or in bringing down on themselves the wrath of the adults and indeed developing early an image amongst adults as undesirable children.

What follows then in this report is a presentation of the ratings for boys and girls in our sample of their aggressive behavior or of their manifestations of anger as an affect closely linked to the likely occurrence of aggression with the patterns of television-viewing they have shown in the four probe periods over the year. As we see later, we have made an effort to look at other available indications of ties between background variables such as social class or IQ with aggression and we have gone a step further by interviewing in the home the mothers of children who showed over the year extremes of overt aggressive behavior and television-viewing.

AGE, SEX, AND PROBE PERIOD TRENDS IN AGGRESSION

The major differences in relation to group or time effects are a function of the sex of the child. Girls show significantly less aggressive behavior than do boys on a three way repeated measure analysis of variance ($F = 20.2$, df = 1,115, $p < .001$). In general there are no differences in aggression between the 3-

year-old and 4-year-old boys and very little evidence of increase over the years' span. In the case of the girls, again, we see little difference between the 3s and 4s and very little indication of increase for the group as a whole over the year's time. If we combine the means for boys and girls there is a slight but nonsignificant trend for our entire sample to increase in the amount of aggression manifested during the year.

Of interest is the fact that there is essentially no difference between TV-viewing patterns of the 3- and 4-year-old boys with respect to the watching of the especially violent shows. Both groups showed some falling off in viewing after the first probe (possibly a general effect of the intervention procedure). Girls show a consistent drop with age with the highest TV-viewing manifested by the 3-year-olds in the first probe and a consistent drop for them throughout the year. The 4-year-old girls already are well below the 3-year-old girls when the watching of action-detective shows and the frequency of viewing drops off considerably so that for this age group by the end of the year one can say that only 30% have watched any action shows at all compared with viewing ratios around 60% for the other groups.

CORRELATIONS BETWEEN TELEVISION-VIEWING AND AGGRESSION

We have already presented a factor analysis of the various dimensions of observed play, television-viewing, language usage, and background variables. A separate factor analysis for the sexes again yields Factor 2 that can clearly be called a television-aggression factor. For boys we see heavy loadings of .84 for weekday TV, .72 for action-detective shows, .72 for adult shows, and so on, whereas aggression loads .55 on the factor, cooperation with adults loads negatively at -.33, anger loads at .525, and socioeconomic status loads .47 (indicating higher loadings for lower SES groups), and ethnicity also loads .32 (indicating higher loadings for Hispanic or Black participants). This factor suggests that for the boys we do find a clustering of variables suggesting that television-viewing is systematically linked to behavioral variables as well as to certain background factors of social class and ethnicity. A boy who watches a great deal of television and therefore would score high on this factor would also be more likely to be aggressive, less cooperative with the adults, and more likely to show flashes of anger during spontaneous play. Essentially the same result emerges for girls with overt aggression loading .603 on this factor but with lower loadings for anger (.283) and with some indication that IQ (-.327) as well as SES are involved.

This factor reflects specific patterns of correlation between television-viewing frequency and also specifically the action-detective television program and overt aggression in spontaneous behavior. Table 6.1 presents the correlations of weekly television-viewing and aggression for each probe of the

TABLE 6.1
Contemporaneous Correlations Of Overt Aggression Ratings And
Television-Viewing

Probe Period	Boys	Girls	Total Sample
Aggression with Weekly Total Television-Viewing			
February 1977	.32***	.04	.24**
April 1977	.26	.26*	.30***
October 1977	.03	.68***	.24*
February 1978	.23*	−.21*	.14
Mean Scores Across Four Probes	.31***	.54***	.35***
Aggression with Viewing of Action Shows			
February 1977	.01	−.11	.05
April 1977	.24*	.17	.25**
October 1977	.19*	.64***	.34***
February 1978	.19*	−.01	.18*
Mean Scores Across Four Probes	.32***	.41**	.33***

Note: Parent intervention began in the spring of 1977 and some of its effects may be influencing results in the October 1977 and February 1978 probes.

*$p < .05$; **$p < .01$; ***$p < .001$.

longitudinal study by sex and for the total sample. From this table correlations for the final means summing correlations across the four probe periods are significant and positive. Thus for aggression and weekly television the correlation for boys is .31, $p < .001$, and for girls it is .54, $p < .001$, with the average correlation for the total sample of boys and girls together of .35, $p < .001$. If we then look at the relationship between overt aggression and watching of the action shows, we obtain correlations of .32, $p < .001$, for boys, of .41, $p < .001$, for girls and a total across sexes of .33, $p < .001$. In effect, we see that our correlations are accounting for from 10 to 25% of the variance, a result that is comparable and indeed stronger than that reported in earlier studies cited (Bailyn, 1959; Lefkowitz et al., 1977).

MULTIVARIATE RELATIONSHIPS

The next step is to examine more carefully whether we can identify which combination of variables best predicts the likelihood that a child will be physically aggressive in school or will show emotions like anger that are likely to be associated with aggressive behavior. For boys the action-detective shows and the watching of news turn out to be significant predictors of aggression ($R^2 = .35$, $F = 10.1$, df = 4,74, $p < .001$) and of anger ($R^2 = .34$, $F = 6.2$, df = 6,72, $p < .001$). For girls watching sports programs, situation-comedies, and cartoons combine to contribute to the prediction of aggression ($R^2 = .45$, $F = 9.24$, df = 5,56, $p < .001$), although the viewing of sports, action shows, situation-comedies, variety/game shows, and adult-family shows all combine significantly to contribute to the prediction of anger ($R^2 = .77$, $F = 10.5$, df = 15.46, $p < .001$). If we combine the sexes, it turns out that the viewing of action shows, news shows, variety-game shows, and the total amount of weekend television-watching are significant predictors of aggression ($R^2 = .489$, $F = 9.3$, df = 13, 127, $p < .001$) and the watching of weekend television, of variety/game shows, the news, and sports all contribute significantly to the prediction of anger ($R^2 = 3.324$, $F = 4.7$, df = 13, 127, $p < .001$).

Of course, demographic or background variables such as SES, IQ, and ethnic background also enter into our prediction formulae. We deal shortly with the extent to which the correlation between aggression and television is a function of a more general relationship between aggression and one of these background factors or whether the relationship between TV and aggression holds up even when we eliminate the effect of such broader variables.

Another form of multivariate methodology involves the use of a canonical correlation analysis. This is a method that in effect correlates *clusters* of variables with each other rather than simply examining individual correlates. One thus generates a matrix from whose patterning we can estimate the extent to which groups of variables in effect line up together. Canonical correlational analysis was carried out, looking at the television-viewing and behavioral variables. It yielded one significant canonical variate ($\chi^2 = 244.59$, df = 175, $p < .001$, eigenvalue = .70, canonical correlation = .84). On the first set of variables, television-viewing, amount of weekly television, cartoons, variety/game shows, adult-oriented shows, and action-detective shows load highly positively (with the action-detective shows showing the highest loading), whereas intensity of concentration during home television-viewing and the frequency of watching Educational TV programs such as "Mister Rogers' Neighborhood" or "Sesame Street" load *negatively* on this variable group. On the second set of variables defining this canonical variate we find aggression, anger, sadness, liveliness, or gross motor activity, the use of television references in spontaneous language, and socioeconomic status all loading positively, whereas IQ, fatigue-sluggishness and the mean length of utterances all load highly negatively. Loadings are presented in Table 6.2. Because frequency of television-viewing and weekend and weekday viewing are all essentially cumulative variables derived from the total of the particular

TABLE 6.2
Canonical Correlation Analyses Of Television-Viewing With Behavior And Language
Variables

Variable	Loadings on First Canonical Variate
Television Variables (Set 1)	
Weekly TV	.78
Cartoons	.69
Variety/Game Shows	.75
Adult Family Dramas	.42
Action/Adventure	.82
TV Intensity (Concentration at Home)	−.19
Public TV Children's Shows (Educational TV)	−.21
Behavior, Language Variables (Set 2)	
Aggression	.46
Anger	.31
Sadness	.20
Liveliness	.28
TV References	.27
Future Verbs	.26
Socioeconomic Status	.61
Race	.39
IQ	−.22
Fatigue-Sluggishness	−.22
Mean Length of Utterances	−.19

types of programming we also carried out the canonical analysis omitting them and also omitting the background variables in order to reduce the number of variables in the analysis and increase its power. The same results were still obtained. When we score the various *categories* of television-viewing not in absolute hours but as proportions of total TV frequency we still obtain similar results.

Essentially this analysis, although not greatly different from the Factor 2 in the factor analysis, does provide even a sharper focus on the pattern of relationships between home television-viewing and overt behavior. Thus we see in the canonical correlation the fact that there is indeed a link between the style of home viewing with a special emphasis of action-oriented shows and with relatively little watching of the more "benign" programming and less intense concentration characterizing viewing being linked to more negative patterns of behavior in general such as aggression, anger, and sadness. The indications are also present that, of the language variables we pick up, the relatively high use of television references in play goes along with aggression.

PARTIAL CORRELATION ANALYSIS:
CAN SOCIAL CLASS, IQ, OR RACE
ACCOUNT FOR THE LINK BETWEEN
TV-VIEWING AND AGGRESSION?

It has generally been reported that children from lower socioeconomic backgrounds are not only more likely to be physically aggressive in play but also more likely to be allowed to stay up late and watch adult programming. Similarly, it might be argued that ethnic background, which of course is in part related to cultural differences that characterize poorer segments of the society, may also play a part in encouraging children not only to be more aggressive but also to watch more television. Finally a similar argument might be made about IQ. We have therefore systematically examined the relationship between TV-viewing frequency and aggression or TV-viewing frequency and anger as well as the relationships between the specific action-detective shows and aggression or action-detective shows and anger. Table 6.3 indicates the first-, second-, and third-order partial correlations between aggression or anger and television. It can be seen that the relationships between aggression and the television variables remain statistically significant even when all the background variables are controlled. The demographic variables seem to be more important as mediators of the relationship between expressions of anger during play and television than they are between aggression and television-viewing. They also seem somewhat more stronger for boys than for girls. These data are essentially comparable to those reported by Lefkowitz et al. (1977) with respect to their findings for background variables. A major difference between our study and the earlier one emerges in the consistent findings of positive correlations between the watching of action shows and aggressive behavior in *girls* even when all background factors are removed. This may reflect an important difference in the television fare now available to girls—the increased emphasis in current programming on aggressive female figures such as "Charlie's Angels" or "Wonder Woman."

In summary, our data suggest that there is indeed a strong and stable relationship between television-viewing and patterns of aggressive behavior in preschool children. This relationship holds for the general frequency of television-viewing and also for most specific types of programming with the exception that those children who are more likely to watch Educational TV shows such as "Sesame Street" and "Mister Rogers'" are somewhat less likely to be aggressive. The data also show parallel patterns for expressions of the emotion of anger during play.

This relationship between television and aggression is equally strong for 3-year-olds and 4-year-olds and also emerges for both sexes even though girls on the whole have been shown to be less aggressive than boys. The finding

TABLE 6.3

Contemporaneous Correlations Of Aggressive And Television-Viewing When Demographic Variables Are Partialled Out (Based on Mean Scores Across Four Probes For TV And Behavioral Variables) [N = 121]

Variable Pair	Original Correlation	1st, 2nd, & 3rd Order Partial Correlations Controlling for:						
		SES	Ethnic Gp.	IQ	SES-Ethnic	SES-IQ	Ethnic-IQ	SES-Ethnic-IQ
School Behavior TV-Viewing								
Total Sample								
Aggression-Weekly TV	.35***	.34***	.32***	.30***	.33***	.30***	.28***	.30***
Aggression-Action Shows	.33***	.31***	.28***	.28***	.29***	.29***	.24***	.25***
Anger-Weekly TV	.24**	.22***	.21**	.22**	.21**	.21**	.19*	.20*
Anger-Action Shows	.20**	.18*	.13	.18*	.13	.16*	.12	.11
Boys								
Aggression-Weekly TV	.31***	.28**	.28**	.22*	.29**	.22*	.22*	.23*
Aggression-Action Shows	.32***	.29**	.29***	.25*	.30**	.25*	.23*	.24*
Anger-Weekly TV	.24*	.23*	.20	.19	.24*	.21*	.19	.23*
Anger-Action Shows	.32***	.32***	.26*	.28**	.30**	.30**	.25*	.29**
Girls								
Aggression-Weekly TV	.54***	.51***	.53***	.54***	.50***	.52***	.53***	.51***
Aggression-Action Shows	.41***	.34**	.39***	.39***	.35*	.33**	.38***	.34***
Anger-Weekly TV	.25*	.18	.24*	.23*	.16	.16	.22*	.15
Anger-Action Shows	.00	-.09	-.04	-.01	-.15	.10	-.07	.18

*p < .05; **p < .01; ***p < .001.

also holds up even across the four probes when we keep in mind that there are great seasonal variations and a considerable drop in TV-viewing during the months of April and October (Probes 2 and 3) when there was more opportunities for children to play outdoors. Brighter children are less likely to show the correlation between TV-viewing and aggression. Children from lower SES or from the groups more subject to prejudice (Hispanics or Blacks) are also more likely to manifest the TV-aggression relationship. Nevertheless, removal of the influence of these background factors does not essentially change the correlations between aggression and TV. Across all of the analyses we find that the correlation between TV-viewing and aggression accounts for between 10 and 25% of all the variance in our data. These correlations are actually stronger than those reported by other investigators who have studied children across time. As Lefkowitz et al. (1977) point out, the likelihood is that younger children should show more direct modeling effects than older children or young adults and this is certainly what we seem to be observing.

Another way of looking at our data is simply to divide our subjects at midpoint on the score of aggression and then look at how they line up on other variables in the study. Those subjects who score high over the year on aggressive behavior in the school turn out to show significantly less persistence in play and cooperation with their peers, significantly more fear, much more anger and sadness and they also turn out to be watching twice as much television during weekdays as well as more overall weekly television. They show significantly more action show watching, cartoon watching and are *less* likely to show imaginative responses on the inkblot test. They also prove to be somewhat less intelligent. For girls the highly aggressive children show significantly more anger in their behavior, they are watching almost twice as much weekend and weekday TV and much more variety and game shows, situation-comedies, action-detective shows, and the like. The high aggressive girls do tend to come from a somewhat lower socioeconomic status group.

DOES TV-VIEWING CAUSE AGGRESSIVE BEHAVIOR IN PRESCHOOLERS?

Our data seem to establish pretty clearly that watching a good deal of television does covary with the likelihood that a child will show a greater amount of aggressive behavior during spontaneous play at the nursery school. Is it possible, however, to ascertain whether the television-viewing has a causal influence on the overt behavior? After all, it might be argued just as well that children who are inherently aggressive might simply prefer to watch aggressive material on television or might be inclined simply to abuse the opportunity to sit up late watching the medium just as they may abuse others' rights or property.

Because we have had an opportunity to observe these children over a year's time, it was possible to link the correlations between television-viewing variables and aggression or anger at different time periods, for example, Probe 1 versus Probe 2, Probe 2 versus Probe 3, and so on. Looking at the correlations of each variable with itself from one time period to the next and then for each variable with aggression across probes we can get some sense as to whether or not the amount of television-viewing at Time 1 leads to perhaps a greater relationship between television-viewing and aggression at Time 2 or whether there is simply a consistent covariation of TV frequency or action shows and aggression. These so-called cross-lag correlations between aggression and weekly TV or aggression and action programming have been carried out for all combinations of the 4 probes in the year. In Table 6.4 one observes that for Probes 1 and 2, the correlations between weekly TV in February and the occurrence of aggression in April is .22, ($p < .05$) and between action shows in February and aggression in April the correlation is .33 ($p < .001$). By contrast, if we look at the amount of aggression shown by children in February, it fails to show any correlation with subsequent weekly TV-viewing in April (r = .02) or with action shows (R = .08).

Similarly, if we look at the correlation between weekly TV in February, it correlates .27 ($p < .01$) with the emergence of aggression in October and action shows in February correlates .35 ($p < .001$) with the emergence of aggression in October. By contrast, there are again zero-order correlations for aggression in the first probe with the subsequent October viewing of weekly TV or of action shows.

Clearly then for these two sets of comparisons encompassing approximately a nine-month period, the initial level of TV-viewing and even more so of the viewing of action shows is more likely to predict subsequent aggression than is the initial level of aggression likely to predict later viewing of TV-action shows. This directional affect is less strong when we compare February 1977 with the following February 1978. Then, the amount of aggression shown in February 1977 turns out to be significantly related to the amount of TV watched in February 1978, r = .25, $p < = .01$). The correlation between TV at the initial time and the later emergence of aggression although positive is not significant. For the second and third probes these results are less conclusive when it comes to prediction of TV watching or the type of program watched in the fourth probe period. The amount of aggression shown in the second and third probes tends to be a better predictor of later watching than the reverse.

On the whole, these results are more or less comparable and indeed even stronger in the earlier probes for girls than for boys. The cross-lag correlation data thus seem to suggest that explanations that emphasize that watching television and in particular the watching of the more violent types of programming represented by the action shows will lead to subsequent

TABLE 6.4
Correlations Between Action Show Viewing And Subsequent Or Prior Behavioral Aggression Ratings

Mean Hours Watching Action Shows Probe	Overt Aggression Probe	Sample				
		Total Sample	Boys	Girls	3-Year-Olds	Control Group
1	2	.33***	.27**	.32**	.21*	.26
1	3	.35***	.28**	.40***	.37***	-.14
1	4	.16	.15	.19	.22*	.27
2	3	.22**	.19*	.24*	.31**	-.21
2	4	.08	-.02	.29*	.11	.20
3	4	.26**	.28**	.15	.43***	.38
2	1	.08	.12	-.14	.07	-.23
3	1	.04	.03	.10	.04	.23
4	1	.09	.11	-.14	.10	.18
3	2	.20*	.11	.23*	.12	.57*
4	2	.28*	.24*	.33**	.29*	.54*
4	3	.43*	.41***	.40***	.55***	.35

Note: Ns on which correlations are based may vary from group to group, thereby accounting for differing significance levels for similar correlation coefficients. Any intervention effects should be most evident between Probes 1-4, 2-4, 3-4. Control group should not reflect intervention effects.

*p < .05; **p < .01; ***p < .001.

aggressive behavior are strongly supported over at least a nine month period of our year study. There seems to be a reversal of direction with the overt aggressive trend leading to greater likelihood of later violent TV-viewing in the last probe period. Nevertheless, the overall trend of the data would seem to rule out the explanation that preestablished patterns of aggression serve primarily as a predisposing factor to the child's preferences for television programming. Rather our data seem to suggest that we cannot rule out the possible causal link between TV-viewing and subsequent aggression.

How are we to explain the trend toward a reversal of direction with aggressive behavior particularly in the third probe more likely to predict subsequent patterns of television-viewing? There seem three possible explanations for this reversal:[1]

(1) As children mature and learn more about mutual relationships and the necessity of give and take or *reciprocity* they may become less directly influenced by the effect of television and therefore less likely to model the violence they watched. If this explanation were appropriate we should expect more "causal" direction between TV-viewing and later aggression for the younger children of our sample than for the older ones. Inspection of Table 6.4 suggests, however, that the same pattern of cross-lag correlations emerges for the 3-year-olds as for the total sample.

(2) The reader should keep in mind that parent training and the intervention study was instituted during the period between the second and third probes of the study. Thus, in this period one might expect any possible influence of the various approaches to the parents to be reflected in the behavior of the children. Because the training was designed either to stimulate imagination or to reduce television-viewing and thus ultimately to reduce more antisocial learned negative behaviors, we should expect some reduction in aggressiveness and some enhancement in positive behavior during this period.

In effect it can be argued that one focus of the intervention was to sever any kind of causal link between TV-viewing and subsequent aggressive behavior. One way of ascertaining this is to compare the correlations for our variables as they emerge for the three experimental groups, cognitive training, imaginative training, or TV control training and the control group that did not receive such training. Inspection of the data for the control group in Table 6.4 does indeed suggest that this group does not show as much of a reversal in causal direction as does the total sample. Because we have of course a much smaller number of subjects involved in this comparison many of the correlations are not significant and the pattern is on the whole not as clear-cut

[1]The authors acknowledge the useful suggestions of Dr. Lonnie Sherrod in developing these explanations and analyses.

as it is for the total sample. Nevertheless, the results are at least slightly confirmatory of this second possibility that the intervention has *weakened* the causal link for some of the children. Future research might look more carefully at this type of comparison with a somewhat larger sample.

(3) We know that television-viewing drops drastically during the April and October probes when children are more likely to be outdoors. This decrease alone may account for the reversal in the direction of the causality relationship; with children who watch less television it may turn out to be only those children who already are interested a great deal in aggression who go on to watch the more violent programming.

In conclusion, our cross-lag analyses bear comparison with those of Lefkowitz et al. (1977) who found the persisting tie between violent-content TV-viewing at age 9 and overt aggressive behavior 10 years later. Our data reflecting a third or fourth of the life span of preschoolers seem to point to the same causal link between watching TV, especially programs with violent content, and subsequent aggression. Certainly our results seem to argue against attributing the later watching of violent TV fare to an aggressive trend in personality or to some third underlying factor.

LOOKING AT EXTREME TV-AGGRESSION GROUPS ACROSS TIME

Still another approach to finding some evidence of a possible causal link between television-viewing and aggression is to look at our subjects when they are broken into four groups based on extreme aggression scores and extreme amounts of television-viewing. We may then surmise that if subjects who show very little aggression during the initial probe but who are watching a good deal of television early go on to show increases in aggression in later probes we are finding further support for the causal link. Table 6.5 presents the results for television-viewing frequency and aggression for boys. The results for girls did not yield sufficiently large Ns in the occurrence of aggression at specific probe periods to provide adequate consistency for this analysis.

Inspection of this table does indeed suggest that those boys who were initially low in aggression but high in television-viewing do show a consistent *increase* in aggression scores over the second, third, and fourth probes. This is roughly comparable to the increase found for the children who are high in television-viewing and also high in aggression at the outset. Children who watch very little television and are high in aggression also show an ultimate increase in final aggression but with a less consistent pattern. There is no special increase evident for the children who are initially low in aggression and who also watch very little television.

TABLE 6.5

Means Of Physical Aggression On Later Probes Based On Extreme Samples; Initial (Probe 1) Aggression And Weekly TV-Viewing For Boys (Probe 1)

Variable Aggression	Low Television Low Aggression	High Television Low Aggression	Low Television High Aggression	High Television High Aggression
Aggression, Probe 1	1.0	1.0	1.4	1.4
Aggression, Probe 2	1.1	1.4	1.4	1.4
Aggression, Probe 3	1.4	1.5	1.2	2.2
Aggression, Probe 4	1.4	1.9	2.1	2.0

These trends are again in the direction one might expect if there were causal links but they cannot be called conclusive. It is also apparent that children who are initially high in aggression but who are watching very little television do show some increases in aggression and there are possibilities that other factors clearly would be related to producing aggressive behavior as well as television-viewing. Nevertheless, our data, viewed on an overall basis, clearly rule out the argument that aggressiveness produces a strong interest in *watching* violent or, generally, a great deal of television; the data do tend to support the possibility that the pattern of television-viewing leads to greater aggression. In our next chapter we examine in greater detail family patterns of our children to see whether we can find further clues about possible links between television-viewing and the likelihood that children will show aggressive behavior in school.

The data summarized in the present chapter do seem to argue that IQ, socioeconomic status, and ethnicity appear to be less influential factors in producing overt aggression in our children than is the sheer amount of time spent watching television and in particular the time spent watching the action-detective-adventure shows that are characterized by considerable violent activity. We cannot from our data conclude whether it is direct modeling or the facilitation of imitation that plays a role here nor can we tell whether it might be the sheer arousal of excitement in the child which leads to hyperactivity and greater likelihood of aggression.

It is worth noting that particular programs that appear especially implicated in the aggressive behavior of children have included the action shows such as "The Bionic Woman," "Six Million Dollar Man," and other action shows that were scheduled between 8:00 and 10:00 P.M. in the East. In addition, we have indications that some of the variety and game shows especially "The Gong Show," which was extensively presented during the week, were watched by significantly more children who scored high in aggression. "The Gong Show," although much enjoyed by college students as a kind of "far out" amateur hour, is in itself characterized by a good deal of physical pummeling of each other by contestants in absurd costumes and also by a generally frenetic quality. Similarly, some of the game shows watched by the children are characterized by adults leaping up and down and shrieking a good deal.

Our data, therefore, cannot resolve the distinction between the more generalized arousal theory and specific aggression modeling hypothesis, although the relationship of overt aggression is most consistent with the viewing of the action-detective category of programming by the children. It is hard to avoid the conclusion that TV-viewing by preschoolers does play an important part, however, in the likelihood that they will show aggressive behavior at school and also in the indications that they will show flashes of anger or other dysphoric moods or uncooperative behavior with adults.

7

Family Interviews: Home Life Style, TV-Viewing, and Aggression

In looking for the "smoking gun" that can link television-viewing to specific behavior at school, we are inevitably drawn to a closer study of the home life of our children. Even though we have indications from our data that family background factors such as ethnicity and social class cannot completely account for the link of TV with aggression it remains possible that other more specific factors within the family setting play a role in determining whether or not a child will be aggressively inclined during school hours. By going into the home and interviewing the mothers we may be able to detect particular facets of the life style that contribute to television-viewing patterns generally and also to the kind of behavior that may be manifest in spontaneous play.

Because research funds were extremely limited it was possible to interview only the parents of 40 children who participated in our study. Families we followed up were those whose children fell into the following categories:

1. Low aggression, low TV-viewing.
2. Low aggression, high TV-viewing.
3. High aggression, low TV-viewing.
4. High aggression, high TV-viewing.

OBJECTIVES OF FAMILY INTERVIEWS

Is it possible that certain characteristics of the family may lead on the one hand to the encouragement of aggressive behavior in the child (perhaps through imitation of the parents' aggressiveness) and at the same time to the encouragement of the child's watching aggressive material on television? If there are fairly clear stylistic differences between families which may foster aggression as well as excessive TV-viewing then these should become apparent once we get into the home and have an opportunity to explore in greater detail the daily routines of the family, the interaction of father and mother and household routine, the patterns of punishment employed in the family, the possible occurrences of life stress situations or of bereavements, and other instigators to emotional distress or aggression in the child.

If the link between television and aggression is *causal* then we ought very likely to find no great difference between the family life styles of children who are high TV-viewers and also high in aggression at school and the family patterns of other children. Thus, if we find no clear indications that the family styles of the high group include unique components of aggressiveness stimulated by parental activity or a consistent frustration of a child then we are in a better position to argue that the sheer amount of TV watching or perhaps the watching of the action shows can be implicated more directly in the child's aggressive behavior at school. By including a group of children who are also low TV-viewers yet who show a good deal of aggression we can determine whether this latter group has a special component in family life, greater home conflict, stress, bereavements, or a special *pattern* of TV-viewing along with a special family life style that may account for their aggression even though they do not watch very much television. A glance into the family can also provide us with some clues about whether there are mitigating circumstances in family life that may moderate the effect of high television-viewing in the group of children that watches a great deal of TV but shows very little overt aggressive behavior.

A closer look into the family life as reported by the mother and indeed a glance around the home itself may offer additional clues about the ways in which different families deal with the television medium. In a sense this more intensive look at the background of our children gives us the chance to validate some of the observations noted in school. Are children who are aggressive in school also likely to be extremely active or aggressive in their home situation? Are the reports of the parents based on the two-week log keeping four times a year consistent with their personal accounts of the way TV is handled in the home setting? To what extent does the way the family is organized with respect to watching television, the daily routines of eating, sleeping, or of maintaining discipline show consistency with the behavior scored either from TV logs kept by the parents or from the overt play responses of the children in school?

In preparing the interview schedule that we employed in this study we considered a variety of possible influences on aggression. We had the interviewers look around the home for signs of guns or other weapons in cases or hanging on the walls in view of the research by Berkowitz on contextual factors that may produce aggression (Berkowitz, 1969). We were interested in the extent to which there were reports by the mothers of parental discord or of acts of overt violence within the home between parents or siblings. We considered the possibility that family break-up or extremely stressful circumstances might be specifically linked to the child's behavior in the school. We looked for indications from the parents' description of fathers' and mothers' daily routines that there were inconsistencies or degrees of hyperactivity shown by parents that might create stress for the children. We also looked for evidence of possible mitigating factors that might reduce the general aggressive potential of the child or might at least mitigate some of the potentially noxious influences of the television medium. Thus we felt it possible that parental emphasis on story-telling, reading, and stimulation of imagination might provide the child with alternative forms of play. We hypothesized that a broader behavioral repertoire would reduce the chances that aggression would be a preferred motor response for a given child. Goldberg (1973) had indeed found that children who showed evidence of greater imagination were less likely to be aggressive than those who showed a paucity of fantasy in their repertory of reactions.

While we were in the home, we took advantage of the opportunity to watch the child's behavior in relation to the mother as it unfolded spontaneously during the interviews that lasted approximately two hours. We also took some time during this visit to administer to the child a *"Television Character Recognition Test"* (to be described in the following) which afforded us an opportunity of checking on the extent to which children who were scored as high or low in television-viewing as reflected in parent logs might also show differences in their ability to identify humans or cartoon figures drawn from current television fare. This technique provided still a further validation of the use of the parent logs, but it might in addition give us some clues about the extent to which television characters have become a part of the current mythology and interchange that goes on between peer groups even as young as three and four in our society. Quite obviously the whole scale emergence recently of the sale of picture cards and toys based on characters in television like the *"Bionic Man"* could conceivably lead to a greater recognition of such TV personalities even by children who were relatively little exposed to them on television itself.

PROCEDURE

Forty children were identified whose observational ratings over the four probe periods consistently reflected either extreme aggression for our sample or a minimum of aggression and who also differed amongst themselves as extremes in the total weekly television-viewing they showed based on the four probe period logs. To meet our criteria, a child must have been above the group median for aggression in at least three of the four probe periods. Wherever possible we chose those children who were consistently above the group median for all probe periods and were also above or below the median in TV-viewing for the four periods. Thus we finally emerged with four groups of ten children each, six boys and four girls in each group, who represented our categories of low aggression low TV-viewing, low aggression high TV-viewing, high aggression low TV-viewing, and high aggression high TV-viewing.

The high aggressive high TV-viewing group perhaps was somewhat more aggressive in its scores than the low TV, high aggressive group. This should be expected, however, in view of the consistently positive correlation between TV-viewing and aggression in our sample. Our high TV-viewers in general averaged more than 50 hours a week of watching television, a staggering average of more than seven hours a day which must be viewed in the perspective of 3- and 4-year-olds who are already spending about five hours a day in nursery school or day-care centers. Our low TV-viewers are averaging less than two hours a day over the week's time. As noted in Chapter 7, however, high aggressive children even though meeting our criteria and distinctly the most aggressive in our sample of 140 can, nevertheless, scarcely be described as *violent* if we look at their means for aggression on a five-point scale. The low aggressive children showed almost no evidence of fighting, pushing, or related activity during the year.

The interview procedure was based on a detailed schedule of questions which were presented by the interviewer to the mother at the home in a semistructured interview format. The mothers were contacted by telephone and individual appointments were made. None of the group solicited turned down the opportunity for the interview. Parents were paid a small additional renumeration for their cooperation in this phase of the study.

The interviewers were trained to look carefully around the house while interviewing the mother and to note indications of the character of the room structure, the commonness of television sets, books, records, weapons, and the like. Actually none of the homes we visited had rifles or other weapons displayed on the walls or in cases, perhaps a reflection of a Northeastern cultural pattern that might contrast with Southern or Southwestern styles. Interviewers marked down the relative orderliness or disorderliness of the house—were toys left lying all around, were dirty dishes piled up in the sink? They took into account the relative affluence of the neighborhood and of the home or the degree to which there were gross signs of poverty.

The mothers were encouraged to talk spontaneously about various categories such as the child's daily routine, the usual daily activities of the parents, or other adults in the home. Narrative protocols were written down by the interviewers and only when the parent failed to give information on a particular topic such as type of punishment were specific questions asked of this kind. Examples of the interview schedule and of the final rating schedule and of the final rating schedule carried out by other raters from the narrative protocols are provided in the appendices. Interviewers were not familiar with what category the children represented, for example, high aggression, high TV, low aggression, low TV, and so on. They were also not familiar with specific hypotheses of the study with the exception of the principal investigators who conducted a very small number of interviews (without knowledge of the child's category, however).

In addition to the interview the Television Character Recognition Test was also administered to the children in the home. This test consisted of a series of 20 sets of four pictures of persons or cartoon figures drawn from current TV fare. Each set of four pictures was presented on a page. The child was asked to pick out from a page which of the four representations was "the Fonz." The child simply responded by pointing to the appropriate picture and this was scored on a special rating sheet. The format of this test was much like that of the Peabody Picture Vocabulary Test. This test was run through once with an answer for each page and then repeated with a new character asked to be identified from each page. Thus we could estimate the reliability of the response pattern of the children from the two run-throughs.

RESULTS

Analyses of variance were carried out for the various categories employed in the questioning of the parents as well as for observational data such as the number of records or books available in the home, etc. By looking at the patterning of the means across the four categories and at the systematic trends it is possible to develop at least to some extent a picture of the special characteristics of the families of children who fall into each of the four groups.

In general the statistical analyses of the study suggest, if anything, greater commonalities across the four types of families than differences between them. We do not find systematic group differences reflecting greater evidence of disorganized or broken families for high or low aggressives nor are there sizable differences in general in types of punishment, in evidence of family fighting or other special indicators that could stimulate aggressive behavior.

The major systematic difference that does emerge is focused chiefly on the high aggressive high television-viewing families who are chiefly characterized by a considerable *laxity in control of the television set* on the part of the parents and a general family lack of *varied outside interests*. In the following section we list family characteristics which seem to identify the home lives of high aggression high TV children. Some of the significant F-ratios will be indicated by *p* values in parentheses.

Children in our group who are characterized as high aggressive and high television-viewing are significantly lower in IQ than the children in the other three groups ($p < .002$). Both high television-watching groups are significantly lower in IQ than the low TV-watching groups but the high television high aggression group that averages an IQ of 104 is clearly the lowest in this respect. The high television-viewing groups are both lower in socioeconomic status than the low television groups but these two high viewing groups are clearly different in aggression. One cannot, therefore, infer that social class differences account for the TV-aggression linkage. Rather, the social class effect seems more linked to the greater TV-watching frequency ($p < .001$).

The home of the high television-viewing high aggression child is characterized as somewhat more disorganized than that of the other families except for the low television high aggression group. It is striking that there are less toys in evidence around the home for the high TV high aggression group and, by far, *the least evidence of books* ($p < .0007$) *and of musical instruments or records* ($p < .05$). Children in this group are allowed to stay up later at night and also wake up later in the morning than the children in the other groups. Indeed, their fathers' patterns also reflect a tendency to wake up later in the morning both on weekdays and weekends ($p < .03, p < .07$) than the fathers in the other groups. Mothers in these families wake up *earlier* than other groups. In general, the high aggressive high TV-viewing families seem to reflect a somewhat more conventional male-female relationship with the father showing less interest in homemaking activities than do the fathers in the other groups ($p < .02$).

What seems to stand out more clearly than anything else for the high television high aggressive child's life style is a gross laxity of control by parents of the TV situation in the home. These families report themselves as generally more likely to watch television while they eat. As might be expected from the television data the mothers report in the interviews as well that children from both high television-viewing groups spend more time watching television both in the morning and at night. The children in the high aggressive high TV group are allowed to stay up later ($p < .04$), are less likely to have a regular bedtime routine ($p < .07$), are less likely to have stories told to them at bedtime ($p = .02$), and are less likely to have a kind of calming down period before going to bed ($p = .09$). They are, however, also much more likely to be required to engage in formal bedtime prayer ($p < .008$). The high aggressive high TV child is more likely than the other children to be watching television with a parent, usually the mother ($p = .02$). Despite this greater amount of joint family watching by children in the high TV high aggression groups, the parents of these children consistently report that it is *the child who controls the TV set* ($p = .007$).

One of our concerns was how families spend time together outside the home. In keeping with our indications that the high television high aggression child's family has less varied cultural interests we see that children from this group are most likely to be spending their time outside with parents going shopping and are less likely than children from the other groups to be taken to parks, picnics, or to museums or other cultural activities. They are more likely, however, to be taken to the movies with their parents. Thus the influence of the popular media and of the potentially arousing or violent components of movies or TV are apparently further emphasized by the nature of family activities with these children.

It is of interest to note that some differences emerge with respect to family sports interests. For the high television high aggression group the father and child together show more interest in team sports of the more widely popular type: football, baseball, and boxing. It is especially with respect to sports involving body contact or aggression that this group stands out, although the results are not statistically significant.

Although the high TV-viewers show more joint watching with parents, the pattern of viewing is of special interest. The high aggressive high TV children are much less likely to be watching educational television children's shows than are, for example, the low aggressive children who also watch a great deal of TV. They are watching more situation-comedies with their families (p = .03) and also more variety/game shows than the other groups except for the low aggression high TV-viewers (p = .06). The high and low aggressive children proved to differ significantly in the watching of the especially "peaceful" "Mister Rogers' show" with greater viewing by the *low* aggressives of this program.

Both of the aggressive groups, high and low TV-viewers alike, are less likely to be watching the adult family shows such as *"The Waltons"* or *"The Little House on the Prairie"* (presumably less violent programming) than are the other two groups. Similarly, and this seems especially striking, the high aggressive low TV-viewers as well as the high aggressive high TV-viewers are both more likely to be watching the action-detective shows. Indeed, if one looks at the means across the four groups, the average viewing of action-detective shows by *both* high aggressive groups is more than four times as great as the viewing of those shows by low aggressive groups (p < .001)! Those high aggression children who watch relatively little TV on the whole are watching more than three times as much of the action shows as the low television low aggression children according to our logs. Thus it appears that even those children who are relatively light viewers of television in our sample but who at the same time show a high level of aggression turn out to be somewhat more likely to be watching the action-detective shows relative to the other types of shows available.

In keeping with the generally somewhat conventional masculine patterns of the family style of high aggression high TV child, the father in this family is especially likely to be watching sports on television (p < .002) and is least likely of the fathers of the various groups to be watching the news (p = .12).

Our data indicate that there is consistency of aggressive behavior from the school reports to the home situation. There is greater evidence of argument occurring between children in the families of both high aggressive groups with the high aggressive high TV group showing the highest score for the total sample in this regard. Again, both high aggressive groups irrespective of TV patterns show greater emphasis of physical versus verbal fighting within the family by the children from our sample and the high aggressive high television group reveals the highest scores in this respect ($p < .01$), which mirrors the fact that the same children also obtained highest aggression scores on the average in the nursery school setting. In this respect, our study is one of the first that reflects indications of continuity from home to school observations with respect to the dimension of aggressiveness.

Can we find any clear indications that there are modeling influences in the home that might play as much of a role in the child's subsequent aggressive behavior at school as the very striking differences in the television-viewing patterns? It is certainly true that children in *both* the high aggressive groups are more likely to be punished by spanking than children in the low aggressive groups ($p = .08$), and they are also less likely, according to mothers' reports, to be rewarded by praise ($p = .01$). Beyond these differences, there are in general few indications of gross family style differences with respect to physical activity, family fighting, family stress or bereavement, or other possibilities of modeling that could differentially influence the children. We do find evidence that the high aggressive high TV children are reported by their mothers as showing more general activity levels and are also more likely to be described by their mothers as having a "fighting problem" ($p = .001$). These children are clearly the least shy of the group whereas the low aggressive low TV-viewers are reported by their mothers as most likely to be shy ($p = .06$). The high aggressive children in general are reported by their mothers as less likely to show humor in their day-to-day patterns of behavior, a result that seems generally in accord with our findings of the generally inverse relationship of positive affects and overt aggression. The high TV-viewing high aggressive children are reported by their parents as somewhat less socially cooperative and less likely to show specific talents. In keeping with the general conventional or conservative style of the family that emerges for the high aggressive high TV-viewing group, we also find this group being rated as lowest on family autonomy in relation to relatives.

Are there any special aspects of behavior that characterize the families of those children rated as high in aggression but who watch very little television? One of the things that emerges in the review of these families is that the children are among the most intelligent in our sample (IQ of 125) and that the family life patterns seem to reflect two intellectually gifted and professionally active parents. The family styles indicate considerable range of interests, cultural and intellectual, for both parents and they are also characterized by the interviewers as "highest activity level," "most competitive," "most autonomous—each going separate ways" and "most disorderly in their family life styles." Thus, the families of these high aggressive but low TV-watching children seem to reflect a good deal of self-directed, varied activities by parents that preclude in the hustle and bustle of their lives much watching of television by the children. Within this low TV orientation it is worth repeating that the children do, however, watch a higher proportion of action-detective shows than do the low aggressive children. It is conceivable, therefore, that these families may provide models for hyperactivity or potential aggressive behavior more clearly than do the other families largely because of their highly active and competitive life styles.

Families of the low aggressive high TV-viewing children also show a greater range of cultural activities than the high aggressive high TV-viewers and they do seem to be much more casual than other groups about children's TV watching. They do not reflect, however, the internal competitiveness or disorderliness that might serve as instigators for aggression and they also seem to be watching proportionately less of the action shows although they watch a good deal of all kinds of programming.

Given the relationship we keep finding between aggression and TV-viewing, how can the existence of a sizable group of children who watch a lot of TV but are low in aggression be explained? For the four groups some of the patterns of television-viewing shown by the children and also their scores of interest provide a clue. For example, high television low aggression children turn out to be watching relatively less of the action-detective violent shows but relatively more than the other groups of the educational or public TV programming and, specifically more of benign TV shows such as *"Captain Kangaroo"* and *"Mister Rogers' Neighborhood."* This result seems to be extremely important for it suggests at least the possibility that programming that is less oriented toward aggression and violence can actually play a constructive role in mitigating some of the more noxious possibilities of extensive TV-viewing. Specific studies carried out by ourselves and by other investigators attest to the positive influences and prosocial value of a show like *"Mister Rogers' Neighborhood"* (Singer, 1978). Keep in mind that action-detective shows have the highest relationship with aggression in our canonical correlation analysis whereas educational TV programming shows a small negative relationship to overt aggression in our significant canonical factor.

It is also worth noting that these children in the high television but low aggression groups tend somewhat to be watching less with their parents than the other groups. This result has important implications because there is much current popular advice that proposes that parents watching with children can play a role in mitigating some of the more negative implications of children seeing violent or frightening television productions. Our data and interview information suggest that if the parents do not play an extremely *active* role by conversing with the children in order to minimize the impact of the violent shows, simply sitting there will not do the trick. If anything, what seems to have happened is that the parents of the high television low aggression children as well as of the low television low aggression children have taken an attitude that there are special programs for children that they can watch alone. These parents have tended to limit opportunities for children to watch adult programming that might include violent or extreme content. Joint viewing of aggression may in a sens there are special programs folent material if the parent does not take an active stance to counteract this possibility (Eisenberg, 1978). In looking more closely at the children in the low aggression but high television-watching group we also find them to be characterized by somewhat higher intelligence than the high TV high aggression group but decidely lower than the other two groups in IQ. Perhaps when other factors of family pressure are not present sheer intelligence can help the child deal better with the stimulation or modeling opportunities provided by frequent TV watching.

An intriguing result that merits further research is the fact that the low aggression high TV-viewers turn out to be the subjects in our study who responded with a significantly greater proportion of human movement responses on the Barron Inkblots. Indeed their scores were more than three times as high on this measure as those of the high TV high aggression subjects and were the highest of the four groups. There is considerable evidence that imaginativeness as measured by Rorschach Inkblots or related projective techniques seems to be inversely related to the likelihood of aggressive behavior in adults and adolescents (Singer & Brown, 1977). Our data obtained with 3- and 4-year-olds seem, therefore, consistent with a broader body of research. In effect this finding suggests the possibility that some form of internalized imaginative capacity is providing these children with an alternative form of dealing with the stimulating material provided by extensive television-viewing.

CHILDREN'S RESPONSES TO THE TELEVISION-CHARACTER PICTURE RECOGNITION TEST

As might be expected, the high television-viewing groups irrespective of aggressiveness show the highest recognition scores on both "passes" through the series of pictures in the TV recognition test ($p = .01, p = .008$). As might be expected, the high TV-viewing groups show more recognition of cartoon characters and of characters from commercial TV children's shows. Supporting the mother's reports based on the logs, the children from the high aggression high TV groups also show less awareness than the other three groups of characters drawn from the educational television children's shows! High TV-viewers are more aware of characters from situation-comedies and it is the high aggressive high TV children who are clearly the highest of the four groups in their recognition of characters from the variety and game shows that include the hyperactive *"Gong Show."* As might be expected, these high TV-viewers are also more aware of the various adult shows and of the characters from the action shows ($p = .003$). With respect to the latter type of show, the high aggressive high TV-viewers are the highest in awareness of action-detective programming. High aggression high TV-viewers are also much more likely to recognize characters drawn from news broadcasts than are children in the other three groups ($p < .004$).

As suggested earlier, it is quite clear that even those children who are reported as low TV-viewers recognize almost 50% of the figures in the TV recognition test. Thus we are turning up evidence of the development of a broad cultural pattern in which, through the use of toys and of trading cards (which all the children report possessing) that are based on TV characters, a commonality of experience around certain personalities is being created. In a sense, we see the origins here of a kind of a common consciousness and mythology being built around television personalities in early childhood much as in other times and cultures children's heroes were drawn from historical and mythological figures whose adventures were told to children at the fireside or in preparation for bedtime. Parents from all groups reported that their children were familiar with commercial jingles. Indeed the commercials seems especially popular with all of the children.

FAMILY INTERVIEWS: A ONE-YEAR FOLLOW-UP

A year after the date of the interviews just described we had the opportunity of reinterviewing 34 of our 40 parents from the earlier study. One parent in each of the low aggressive groups could not be seen because of moves from the community and two parents from each of the high aggressive groups were unavailable for the same reason. Interviews were conducted by staff members (Rhoda Brownstein and Rena Repetti) without knowledge of children's scores on aggression or TV-viewing.

The children were readministered the Peabody Picture Vocabulary Test for IQ estimates. Although all scores increased, the relative positions remained the same, the high TV watchers as a group were lowest in IQ with the high aggression high TV groups significantly below the low TV watchers ($p < .05$). The high aggression low TV group continued to be the group with children showing the highest IQs in the sample.

Once again patterns for the four groups showed more similarities than differences in most daily life patterns according to mothers' reports. The homes of the high aggression low TV group were again rated as the most disorderly. The high aggression, high TV group was again rated significantly deviant from the sample in showing least evidence of "cultural" artifacts, books ($p = .002$), musical instruments ($p = .001$), and so on. This time around one rifle was actually observed hanging on the wall—in the home of a high aggression low TV-viewing family! Although some marriages had been disrupted this pattern was not significantly different between groups. Daily routines resembled each other across groups somewhat more than previously, although fathers' wake-up times for high aggressive high TV children's families still were the latest. The children from the two high TV groups again were reported by their mothers as watching TV earliest in the day on weekdays and weekends ($p = .003, .002$). The high aggression high TV group again was described as most likely to be watching TV during mealtimes ($p = .03$). The low aggression high TV group did differ from other groups in reflecting a pattern in which a caregiver other than the mother significantly more often took the child to school or brought it home. No differences in sleep patterns, sleep disturbances, and the like emerged across groups. If anything both high aggressive groups were reported as having the most hours of sleep, an important finding because it might be thought that their heavier watching of action TV (which airs later at night) might lead to a lack of sleep that could explain their restless or aggressive behavior at school. The low aggression high TV children were clearly the lowest sleepers in the sample.

Although we had no opportunity this second year to observe children at school the parents again reported more evidence of conflict around the house and over TV for the high aggressive children ($p = .06$). The high aggressive high TV families continued to show less varied activities and more involvements in visiting relatives, etc. than the other groups, although many of these differences were not as great as last year. The high aggression high TV families were still most likely to go to movies and fathers of these families were again most interested in watching conventional sports, as were the mothers ($p = .02, .04$). Family joint watching of TV was still much greater for both high TV groups ($p < .001$), suggesting that results from logs prepared more than a year ago were still predictive of current TV-viewing patterns. The high aggression high TV group continued to reflect much less parental involvement in hobbies or outside interests.

The children from the high aggression high TV group were again described by parents as showing more "physical" arguments in the home ($p = .009$), again confirming a continuity in aggressive behavior. It is of interest that both low aggression groups reported more *arguments between parents* being witnessed by children than did the high aggressive group parents ($p = .02$). The greatest amount of parental disagreement over child-rearing was reported by the low aggression high TV group mothers ($p = .04$). Although the groups did not differ in psychological restrictions or punishments, both high aggression groups differed from the others in reporting more scolding and physical punishment of the children, with the high aggression high TV-watching groups showing highest scores on these variables again ($p < .05$, .0005). No differences in praise or material rewards to children were reported.

As was found before the groups differed very significantly in the importance attached to TV in the home. Both high TV groups reported much more emphasis on the medium as a focus of daily life and interest, with the high aggression high TV group showing the highest score in this category ($p < .00001$.) It was evident, as in the previous year, that continuity in heavy TV-viewing continues and that the high aggression high TV child continues to control the TV set in the home.

In summary, a one-year follow-up of our families contrasted on the basis of children's TV watching and aggressive behavior at school reveals an essential continuity of pattern in both of these areas. Family styles still reflect a much greater investment in TV-viewing by the high aggression high TV parents and children with little outside or alternative activities. Whereas the high aggression groups are both more "physical" with children this may reflect a continuing response to aggressive behavior by the children. There was little evidence that the high aggressive high TV families can be characterized as more grossly disorganized, stressful, or violent, but it is clear that they are oriented much more to a kind of subtle, perhaps unwitting sanctioning of cultural emphases on violence by allowing children to watch TV indiscriminately, by resorting to physical punishment, and by an interest of both parents in the more violent of popular sports.

IMPLICATIONS OF THE FAMILY INTERVIEW STUDY

Our peek into the home life of about a third of our total sample again does not lead to an unassailable set of data linking television-viewing to overt aggression. It does, however, seem on the whole to rule out indications that children who are watching a great deal of television and who are also aggressive come from families that stand out glaringly as disorganized, under considerable stress, or reflect a good deal of daily parental violence that children could model. Quite the contrary. The family lifestyles of the high aggressive high television-viewing children seem to be the most conventional and traditional of our four groups. The high TV high aggression children's families seem to be mostly characterized by a reliance on the popular media for entertainment and on a minimum of provision of alternative interest patterns for the children. Both high and low TV-watching high aggression groups do show somewhat greater emphasis on physical punishment for the children and somewhat less emphasis on positive reinforcement or praise in motivation. The difference between the two groups seems to be that the low

TV-viewing but high aggressive children come from families of considerable intellectual attainment and variety of interests but with a somewhat more disorganized and disorderly day-to-day life style and with evidence of considerable competitiveness and pressurized family living. This might account for the fact of greater aggression in the children from these families even though TV-viewing is not very great by the children. It is worth noting, however, that the proportion of watching of the more violent forms of TV is greater for this group relative to its small total number of hours spent before the set.

It is also apparent that those children who are allowed to watch considerable amounts of television but who show very little overt aggression seem to come from families that are otherwise rather tightly organized, quite neat and tidy, and which follow fairly regular routines. The children also are somewhat more intelligent than the high aggressive high TV-viewing children and they show in particular a greater imaginative tendency as measured on the Barron Inkblot test. They also are more likely to be watching the less violent, more benign, and pro-socially oriented educational children's TV or commercial channel children's fare like "Captain Kangaroo." These findings would seem to suggest that sheer amount of television-viewing can be counteracted by other factors in family life or by the type of programming watched.

One cannot avoid the thought that a greater variety of pro-socially oriented, less aggressive fare directed at children might be a valuable addition to the available material on television. Were a greater choice of children's shows available it might cut down some of the inclination of children to watch the violent programming that characterizes so much of the material predominantly oriented toward adults. Perhaps with the advent of cable television we can see the day when there will be whole channels devoted primarily to constructive and benign programming directed at children.[1]

In conclusion we must assert that our exploration of the relationship of TV to aggression has not been able to come up with the kind of "smoking gun" that would satisfy the most severe critics of television research and certainly the most enthusiastic advocates for the TV industry. It seems likely, however, that we can rule out the widespread belief that television-viewing of aggressive material is simply a consequence of an aggressive tendency in the child. Rather our data suggest the reverse tendency as having stronger support. In addition, we cannot assert that there is simply no relationship between what children watch on television and the way they behave in school. Our data again and again point to a linkage even if we cannot demonstrate absolutely

---

[1]In a separate research project we have explored a series of "age-specific" programs intended for the cable TV and our research demonstrated that such programming had a good combination of educational and entertainment value.

the causal direction. Thus what children watch on television is not simply something that passes over their heads and has little relation to the way they act in other respects. It clearly is linked in particular to aggression and to a somewhat lesser extent to less cooperative behaviors with adults and more evidence of distress in the course of spontaneous play.

Our search for causal sequences through the cross-lagged analysis is perhaps too simplistic an approach for the description of many developmental processes. It is quite possible that many contemporaneous events and sequential interactions or what might be termed transactions are more representative of normal developmental process. Contemporary, sequential, and cross-lag relations coexist at each point in time and they may in effect zigzag in direction across time resulting in a spiral view of development, a conception of growth more akin to the extensive developmental theorizing of Heinz Werner (1948).

It is perhaps much too simple-minded to assume that a child who is already somewhat prone to aggression watches a violent TV program, gets an idea of "how to get even with the kid next door," and then proceeds to act on this and perhaps get reinforced for this aggression. It seems more likely that the process is one in which children may be aroused or given ideas about possible activities through the watching of television and may indeed occasionally act on these. In the course of expressing interest in and receiving reinforcement for aggressive behavior they find themselves more attracted to and intrigued by aggressive actions of others especially as represented on television. Thus we find transactional developmental processes perhaps being more typical in the short run.

The important findings of Lefkowitz et al. (1977) indicating a long-term result cannot be ignored, however, and our own data certainly for the first nine months of our study seem to be generally comparable to their findings. Our data suggest that whereas industry has a responsibility in providing a greater range of more benign and socially constructive programming directed at children, parental involvement is crucial. The striking fact for our high aggression high TV-viewing children is that their parents allow them to control the TV set. Indeed this is the single most dramatic indication from our family interviews—the willingness of the families of these children to give up their personal responsibility for the viewing patterns of their children. In the next chapter we look at the efforts we made in the study to influence parent attitudes and to see if we could produce changes in children's behavior and TV-viewing patterns as a consequence of parent intervention procedures.

8 Parent-Intervention Study: Rationale, Method, Results

INTRODUCTION

As far as we can determine, our attempt to train parents of the children in our study is one of the first systematic approaches to the parental control of television-viewing. Suggestions for parent training in regard to television have been presented by Leifer (1975) and Smart (1976), but these projected studies have not yet been completed. The Parent Teachers Association has been instrumental in its campaign to raise the awareness of parents to what the PTA claims are violent and aggressive programs and to point out the deleterious effects of such programs on young children. The PTA suggests that parent intervention is important, but they have not yet carried out a large-scale training program for parents.

An important component of Head Start as well as other such projects has been the education of the parent regarding child care concepts, or cognitive skill concepts as described by Boger (1969), Filep (1971), Karnes, Teska, Hodgins, and Badger (1970), Schaefer and Bell (1958), and White (1975). The Toy Library Resource Program of New Haven has attempted to teach mothers in their homes how to play with specific toys in order to develop certain cognitive concepts. To our knowledge, the training of parents in conjunction with a complex television study such as ours appears to be a pioneering endeavor.

Three parent intervention groups, *Television Training, Imaginative Training,* and *Cognitive Training,* were designed to influence subsequent child behavior and on television-viewing patterns. The parent training groups were also necessary to balance the amount of attention provided to parents by the researchers and also to equalize roughly the amount of attention provided by parents for their children in response to the training.

A nonintervention control group was also set up. Because this group was less motivated since they did not have regular meetings, there were some parents in the group who failed to keep logs for all periods. Therefore comparisons between the three intervention groups and the control group must be viewed with greater caution. The untreated control does provide an opportunity to evaluate over a year the impact of so much staff attention to parents in the intervention groups on the subsequent response patterns of the children.

Because of the late start of the project occasioned by a delayed receipt of research funds and the large number of subjects in each intervention group, it was decided to limit the number of intervention training sessions to three. This decision was also based in part on responses from parents about how much time they would be willing to offer in the evening. In addition, extensive supplementary materials were prepared and set out systematically to parents during the months following completion of training. These supplements were continued through the summer of 1977 and into the fall of 1977 at which time an additional parent training session took place. Material relating to the holiday season was also sent out before Christmas 1977.

PART I: PREPARATION OF MATERIALS FOR PARENT-TRAINING MANUALS

Because the design of the intervention called for three groups of parents, Imagination Training, Cognitive Training, and Television Training, materials had to be specifically designed for each group.[1]

Imagination Training Manual

Exercises as well as theory are presented so that parents can work with their children for a few minutes each day in order to stimulate imagination and creativity. Sociodramatic play, fantasy games, games imitating animals, using sense modalities, and so on are included. Emphasis in the manual is on use of the total body, a few structured toys, creating toys and games out of readily available materials, lists, and instances of the benefits of play and make-believe, "how to become a playful adult," and how to encourage make-believe. The games and exercises were used in earlier research and are

---

[1]Copies of the three manuals and the supplementary material are available from the Yale University Family Television Research and Consultation Center at the cost of reproduction and mailing.

presented in D. Singer & J. Singer, *Partners in Play: A Step by Step Guide to Imaginative Play in Children.* The first training session began with a film, *Pretending,* produced by Dr. Robert Abramowitz and Mr. Arthur Greenwald of the Yale Child Study Center. This film depicts children in a nursery school engaged in socio-dramatic play. Based on the content we asked parents to think about the different roles and characters the children assumed in the film, the kinds of materials they used in imaginative play, and the ways in which teachers assisted the children in their imaginative play. The introduction to "play" served as the steppingstone to our later discussions about the benefits of play and the purpose of play in a child's life.

Parents were encouraged to recall their own childhood events, private games, magical rhymes, childhood impressions in order to get closer in touch with their child's world. Parents were also directed to try and remember their dreams and to become sensitive to separating realities from fantasies in dream content in order to understand how difficult a task it is for a child to make such separations. The adults were also encouraged to watch their children and to play with them. Watching a child struggle with a problem enables a parent to gain perspective about the parent's own difficulties as well as the parent's own possibly rigid and inflexible approach to a situation.

Three roles were suggested for the parent: onlooker, participant, and stimulator. We encouraged parents to note a child's speech patterns, play themes, signs of fear or hesitancy, indications of imagination by observing how simple or complex the games became. We provided parents with suggestions of how to discuss things with their children, and how to pay special attention to naptime or bedtime conversations. Above all parents were urged to be unobtrusive while they observed their children and to avoid rushing in too hastily to help pick up a fallen construction or to assemble a playhouse in a more orderly fashion.

In order to be a parent participator in play, suggestions were made concerning cautions such as maintaining one's adult status while going along with the game. It was pointed out that children become confused and distressed when an adult begins to act like a "baby" or became too silly. Parents were also cautioned to play only for a short time and then withdraw so that the child could develop a sense of his or her own mastery of the game. Finally, as a stimulator of imaginative play, parents were advised to offer suggestions for games by either telling a story, or setting up a few toys to start a theme, or to offer some help in imitating voices or noises as they initiated a game. In order to help develop the imagery needed for imaginative play, steps were provided for use of pictures and models to illustrate a particular game or story.

At the end of the first session, the film *Pretending* was shown again in order to find out if the group would be more sensitive after the short training session to the actions of the children. The general response was enthusiastic. The discussion after the second showing led to an increased sensitivity to the complexity of a child's imaginative play. The following two sessions expanded on the concepts laid down at the opening session. Session 2 focused on emotional awareness and sensitivity. Parents received information about how recognition of a child's own emotions and those of others enables it to engage in symbolic play. The tape that was shown portrayed children changing their facial expressions to reflect particular emotions such as joy, anger, surprise, disgust, and so on. Ideas were offered to parents dealing with a variety of ways in which they could discuss and act out "feelings."

Concepts of size and shape were discussed at Session 2; again, the parents were given ideas on how they could play imaginatively to learn about size. For example, making-believe the child is "small like a ball," "an apple," or "a pebble," or "tall as a giant" again enables the child to experience motorically change and transformation and use the child's imagination simultaneously. The tape showed children playing games where they changed their size by pretending they were different objects.

This second session also included demonstrations of role-playing through the use of simple props in order to make transformations. A "bag of hats" was introduced and parents were given the opportunity to try on a hat and play a character such as a "fireman," "policeman," "cowboy," "fancy lady," "conductor," and so on. Familiar stories, poetry, and word stimulators were also presented so that parents could begin to see how they could engage their children in sociodramatic games. Simple poems, scripts, and story line ideas were made available to the parents.

Finally, Session 3 dealt with imaginative activities that parents could carry out on special occasions with their children. Games for "waiting" situations such as doctor or dentist visits were suggested. A simple technique of the "special bag" was described whereby a box or bag of simple plastic toys or construction materials was kept and only brought out for use on these occasions when waiting became a necessity. Descriptions of games to be played with these materials were offered to the group such as playing miniature "Parking Lot," "King and Queen," "Space Trip to a Planet," "Fire House." Paper and pencil games were suggested; games that required no props such as songs utilizing body movements; imagery games such as "make-believe we're in the grocery store—here's what we see"; or "captive" allowing the child to imagine the child's cowboy tied up by rustlers. All the events were suggested through imagery.

Parents were also offered ideas for outings; ideas to use on car trips; in supermarket shopping; department store; bank or post office visits. Finally, ideas for bedtime, bathtime, meals, sick-in-bed occasions, and even how to prepare an imaginative birthday party were presented.

Cognitive Training Manual and Group Training Procedures

Theory and exercises are again presented in the manual and supplementary materials with an emphasis on cognitive skills such as language acquisition, concept formation, conservation ordering, and the like. Parents were offered games to help children develop number and reading readiness skills. A Piagetian cognitive framework served as the basis for much of the material. Care was taken in writing the material for the cognitive group so that the skills presented relied more on a structured approach, minimizing imaginative content.

Session 1 concerned the child's senses—*smell, taste, touch, hearing, sight.* Parents were encouraged to keep a small shelf for plastic containers filled with things to smell such as ammonia, mustard, pepper, onion, coffee, perfume, vanilla, and the like. A "touching bag" was also suggested with items in it such as cord, cellophane, rubber, velvet, sandpaper, some pebbles, etc. We described how a child could shut eyes, reach in the bag, and tell what was felt. The tape we prepared demonstrated these "sense" games with nursery children. Hearing involved a sound effects record, use of a bell, metronome, and the like. In this way the other sense modalities were discussed along with exercises to teach the child how to become more aware of these sensations.

Shapes and forms were discussed along with suggestions as to how to find differences among circles, ovals, squares, triangles. Recognition of shapes and forms would be necessary before introducing the alphabet. We presented ideas for the parents to use with their children in order to teach the names of the letters such as an "alphabet line" made of 26 clothespins each holding a picture of an object depicting the appropriate letter and several different examples for each letter; sandpaper letters to develop a kinesthetic sense of form; and a go-fish game whereby a child has to "fish" for a particular letter with a small pole and magnet. Each letter has a paper clip attached to enable the magnet to work.

The second session dealt with relationships such as size, position, space, amount, weight, and direction. Another tape enabled the parents to once again see young children manipulating objects according to size; moving them to determine direction; testing out whether objects would sink or float; and whether or not they understood classifications by size, color, shape. Fortunately one parent brought her little girl to the second session. It gave the instructor the chance to demonstrate some of Piaget's conservation experiments—those of quantity, liquid, and mass.

Number familiarity was emphasized at this session, too. The parents were inducted in ways in which they could present number concepts to their children. It was stressed in this session that children in the preoperational stage counted by rote and that the one-to-one correspondence of number with object came later. The session was devoted primarily to Piaget's theories of intelligence and his four stages were briefly outlined with emphasis on Stage II—Preoperational.

Session 3 focused primarily on language. The parents were given a short review of grammar and activities were presented to help them encourage language growth with their children. Activities were presented that involved making picture-vocabulary books; card collections containing words and pictures; riddle games; answering questions; making up songs; tell a story game, and so on. Parents were encouraged to talk to their children frequently about the most simple topic; to encourage their children to use sentences; name things around the house; in a car on trips; or on visits to the store, bank, post office.

Although both the imaginative and cognitive groups received information concerning concept formation, language, numbers, sense modalities, and the like, the techniques employed in conveying the information were different for each of the groups. It is important to emphasize this distinction—the focus on imagery and make-believe in the imaginative group and on the more formally pedagogic and structured approach in the cognitive sessions.

Television Training Manual and Group Training Procedures

Materials in this manual and supplement deal with some research concerning effects of television in children; suggestions concerning how to begin to use TV with children; negative effects of TV; positive aspects of TV; kinds of programs to avoid; kinds of programs to watch; and some typical questions parents ask about TV with possible answers. In addition, during training parents were given suggestions about controlling TV, names of action groups that lobby for better TV, copies of the "Children's Review Unit" of the Better Business Bureau's self-regulations concerning commercials directed to children on TV, and so on. They were shown a film from Action for Children's Television that dealt with the effects of commercials on children.

Session 1 presented the research in the area of violence and aggression as well as the pro-social data. Tapes of TV clips of violent program content as well as pro-social content were shown. Emphasis in this session was on the accumulated evidence demonstrating the negative effects of television on children, and the controversy that currently exists concerning this evidence. Much of the discussion centered on violence rather than on the pro-social content because two particularly vocal parents seemed most concerned about the position of the various researchers on this topic.

The second session dealt with guidelines for television-viewing for the preschooler. Suggestions were given to the parents in what they should look for in a children's show; amount of viewing time deemed desirable; how to become more active rather than passive viewers; setting schedules for TV-viewing, and so on. A discussion about reality and fantasy dimensions related to television also took place during that meeting. Some parents were angry about any suggestions made to limit TV-viewing and one parent particularly was still adamant about our emphasis on aggression.

The final session focused on commercials and their effect on preschoolers. The ACT film was shown at this session and parents had an opportunity to brainstorm about making up commercials. The guidelines prepared by the Children's Advertising Review Unit of the Better Business Bureau were distributed and discussed. Parents were alerted to notice ads that did not carry disclaimers such as "batteries not included" or "assembly is required" when directed at young children.

PART II: PREPARATION OF TRAINING TAPES

The University of Bridgeport audio-visual staff contracted with us to prepare four training tapes. These were video tapes made in the university nursery schoolroom utilizing four volunteer children and a "teacher." Using the materials from our manuals, this young woman actually played the exercises and games that we prepared for the parents with the unrehearsed children. We prepared two tapes dealing with *imaginative* play training and two tapes dealing with *cognitive* training. The reason for the use of training tapes was that because our parent sessions were to be held in the evening, obviously we could not expect preschoolers to perform for such large groups. Thus we could actually show the parents how these games would look when used with their own children. The content on these tapes was derived from the training manuals and thus served as additional reinforcements of the written material.

Preparation of the tapes took one afternoon of work in the nursery school. The "teacher" had been a music teacher and was currently a graduate student in school psychology. She had experience also in working on an earlier research study with the directors of this project. Another day was spent editing the four hours of shooting down to four tapes, each 20 minutes long.

In addition to making these video-tapes, a staff member in charge of audio-visual material on our project began to tape selected portions of television programs and commercials from television shows. Samples of violent cartoons, pro-social cartoons, educational television, family situation programs, fantasy programs, violent adult shows, pro-social shows, commercials were taped and edited to make two tapes: one with examples of antisocial content and stereotypes and one with pro-social content.

PART III: TEACHER TRAINING

The female director and two female staff members met for four training sessions prior to the parent meetings. Materials in the manual tapes and films were previewed and discussed. "Lesson plans" were prepared so that each instructor knew what she was to teach and to discuss during each parent session. Instructors were rotated in a Latin square so that each group had a different instructor each evening in order to counterbalance the teacher variable. An *Instructor Evaluation Form* was prepared in advance so that parents could rate the instructors each session on their knowledge of the material and delivery as well as the parents' prior knowledge and familiarity of the material and their willingness to use the material. These forms were anonymous and were filled out by parents at the end of each session, collected, and entered on data sheets to assess instructor variability.

PART IV: PARENT TRAINING SESSIONS

There were three parent training sessions held in February and March after observation data had been collected on the sample. These sessions took place once a week consecutively from 8:30-10:00. Parents received a letter inviting them to attend and a follow-up reminder. Attendance averaged about 55 parents per group; many fathers attended despite our expectations that only mothers would show up. Our staff assisted at these sessions by taking attendance, taking minutes, setting up seating, helping with audio-visual equipment, passing out and collecting the Instructor Evaluation Forms, and at the end of each session distributing the appropriate section of the training manual.

All three groups, imaginative, cognitive, and television met in the same building, the same evenings. We asked the groups not to discuss their training with other parents. Attendance was excellent.

The format of each session involved some lecture, some film or tapes, some brainstorming, specific activities for parents, question and answer periods. The instructors introduced themselves, spoke only in general terms about the nature of the project, and requested that parents utilize our suggestions with their children for a few minute each day.

At the end of each of the sessions, the parents received material from the manual that had been discussed that evening so that they could work on the games, exercises, and use the suggestions. At the end of the three-week period the groups seemed more cohesive and more relaxed. We felt that we would have liked at least three more sessions although initially, parents balked at the proposed original six-week training period. Comments about the sessions are on the *Instructor Evaluation Forms* and in general were favorable. Most criticism was directed towards the instructors of the television group. The parents in this group were resistant about controlling TV, although our results indicate that the children of these parents actually showed a greater drop in their amount of TV-viewing during the April probe when compared with the other intervention groups. It was apparent that although parents clearly were more concerned about the nature of the TV medium after exposure to our presentation, they relied heavily on TV as a "baby sitter" and were reluctant to confront the problem of controlling the children's viewing frequency or pattern.

When the *Instructor Evaluation Forms* were examined for the three sessions, *t-tests* were carried out to determine whether or not there were significant differences among instructors. One of the instructors, an experienced college teacher, received consistently higher ratings from parents than the other group leaders. Leaders were rotated through the three training conditions, however, so that this teacher effect did not lead to higher ratings for any specific training condition.

PART V: DESIGNING THE SUPPLEMENTAL MATERIALS

Parents received additional training materials. Four supplemental training sections of the manual were sent out. The first went out a month after the training sessions ended. The second one was sent out the third week in July, and the third was sent out in October after the third observation period.

Just before Christmas 1977, we sent out our last supplement. Both the imaginative and cognitive group received materials relating to activities that could be carried out during the holidays, with the appropriate training emphasis for each group. The television group received guidelines related to advertising, especially concerning the toy ads that were heavy during the holiday season. Each supplement offered the parents additional games, ideas, and exercises pertaining to their group.

In the summer of 1977, we asked for comments from the parents concerning their reactions to the materials in the manual. In general, most of the comments were favorable and parents reported that they used the materials with their children. The parents in the Television Training group reported more control over their children's TV-viewing. Some minor negative comments were reported, and these comments were heeded in our preparations for the September review sessions.

PART VI: REVIEW SESSION

In September 1977 we invited the parents to attend a fourth session in order to discuss their use of materials to date. Each intervention group met on a separate night and all teacher trainers were present. In general, the parents commented favorably on the usefulness of the manual. The parents also asked many questions related to child development and seemed to be seeking information about child-rearing practices. It appeared as if our trainers had raised the consciousness level of these parents concerning alternate ways of using materials with their children. At these sessions, we also showed a short film related to each of the two group's particular training. Thus the imaginative group was shown a film dealing with sociodramatic play; the cognitive group viewed a film dealing with language. The television group also received further research material and suggestions concerning the effects of TV.

EXPERIMENTAL EXPECTATIONS

The intervention study was designed to provide parents with means of coping more effectively with the influence of television on the development of their children. Two major strategies were involved—an indirect but active approach in which stimulation of the child's imaginative play would presumably minimize some of the direct effects of TV and a direct, TV-control training procedure. The Cognitive Training group was an active approach, offering parents something useful but essentially unrelated to the control of TV or to the encouragement of imagination. The control subjects served as a kind of baseline group.

If the training approaches were effective, there are several procedures for obtaining evidence of this: (1) Children whose parents received imagination training should reflect this by increases in their spontaneous imaginative play during the post training period, Probes 3 and 4. They should also show increases in positive affect, cooperation with peers, and language usage. Reductions in overall TV-viewing or at least in viewing of more indiscriminate or violent programming might be expected. (2) Children whose parents received training in television control should show a systematic drop in TV-viewing frequency and should also manifest a shift away from "less desirable" shows such as action detective toward the educational TV shows or toward children's shows generally or perhaps toward nonviolent adult family shows if anything. Such viewing shifts might also be reflected in behavioral changes in the direction of more pro-social behavior and in more extensive language usage (if TV-viewing is indeed associated with less adequate language development).

To the extent that sheer intervention with parents is a factor in motivating parental action (a "Hawthorne" effect) one might expect more behavioral, language, and TV-viewing changes to be reflected by children whose parents were in the three intervention groups relative to the control group. After all the parents all knew that the study was related to television and its presumed effects.

Following randomization in assignment of parents to groups there were no significant differences between the children of these parents on the major independent variables or in the relative distribution of the sexes or social classes for the three treatment groups or for the untreated control group.

RESULTS

In general, the statistical results of the intervention study can be described as somewhat disappointing. Extensive statistical analyses for experimental effects carried out using ANOVAs for boys, girls, and the groups combined, employing difference scores rather than absolute scores, reveal little evidence of significant main effects or even anticipated interactions. Imaginative and cognitive training both yield increases in the spontaneous imaginative play of children, but results for other behavioral variables are less clear.

Especially unsatisfactory were the findings for the TV-control training group. Examinaton of the patterns of results suggests that this group is often almost indistinguishable from the control group. The two groups receiving training in interaction with children around imagination and cognitive skills do, indeed, cluster together in effects and suggest that parents welcomed the opportunity to learn things they could do with their children. By contrast, the TV group (which was actually more resistant during training) was receiving information and methods for controlling or limiting their children's behavior.

If we examine our data when we combine the Imaginative and Cognitive Training groups and compare them with the TV and control groups, the results are somewhat more encouraging. Whereas, again, statistically significant results do not emerge, the pattern of difference are on the whole in the anticipated direction. This is especially true for the language and TV-viewing variables. For example, we find that after parent training the children whose parents were in imaginative and cognitive groups are watching significantly less variety/game shows, using significantly fewer TV references in their language than children fron the TV or control groups. Boys from the imagination and cognitive groups used significantly more words and make more utterances and make fewer TV references during play than do boys whose parents were in the TV or control groups. Girls from the imagination and cognitive groups are showing significantly better concentration and are watching significantly less sports and news TV shows.

The overall pattern suggests that for the behavioral variables the imagination-cognitive group children are showing more imaginativeness of play, better concentration, more peer and adult interaction; they dropped off less than did the TV-training and the controls in signs of elation during play whereas the TV-control children show more fatigue or sluggishness during play. For the language variables the children whose parents received training in imagination or cognitive skills are showing more words used, more utterances, longer mean lengths of utterances, fewer TV-references, and more use of future verbs. With respect to TV, the imagination-cognitive groups have declined more in weekly TV-viewing from their initial levels, but are concentrating better when they do watch TV. They are watching fewer cartoons, have dropped off less in watching children's shows, are watching fewer situation comedies, variety/game shows or other adult fare including news and sports.

The Imaginative and Cognitive Training groups show the anticipated or "desirable" changes in 6/14 behavioral variables, 9/11 TV-viewing variables, and 5/6 language variables. Overall, then, there are changes in 20/31 variables of importance which reflect the influence of the active intervention methods with parents compared to the television-training or control conditions. These effects are not strong enough to yield many statistically significant results but they do suggest that four parent-training sessions and the distribution of manuals can begin to have some influence on the subsequent behavior of children. The control group did show (for boys) an increase in TV-viewing and (for girls) only a very slight decline compared with larger declines in overall viewing for the three intervention groups. We have reason to believe, therefore, that on an overall basis intervention with parents can begin to lead to some constriction of their children's TV-viewing frequency. We have already mentioned the finding that the shift in the direction of the cross-lagged correlations between TV-viewing and subsequent aggression on a later probe does not appear for the control subjects. Thus it is possible that our intervention efforts did moderate the possible causal link between TV-viewing and aggression.

Our data on the whole seem to support a view that direct efforts at training parents to control and limit children's TV-viewing (even when the children are just 3 and 4) may not be as effective as giving the parents more active things to *do* with the children, games and exercises to foster imagination and language usage. Our data as well as qualitative indications from talks with parents and letters received from them suggest that parents are uncomfortable with an emphasis on controlling the child's TV-viewing. It seems clear that by even 3 and 4, the TV habit is so well established and the use of TV as a "companion" and baby sitter is so much a part of family life that direct efforts at change may not only be ineffective, but may be actively resisted by the parents. It is likely that three training sessions of two hours each with a "booster" a few months later may not be sufficient to accomplish such a goal.

QUALITATIVE FINDINGS

Comments regarding the materials sent to the parents were solicited through the mail. In general the parents reported favorably on the training (see appendix for samples). Parents in the imagination and cognitive groups expressed general appreciation with such statements as "Very helpful—loved the parent sessions; hope we hear from you again"; "Very informative—new insights at playtime"; "They have provided many interesting and useful ideas which I have modified for our own use"; "I find them very informative. Our dependence on TV has not been as excessive, because we are finding more things to do." More negative comments came from the Television Training group, and some parents in the other groups felt the games were "obvious" and "inane," but a significantly larger percentage reported that they could enjoy the games, saw some changes in their children as a result of less TV-watching, and as one parent stated: "We have more things to do together now."

Many of the parents reported that because of the training sessions, they began to watch TV with their children. One parent, for example, wrote: "Primarily as a result of the training sessions, we are watching more TV with our son now and are making more comments to interpret what he sees. I have also tried to discourage Saturday morning cartoon viewing, but haven't been too successful!"

Finally, some of the parents commented on our inclusion of their own brainstorming materials at the sessions and some asked for further contact with the center. On the whole parent reports indicate that training is of value, and from this experience with parents our future studies will substantially increase the number of parent contacts. It seems that presenting parents with ideas for play can produce a less passive child. One parent from the imaginative group commented: "John is no longer in the TV syndrome. He comes in and starts playing by himself (not too quietly)."

Training manuals for use by parents in encouraging imaginative play and cognitive growth in their children are now available for further use as a result of this study. The television-control manual is also available although its efficacy is less certain. The efforts to change overall viewing patterns may have to start with younger children or may require a *combination* of cognitive, imaginative, and TV-training for parents as well as for nursery school teachers. An evaluation of such a more massive effort is currently underway with a new sample of preschoolers from lower socioeconomic backgrounds.

In conclusion, despite our serious concern about influencing behavior, language, and viewing patterns through intervention with parents, we lacked the resources to provide a sufficiently intensive experience for the parents. We must also admit that our feeling is that television has become so entrenched in the daily life of children and families that direct efforts to influence parents to restrict viewing in any drastic way are doomed to meet strong resistance. Training efforts need to be integrated more with school activities; cooperation from the industry and from parent groups is also necessary. We believe our procedures for providing parents with cognitive and imaginative exercises were especially well received but it remains to be seen whether more extensive work along this line can make a change in the ingrained TV-viewing patterns of children.

9 Television and Imagination: What We Have Learned and What Still Lies Ahead

LARGE-SCALE FIELD RESEARCH: SOME IMPLICATIONS

In carrying through a large-scale research, one often learns much more than is expressed in the statistical analyses and formal presentations of data. We have during the two years of the study visited dozens of nursery schools and daycare centers, talked with scores of teachers, and met with more than 200 parents of preschoolers. Although we could not, for methodological reasons, serve as formal observers and raters of the children in our study, we have spent hours watching the groups at play and we have also read over hundreds of written protocols of interviews and play observations of the 3- and 4-year-olds.

Our work has involved a mixture of basic *developmental psychology* as we have studied processes of language and play in 3s and 4s over a year, of *clinical psychology* as we have pondered family interview data and the play patterns of individual children, and of *community psychology* as we have sought through our intervention procedures to raise the consciousness of groups of families concerning imagination, cognitive skills, and the possible impact of television. In concluding this work we are taking the liberty, therefore, of moving somewhat beyond the formal data of the previous chapters to present more speculative interpretations and implications drawn from our broader experiences.

Principal investigators of social science field researches usually report their results in rather formal and much too abbreviated formats, dictated by the financial exigencies of page limitations in professional journals. What gets left out are the day-to-day contacts with the "real" people who are the "subjects" or "participants" in the research or the numerous staff members who have to go out day after day to field settings and, as unobtrusively as possible, carry out careful observations or engage in testing and interviewing in cramped quarters or under other often uncomfortable circumstances. In leading a large-scale study one must be especially careful to adhere to ethical standards in dealing with human beings that conform to personal, professional, or government-decreed principles. And there are community relationships that must be maintained if so large a study is to continue over a period of time. We have taken great pains to train our observers about unobtrusive interventions and to meet as much as possible with school authorities to insure that our research was not disrupting their own routines. An observer who stretched out in a skimpy bathing suit on the lawn of a church housing one of the nursery schools in our study had to be confronted summarily not only with the impropriety of the behavior but with the danger it presented to the overall continuation of the project.

Carrying on research of this kind necessitates constant preoccupation with issues of ethics, public relations, some skill at diplomacy, and even salesmanship. Indeed in the numerous preliminary meetings we hold with potential-participant school personnel or parents we find ourselves sometimes having to insist that we are not pitchmen who, after a lively spiel on the pervasiveness of television, will turn around and try to sell some electronic gadgetry to the audience. As serious scientific investigators we have come to feel that participation in research ought to be a basic obligation of a citizenry that would certainly wants its officials ultimately to draw on reasonably solid information in generating social policies. If government bodies like the Federal Communications Commission or the Federal Trade Commission or the state or local school boards as well as educational authorities are to have available a substantial body of systematized information or adequately tested theories then qualified researchers must have continuing access to settings and to people whose behavior can be studied under appropriate ethical constraints. Too much of what has been said pro and con about television's impact on children has been derived from casual observation, the overgeneralizations of a few physicians who have talked with a small number of children or parents in clinical settings, the frustrated reactions of some exasperated teachers, or the defensiveness of some television industry representatives. There is no alternative to careful research and such work necessitates broad public cooperation.

In the work carried out at the Yale Family Television Center we have sought wherever possible to intermingle research on basic theoretical questions with work that can be of direct use to participant schools or parents. We have also tried to feed back as much information as possible to parents and teachers at the conclusion of the study as was feasible. At the same time we continue to believe that research participation should be more regularly accepted by schools and parents as an inherent feature of the educational experience. The experimenting society (Campbell, 1975) is, we believe, ultimately the freest and healthiest one.

IMAGINATION AND PLAY IN THE PRESCHOOLERS' DEVELOPMENT

We began this investigation with some assumptions and hypotheses about the origins of imagination and its possible adaptive value for the growing child. If one takes into account the technical difficulties of obtaining information about this most private form of human expression we believe our investigation has carried us along a good deal further in understanding children's fantasy behavior and its implications. We can identify two basic forms that childhood imagination takes in the third and fourth years. One pattern we can identify through watching the child's spontaneous activity: *imaginativeness* as reflected in setting up pretend games; talking to blocks as if they represented persons; transcending or transforming time and space. By 3 years of age enough children show consistency in the extent to which they will demonstrate pretend elements in their play to suggest that we can regard imaginativeness as a personality trait or style. Contrary to some popular concerns, such make-believe play seems to be a part of a kind of healthy, exuberant playful style that includes signs of joy, constructive interpersonal contact, and expressive language usage.

The second form imagination takes, as we can measure it, seems a more private one. It seems reflected in an inner sensitivity to "movements in the mind's eye" and emerges in the child's seeing of humans in motion when asked to give responses to inkblots, the M responses on the variant of the famous Rorschach Test which we employed. The imaginary or invisible playmate as reported by parent or child is still another manifestation of this private capacity or inclination. Piaget (1932) long ago speculated that the egocentric speech of the child as it plays is gradually internalized into private fantasy so that only socialized communication intended for others emerges. We suspect that it is this internalization process that we are picking up from the fact that M responses and imaginary playmates load on a separate factor along with cooperation with peers.

It is the older children and especially the older girls (already somewhat more socially and cognitively advanced than boys) who show more of the inner imagination. It may well be the case that the drop in spontaneous language use we find in the older girls of our study during the fourth probe (when some are now well into their fifth year) reflects just the process suggested by Piaget. They may no longer "need" to talk out all their thoughts or to manifest imagination only by the direct actions we can score as imaginativeness of play.

It does seem likely that our 5-year-old girls are indeed becoming "little women," more judicious in speech, less inclined to manifest their fantasies in overt, flamboyant play, less dependent on television as their own inner resources crystallize. Whereas imaginativeness of play as a variable loads slightly positively with television-viewing and aggression we know that the inner imagination measures are inversely related to TV and aggression. More subtle analyses do suggest that our measure of inner and overt imagination are related (a finding also reported by Shmukler, 1978). It seems possible that the overt expression of fantasy play may indeed reflect an earlier stage of development that can eventually be transformed into private fantasy. It is the later stage of such a development that may make for the imaginative child's greater resourcefulness in situations of delay or frustration or in the possibly reduced susceptibility to the more noxious influences of television.

The shift from overt to private imagery which we seem to see in its incipient phases during the child's fifth year bears comparison with psychoanalytic speculations about "the internalization of the object" as a critical phase of ego development (Blatt & Wild, 1976). In simplified terms, this theory proposes that maturity and the ability to avoid thought disorder or breakdown under stress depend on the extent to which a child (or the later adult) has incorporated the representation of parental images, morality, or values as part of an organized self-directing system. A feature of such internalization is the establishment of clearer "boundaries" between self and others. Such boundaries presumably allow for independent differentiation of schema for internal experiences, memories, plans, wishes, and of externally generated experiences with fathers, mothers, friends, authorities, lovers.

We are inclined to feel that the internalization process is indeed a critical feature of a child's development although we are uncomfortable about phrasology, the seeming impersonality of the term "the object," and the implication that it is one "object," presumably the mother, whose incorporation is so important. We are more inclined to believe that the developing child needs to learn how to be comfortable with its own thoughts, how to step back from direct action to contemplate through its own memories and fantasies the realm of the "possible." Certainly imagery seems a basic component of human information-processing capacities. Still it seems likely that children need to learn through imitation, example, encouragement and practice how to attend to their own ongoing thoughts, how to transform the objects of the environment into playthings they can at least temporarily control, and how to recreate in miniature, accessible form some of the many complex, confusing, or frightening scenes they have experienced.

The role of a benign adult seems essential to help the child accomplish this development of imaginative skill. The parent or grandparent who lovingly tells a bedtime story establishes a basis for the child to start telling stories to itself with the sense that such activity is sanctioned and is indeed a part of the security and closeness in one's life. Even frightening material presented in the warmth of a bedtime relationship may have benign effects as Bettelheim (1975) has proposed. Was it an accident that Dickens used the same family name as his childhood story-telling nurse, Miss Weller, (Mankowitz, 1976) for the name of one of his warmest and most delightful characters, Mr. Pickwick's servant, Sam?

Earlier research has suggested that more imaginative older children do indeed report that their parents tell them stories or play fantasy games with them (Singer, 1961, 1973). In our present study one of the statistically reliable differences between the families of the high TV-viewing high aggression children and the other families according to mother's accounts was that there was very little bedtime story-telling or reading in these children's homes. There was, indeed, no quiet, settling-down time described, compared with other groups. Instead, after a late night of TV, the child was packed off to bed with the requirement of a prayer. Prayer may be soothing and encouraging of meditation for adults but for preschoolers it is often a lonely and rapidly repeated ritual whose words convey little meaning to so young a child. We wonder if the susceptibility of our high TV high aggression children to imitation of violent TV content might not reflect the fact that they lacked parental endorsement and demonstration of inner imaginative behavior. Perhaps lacking such preparation for making-believe and for identifying fantasy they simply copied the violence they saw on TV rather than incorporating it into a story format in which other children could share or by means of which they could entertain themselves.

We have referred to a study by Dr. Diana Shmukler (1978) carried out in South Africa during the same period as our own work. Dr. Shmukler analyzed her data on imagination in preschoolers in relations to the mothers' attitudes. She found that children who showed more imaginativeness and positive affect also had mothers whose own behavior was rated by observers as reflecting more imagination, warmth, and involvement. A Boolean statistical analysis that looks at the patternings of groups of statements from interviews or questionnaires as they best discriminate certain play patterns revealed that the single best predictor of the child's imaginativeness from a group of background variables was the report that *mother tells stories*. The best pair of predictors were *mother tells stories* and *mother accepts child*. We have already mentioned our earlier findings that the mothers of children who played imaginatively in nursery school rated themselves higher on adjectives such as independence and creativity than did mothers of less-imaginative children. Even stronger findings indicating that the self-ratings of *both* parents for values like imagination and creativity predict spontaneous imaginative play by their preschoolers have recently been obtained by Tower (1980).

Clearly the establishment of an atmosphere at once warm and also encouraging of imagination by story-telling is a significant part of the internalization process. Further encouragement of spontaneous make-believe activities may aid the child in developing private resources. Initiation of fantasy games and then *stepping back* (Shmukler, 1978; Singer, 1973; Singer & Singer, 1977) may be important in allowing the child to continue to develop fantasy skills.

TELEVISION, IMAGINATION, AND AGGRESSION

If story-telling is so useful in generating an imaginative tendency then television in the home should be a powerful stimulant towards fantasy and imaginative resourcefulness in the child. Our data and our more general observations suggest that a major consequence of television-viewing is the creation of a common consciousness—a widespread equivalance of experience on which imagination and communication may be constructed. Never before in history have so many children from diverse subcultural backgrounds grown up with such similar experiences. In Ancient Greece, perhaps, the oral learning of the *Iliad* and the *Odyssey* and of a common mythology of gods and heroes made for some comparability of consciousness. Today the preschool child whether an American Indian from South Dakota or New Mexico, an Italian-American from East Haven, Connecticut, a Jewish-American from New York City, an Anglo-Saxon Southerner from Plains, Georgia, or a Black-American from Detroit, Michigan, all can sing the McDonald's jingle, the United Airlines song, can identify O. J. Simpson, Hertz Rent-a-Car, the Fonz, and Wonder Woman. Twenty or 30 years from now a novelist or TV script writer will probably produce a national shock of recognition or nostaligia-wave by suddenly introducing a character like The Fonz, instantly recognizable to 100 million aging citizens.

But if television is contributing to the *content* of consciousness, is it having an impact on the structural properties of thought, the capacity to attend to and to manipulate the stream of consciousness (Pope & Singer 1978)? Our data and observations indicated that heavy TV-viewing did not seem to be conducive to the development of the imaginative capacities of our middle-class preschoolers. The heavy viewers seemed less likely to be our most imaginative children. The pattern we found was that TV references during play did reflect frequent viewing but it went along with less expressiveness in language and with a greater trend toward overt aggression or uncooperative behavior with the teachers. Indeed our heavy viewers, although not concentrating on the set as intensely as some of the low frequency watchers, spent more than seven hours a day watching TV. With five or more hours at school these 3- and 4-year-olds were spending very little time in just exploring their physical environment or in developing games of mastery, rules, or pretend that can be so enjoyable and adaptive a part of the growth process. With so little being tried in the way of alternatives one wonders if such children are not growing up poorly equipped to discriminate social reality from the fantasy of TV and are failing to acquire the skills of complex interchange because one does not really converse with an electronic box. Their *recognition memory* may be great but they have little practice in rapid retrieval of words and concepts because such processes require active practice.

And, of course, there is aggression. True, none of our children were "monsters" or presented major examples of serious violence. But the link of heavy viewing to attacking other children or property as a consistent pattern cannot be denied. Frankly, we had not anticipated so clear a result as we obtained. Our finding, too, that specific programs, the action shows that more than others present a model for violence, were the most discriminating predictors of a child's aggressive behavior in school confirm the results of Lefkowitz et al. (1977) and support the theoretical and experimental analyses of Bandura's (1973) social learning theory. We obtained such data from a relatively middle-class sample. Subsequently we have had the opportunity to study 200 children from a lower socio-economic group, working-class, and more innercity-oriented backgrounds. Our results still under analysis confirm the link between viewing of action shows, aggressive cartoons, and overt aggressive behavior.

We had hoped to use the stimulation of imagination in children through parent-training as a means of mitigating possible noxious influences of TV-viewing. Our developmental data do offer some support to the possibility that the more imaginative preschoolers will either watch less TV or, if they do watch a lot (as in our high TV low aggression sample) may prove to be less overtly aggressive. Our parent-training efforts did not produce statistically powerful effects, however, and we need to reexamine our methods. Very likely the number of training sessions for parents were too few and the reliance on very large group sessions probably somewhat less than optimal as a teaching device.

We have decided to move beyond parent-training alone. Our current study with several hundred preschoolers includes training of nursery school teachers to employ a series of 30 lesson plans that can stimulate cognitive skills, imagination, and pro-social behavior in children. Parents can also be provided with similar training. Ultimately we need to develop some techniques designed to help children to adopt a more active orientation toward the TV they watch, encouraging parents and teachers to help children use new concepts and play theories from whatever current TV program they happen to be watching. It remains to be seen whether such an approach will work to increase imaginativeness, language expression, and reduce aggression.

USING TV CONSTRUCTIVELY

We have been stressing the relationship between TV-viewing and imaginative play or aggression. There is also a small but impressive body of evidence that TV-viewing can increase what have been called pro-social behaviors, sharing, helping, cooperating, offering positive reinforcement to others (Stein, Friedrich, & Vondracek, 1972; Friedrich & Stein, 1975; Coates, Pusser, & Goodman, 1976). These effects have been particularly demonstrated with exposure of preschoolers to *"Mister Rogers' Neighborhood,"* a program developed with considerable thought about the development level of preschool viewers and their cognitive and affective needs. It is important to note that in our own studies with this program when children watched in small groups with an adult present there were positive changes in affect and social cooperation after two weeks of exposure (Tower, Singer, Singer, & Biggs, 1979).

In the investigation described in this book our data are based on a more naturally occurring situation. We found, for example, that after the first probe, high and low aggressive children differed significantly on a number of particular programs they had watched regularly according to the parents' logs. Most of the differences reflected heavier viewing by the high aggressives of a specific show. Only with *"Mister Rogers"* did we find that low aggressives were watching significantly more than highs. The factor analysis data based on a year-long analysis of TV-viewing and overt behavior indicates that watching of educational TV, for example, specifically those programs especially designed for children with special advice on constructive social behavior, loaded positively along with cooperativeness with peers, low aggression, and the inner imagination variables. Although we cannot definitely pin down the "causal" link it is also the case that our high TV-viewers but low aggressives are watching relatively more of these "benign" shows whereas the high aggressives are watching relatively less of them and more of the action shows.

It is hard to avoid the implication that we need much more in the way of thoughtful programming for young children—literally dozens of creatively developed interesting shows that dare to have somewhat slower formats, more repetition, considerable positive reinforcement, more emphasis on helping, sharing, and befriending, more clear-cut emphasis on reality-fantasy distinctions. In our current work with preschoolers we have developed brief TV segments to be used experimentally with teachers' lesson plans that highlights examples of increased sensory awareness, cognitive skill development, imagination, and pro-social behavior. Our hope is that we can alert even preschoolers toward dealing more actively with whatever is presented on TV.[1]

We are also currently evaluating some commericially developed programming designed for preschoolers that is strongly oriented toward providing the child with a constructive social perspective. Examples include men doing housework alongside women and a quiet, slow pace of presentation and a fantasy figure who responds to questions by pantomime rather than speech. Our preliminary obesvations suggest that children do enjoy this format and that preschoolers call out the words that the fantasy character mimes, thus taking a more active stance in relation to the program.

Still another approach we have undertaken at the Yale Family TV Center[2] has been to prepare lesson plans for use by teachers in social studies or language arts curricula for third, fourth, and fifth graders. Here our intent is also to help children develop a more active and discriminating stance toward the TV they are likely to watch in any case. Lesson plans include presentations of how TV works, how shows are put together and the different *genre,* for example, documentaries, news, fiction, cartoons, game shows, commercials, and so on. We discuss reality-fantasy distinctions, the role of stereotypes, and the nature of commercials. We have produced brief TV segments to demonstrate points in the lesson plans. We have tested the efficacy of these plans with experimental and control classes in a local school district. Results were excellent and we would hope to see schools generaly adopting comparable materials. TV is an institution of our society so pervasive that our children need to learn about it much as they learn about the government, the stars and planets, or the ecology of their communities.

WHO CONTROLS THE TV AND WHO SHOULD CONTROL IT?

One of the most impressive features of our overall experience in directing this study was of the widespread and heavy use of TV by preschoolers. Keep in mind that our parent group was largely of a moderately comfortable middle-class background and reasonably well educated. The extensive use of TV as a

[1]Study supported by the Spencer Foundation and by the National Science Foundation.
[2]With the support of a grant from the American Broadcasting Company.

baby sitter was simply astounding to us. As a matter of fact we received the most "flack" from the parent groups whose consciousness we were trying to raise about the nature of the medium with the obvious intent of getting them to cut down their children's viewing. It is true that viewing frequencies were reduced somewhat from the initial high levels for our participants but we were struck by how resistant families were to shutting off the set. We can only ask, then, if parents will not pull the plug are they prepared to let a small number of network executives make the decisions about the influences to which their preschoolers are exposed?

In a certain sense, the U.S. government has control over television but in an extremely limited way: the Federal Communications Commission could refuse to renew a station's license—an occurrence almost unthinkable in the nearly 50-year history of that commission. The Federal Trade Commission has recently raised a question about whether commercials should be permitted in association with programming directed at children. Even if such a ruling were forthcoming and could stand up under constitutional test the facts from our research and the Nielsen ratings make clear that our most susceptible viewers are watching a considerable amount of adult programming at hours other than on the Saturday morning "children's ghetto."

Because few people would really welcome government censorship we might still hope that federal agencies could emphasize more extensive and thoughtful children's programming as an expectation for local stations or networks. Industry self-regulation seems to have worked (often after consumer pressure) in the adherence of networks and advertisers to codes of fairness to children in advertising developed by the National Association of Broadcasters and by the Children's Advertising Review Unit of the Council of Better Business Bureaus (which monitors network children's commercials). Industry has recently been more responsive to outcries against violence and the 1978-1979 programming called for fewer regular direction action series than in a long while. But the evening movies promised for the year on TV are still full of disasters and violence! Perhaps industry could continue to examine its offerings carefully and encourage artists to develop drama with action but will less realistic on-screen aggression capable of direct imitation by susceptible viewers.

Industry could use a tiny fraction of its enormous profits to provide a regular pool of funds for research on the medium and for evaluation of innovative writing and production of specialized material for children. At least then we could begin to consider a variety of creative formats that might capitalize on the medium's attraction to children.

Finally, however, we come back to the family. Somehow or other parents have to resume their responsibilities for how their child's consciousness is formed. True we no longer live in extended families and grandparents, uncles, or aunts are not around to entertain children with legendry or history tales.

Television certainly has a useful part to play and is a most welcome baby sitter in the single-parent family or in the harassed household of working parents. Wouldn't it make more sense though if parents knew what their children were watching and under what circumstances? Wouldn't it be better if they did some of the story-telling or at least shared some of the TV-watching of carefully selected programming with their children—not just sitting passively with the child but actively discussing, explaining, and even teaching? The human imagination is one of our greatest resources. We believe this exciting capacity of the growing child is nurtured best through the relationship with a warm, communicating parent and not through passive exposure to an electronic screen.

References

Ames, L. B., & Learned, J. Imaginary companions and related phenomena. *Journal of Genetic Psychology,* 1964, *69,* 147–167.

Anderson, R. M. *Imaginary companions among fourth and fifty grade children as related to selected psychological and demographic variables.* Unpublished Master's dissertation, Ohio State University, 1977.

Ardrey, R. *The territorial imperative.* New York: Dell, 1966.

Bailyn, L. Mass media and children: A study of exposure habits and cognitive effects. *Psychological Monographs,* 1959, *73,* (1, Whole No. 471).

Bandura, A. *Psychological modeling: Conflicting theories.* Chicago: Aldine-Atherton, 1971.

Bandura, A. *Aggression: A social learning analysis.* Englewood Cliffs, N.J.: Prentice-Hall, 1973.

Baron, R. A. *Human aggression.* New York: Plenum, 1977.

Belson, W. A. *Television and the adolescent boy.* Hampshire, England: Saxon House, 1978.

Berkowitz, L. (Ed.). *Roots of aggression.* New York: Atherton Press, 1969.

Bettleheim, B. *The uses of enchantment.* New York: Random House, 1975.

Blatt, S., & Wild, C. *Schizophrenia; A developmental analysis.* New York: Academic Press, 1976.

Bloom, L. *Language and play as developmental correlates.* Paper presented at the meeting of the American Psychological Association, New Orleans, August, 1974.

Boger, R. P. *Parents as primary change agents is an experimental Head Start Program language intervention.* Experimental program report, November 1969, ERIC Document Reproduction Service, No. ED 044168.

Branch, T. New frontiers in American philosophy. *The New York Times Magazine,* August 14, 1977, 12–22.

Brodzinsky, D. M., Messer, S. B., & Tew, J. D. Sex differences in children's expression and control of fantasy and overt aggression. *Child Development,* 1979, *50,* 372–379.

Buss, A. H. Aggression pays. In J. L. Singer (Ed.), *The control of aggression and violence.* New York: Academic Press, 1971.

Caldeira, J., Singer, J. L., & Singer, D. G. *Imaginary playmates: Some relationships to preschoolers' spontaneous play, language and television-viewing.* Paper presented at the meeting of the Eastern Psychological Association, Washington, D.C., March 1978.

Campbell, D. T. Assessing the impact of planned social change. In G. M. Lyons (Ed.), *Social research and public policies.* Hanover, N.H.: University Press of New England, 1975.

Chaffee, S. Television and adolescent aggressiveness. In J. P. Murray, G. A. Comstock, & E. A. Rubinstein (Eds.), *Television and social behavior* (Vol. 3). Washington, D. C.: Government Printing Office, 1972.

Church, J. (Ed.). *Three babies: Biographies of cognitive development.* New York: Random House, 1966.

Cicchetti, D. V. Assessing interrater reliability for rating scales: Resolving basic issues. *British Journal of Psychiatry,* 1976, *129,* 452–456.

Cline, V. B., Croft, R. G., & Courrier, S. Desensitization of children to television violence. *Journal of Personality and Social Psychology,* 1973, *27,* 360–365.

Coates, B., Pusser, H. E., & Goodman, I. The infuence of "Sesame Street" and "Mister Rogers' Neighborhood" on children's social behavior in the preschool. *Child Development,* 1976, *47,* 138–144.

Comstock , G., Chaffee, S., Katzman, N., McCombs, M., & Roberts, D. *Television and human behavior.* New York: Columbia University Press, 1978.

Dansky, J. L. *Cognitive functions of sociodramatic play: A training study.* Unpublished doctoral dissertation, Ohio Dominican College, 1976.

Dennis, L. G. *Individual and familial correlates of children's fantasy play.* Unpublished doctoral dissertation, University of Florida, 1976.

Dollard, J., Doob, L., Miller, N., Mowrer, O., & Sears, R. *Frustration and aggresstion.* New Haven: Yale University Press, 1939.

Eisenberg, G. J. *Effect on subsequent behavior of seven year olds after observed film aggression with sanctioning adults.* Unpublished doctoral dissertation, Fordham University, 1978.

Feilitzen, C. von. The functions served by the media: Report on a Swedish study. In R. Brown (Ed.), *Children and television.* Beverly Hills, Ca.: Sage, 1976.

Fein, G. A transformational analysis of pretending. *Developmental Psychology,* 1975, *11,* 291–296.

Feshbach, S., & Singer, R. D. *Television and aggression.* San Francisco: Jossey-Bass, 1971.

Fiedler, L. *Love and death in the American novel.* New York: Stein & Day, 1966.

Filep, R. T. *The Sesame mother project.* Final report, Augusut 1971, ERIC Document Reproduction Service, No. ED 055676.

Fraiberg, S. *The magic years.* New York: Scribners, 1959.

Freud, S. [Beyond the pleasure principle.] In J. Strachey (Ed. and trans.), *The standard edition of the complete psychological works of Sigmund Freud.* London: Hogarth, 1955. (Originally published in 1920.)

Friedlander, B. Z., Wetstone, H. S., & Scott, C. S. Suburban preschool children's comprehension of an age appropriate informational television program. *Child Development,* 1974, *45,*561–565.

Friedrich, L. K., & Stein, A. H. Aggressive and prosocial television programs and the natural behavior of preschool children. *Monographs of the Society for Research in Child Development,* 1973, *38* (4, Serial No. 151).

Friedrich, L. K., & Stein, A. H. Prosocial television and young children: The effects of verbal labeling and role playing on learning behavior. *Child Development,* 1975, *46,* 27–38.

Friedrich, L. K., Stein, A. H., & Susman, E. *The effects of prosocial television and environmental conditions on preschool children.* Paper presented at the meeting of the American Psychological Association, Chicago, September 1975.

Gardner, H. What is play? In P. Chance (Ed.), *Learning through play.* New York: Gardner Press, 1979.

Garvey, C. *Interaction structures in social play.* Paper presented at the meeting of the American Psychological Association, New Orleans, August 1974.

Gerbner, G. Television and the family. *Prix Jeunesse Seminar,* Munich, West Germany, 1977.

Gerbner, G., & Gross, L. Living with television: The violence profile. *Journal of Communication,* 1976, *26,* 173–199.

Gershowitz, M. *Fantasy behaviors of clinic referred children in play environments with college undergraduates.* Unpublished doctoral dissertation, Michigan State University, 1974.

Goldberg, L. *Aggression in boys in a clinic population.* Unpublished doctoral dissertation, City University of New York, 1973.

Gould, R. *Child studies through fantasy.* New York: Quadrangle Books, 1972.

Graham, H. D., & Gurr, T. R. (Eds.). *The history of violence in America.* New York: Bantam Books, 1969.

Green, G. H. *Psychoanalysis in the classroom.* New York: Putnam, 1922.

Griffing, P. Sociodramatic play among young black children. *Theory into Practice,* 1974, *13,* 257–264.

Halpern, W. Turned-on toddlers. *Journal of Communication,* 1975, *25,* 66–70.

Hollenbeck, A. R., & Slaby, R. G. Infant visual and vocal responses to television. *Child Development,* 1979, *50,* 41–45.

Hollingshead, A. B., & Redlich, F. C. *Social class and mental illness: A community study.* New York: Wiley, 1958.

Hornick, R. C. Television access and the slowing of cognitive growth. *American Educational Research Journal,* 1978, *15,* 1–15.

Hurlock, E. B., & Burstein, M. The imaginary playmate: A questionnaire study. *Journal of Genetic Psychology,* 1932, *41,* 380–391.

Hutt, C. Play in the under-fives: Form development and function. In J. C. Howells (Ed.), *Modern perspectives in the psychiatry of infancy.* New York: Brunner/Maazel, 1979.

Izard, C. *Human emotion.* New York: Plenum, 1977.

Jersild, A. T. *Child psychology.* Englewood, N.J.: Prentice-Hall, 1968.

Jersild, A. T., Markey, F. V., & Jersild, C. L. *Children's fears, dreams, wishes.* New York: Teachers College Press, 1933.

Karnes, M. B., Teska, J. A., Hodgins, A. S., & Badger, E. D. Educational intervention at home by mothers of disadvantaged infants. *Child Development,* 1970, *41,* 925–935.

Lefkowitz, M. M., Eron, L. D., Walder, L. O., & Huesmann, L. R. *Growing up to be violent.* New York: Pergamon, 1977.

Leifer, A. D. *How to encourage socially-valued behavior.* Paper presented at the Society for Research in Child Development meetings, Denver, 1975.

Lesser, G. S. *Children and television.* New York: Random House, 1974.

Lewis, M., & Rosenblum, L. *The development of affect.* New York: Plenum, 1978.

Lewis, P. H. The relationship of sociodramatic play to various cognitive abilities in kindergarten. (Doctoral dissertation, Ohio State University, 1973.) *Dissertation Abstracts International,* 1973, *33,* 6179.

Liebert, R. M., Neale, J. M., & Davidson, E. S. *The early window: Effects of television on children and youth.* Elmsford, N.Y.: Pergamon Press, 1973.

Lieberman, J. N. *Playfulness.* New York: Academic Press, 1977.

Lorenz, K. *On aggression.* New York: Harcourt, Brace & World, 1966.

Lyle, J., & Hoffman, H. R. Children's use of television and other media. In E. A. Rubinstein, G. A. Comstock, & J. P. Murray (Eds.), *Television and social behavior* (Vol. 4). Washington, D.C.: U.S. Government Printing Office, 1972.

Lyle, J., & Hoffman, H. R. Television viewing by preschool-age children. In R. Brown (Ed.), *Children and television.* Beverly Hills, Ca.: Sage, 1976.

Maccoby, E. E. Why do children watch television? *Public Opinion Quarterly,* 1954, *18,* 239–244.

Maccoby, E. E. *Social Development.* New York: Harcourt Brace Jovanovich, 1980.

McCord, W., Mc Cord, J., & Howard, A. Familial correlates of aggression in nondelinquent male children. *Journal of Abnormal and Social Psychology,* 1969, *62,* 79–93.

McDougall, W. *An introduction to social psychology.* London: Methuen, 1908.

Mander, J. *Four arguments for the elimination of television.* Caldwell, N.J.: Morrow, 1978.

Mankowitz, W. *Dickens of London.* London: Weidenfeld & Nicolson, 1976.

Manosevitz, M., Prentice, N. M., & Wilson, F. Individual and family correlates of imaginary companions in preschool children. *Developmental Psychology,* 1973, *8,* 72–79.

Marcuse, H. *Eros and civilization.* Boston: Beacon Press, 1966.

Masih, V. K. Imaginary play companions of children. In R. Weizman, R. Brown, P. Levinson, & P. Taylor (Eds.), *Piagetian theory and the helping professions* (Vol. 1). Los Angeles: University of Southern California Press, 1978.

Milgram, S., & Shotland, R. L. *Television and antisocial behavior: Field experiments.* New York: Academic Press, 1973.

Miller, G., Galanter, E., & Pribram, K. *Plans and the structure of behavior.* New York: Holt, 1960.

Murray, J. P., Comstock, G. A., & Rubinstein, E. A. (Eds.). *Television and social behavior* (Vol. 3): *Television and adolescent aggressiveness.* Washington, D.C.: Government Printing Office, 1972.

Nabokov, V. V. *Speak memory.* New York: Putnam, 1966.

Nahme-Huang, L., Singer, J. L., Singer, D. G., & Wheaton, A. B. Imaginative play training and perceptual-motor interventions with emotionally-disturbed hospitalized children. *American Journal of Orthopsychiatry,* 1977, *47,* 238–249.

Noble, G. Film-mediated creative and aggressive play. *British Journal of Social and Clinical Psychology,* 1970, *9,* 1–7.

Noble, G. Effects of different forms of filmed aggression on children's constructive and destructive play. *Journal of Personality and Social Psychology,* 1973, *26,* 54–59.

Noble, G. *Children in front of the small screen.* London: Constable, 1975.

Olweüs, D. Stability of aggressive reaction patterns in males: A review. *Psychological Bulletin,* 1979, *86,* 852–875.

Paivio, A. *Imagery and verbal processes.* New York: Holt, Rinehart & Winston, 1971.

Pervin, L. A. The representative design of person-situation research. In D. Magnusson & N. S. Endler (Eds.), *Personality at the crossroads: Current issues in interactional psychology.* Hillsdale, N.J.: Lawrence Erlbaum Associates, 1977.

Piaget, J. *Language and thought of the child.* New York: Norton, 1932.

Piaget, J. *Play, dreams and imitation in childhood.* New York: Norton, 1962.

Pope, K., & Singer, J. L. (Eds.). *The stream of consciousness.* New York: Plenum, 1978.

Rohwer, W. D., Jr. Images and pictures in children's learning: Research results and educational implications. *Psychological Bulletin,* 1970, *73,* 393–403.

Rosenberg, B. *Mental activity and environmental responsiveness: Optokinetic nystagmus during mental tasks associated with the left and right cerebral hemispheres.* Unpublished doctoral dissertation, Yale University, 1977.

Rubin, K. H., Maioni, T. L., & Hornung, M. Free play behaviors in middle and lower class preschoolers: Parten and Piaget revisited. *Child Development,* 1976, *47,* (2), 414–419.

Saltz, E. *Training for thematic-fantasy play in culturally disadvantaged children.* Annual report to the Spencer Foundation, Wayne State University, 1976.

Saltz, E., & Johnson, J. Training for thematic-fantasy play in culturally disadvantaged children: Preliminary results. *Journal of Educational Psychology,* 1974, *66,* 623–630.

Schaefer, C. E. Imaginary companions and creative adolescents. *Developmental Psychology,* 1969, *1,* 747–749.

Schaefer, E. S., & Bell, R. Q. Development of a parental attitude research instrument. *Child Development,* 1958, *29,* 339–361.

Schramm, W., Lyle, J., & Parker, E. *Television in the lives of our children.* Stanford: Stanford University Press, 1961.

Scott: J. P. *Animal behavior.* Chicago: University of Chicago Press, 1972.

Shmukler, D. *The origins and concomitants of imaginative play in young childhood.* Unpublished doctoral dissertation, University of Witwatersrand, Johannesburg, South Africa, 1978.

Singer, D. G. Television and imaginative play. *Journal of Mental Imagery,* 1978, *2,* 145–164.

Singer, D. G., Caldeira, J., & Singer, J. L. *The effects of television viewing and predisposition to imagination on the language of preschool children.* Paper presented at Eastern Psychological Association, April 1977.

Singer, D. G., & Lenahan, M. L. Imagination content in dreams of deaf children. *American Annals of the Deaf,* February 1976, 44–48.

Singer, D. G., & Revenson, T. *A Piaget primer: How a child thinks.* New York: International Universities Press and New American Library, 1978.

Singer, D. G., & Singer, J. L. *Partners in play.* New York: Harper & Row, 1977.

Singer, J. L. Imagination and waiting behavior in young children. *Journal of Personality,* 1961, *29,* 396–413.

Singer, J. L. The influence of violence portrayed in television or motion pictures upon overt aggressive behavior. In J. L. Singer (Ed.), *The control of aggression and violence: Cognitive and physiological factors.* New York: Academic Press, 1971.

Singer, J. L. *The child's world of make-believe.* New York: Academic Press, 1973.

Singer, J. L. Imagination and make-believe play in early childhood: Some educational implications. *Journal of Mental Imagery,* 1977, *1* 127–144.

Singer, J. L. The power and limitations of television: A cognitive-affective analysis. In P. Tannenbaum (Ed.), *Television and entertainment. Report of an SSRC Conference.* Hillsdale, N.J.: Lawrence Erlbaum Associates, 1980.

Singer, J. L., & Brown, S. The experience-type: Some behavioral correlates and theoretical implications. In M. C. Rickers-Ovsiankina (Ed.), *Rorschach Psychology.* New York: Krieger, 1977.

Singer, J. L., Greenberg, S., & Antrobus, J. S. Looking with the mind's eye: Experimental studies of ocular motility during day-dreaming and mental arithmetic. *Transactions of the New York Academy of Sciences.* 1971, *33,* 694–709.

Singer, J. L., & Singer, D. G. Imaginative play in early childhood: Some experimental approaches. In A. Davids (Ed.), *Child personality and psychopathology.* New York: Wiley, 1976a.

Singer, J. L., & Singer, D. G. Can TV stimulate imaginative play? *Journal of Communication,* 1976b, *26,* 74–80.

Singer, J. L., & Singer, D. G. *Television viewing and imaginative play in preschoolers: A development and parent-intervention study.* Progress Report #1, National Science Foundation, No. DAR 6-20772, Yale University, July 1977a.

Singer, J. L., & Singer, D. G. Television: A member of the family. *The National Elementary School Principal,* 1977b, *56* (3), 50–53.

Singer, J. L., & Singer, D. G. *Television-viewing and imaginative play in preschoolers: A development and parent-intervention study.* Progress report #2, National Science Foundation No. DAR 6-70772, Yale University, May 1978.

Singer, J. L., & Streiner, B. F. Imaginative content in the dreams and fantasy play of blind and sighted children. *Perceptual and Motor Skills,* 1966, *22,* 475–482.

Smart, M. E. *Rationale and activities of project on television in early education.* Progress Report, University of Southern California, 1976.

Smilansky, S. *The effects of sociodramatic play on disadvantaged preschool children.* New York: Wiley, 1968.

Stein, A. H., Friedrich, L. K., & Vondracek, F. Television content and young children's behavior. In J. P. Murray, E. P. Rubinstein, & G. A. Comstock (Eds.), *Television and social behavior* (Vol. 2). Washington, D. C.: U.S Government Printing Office, 1972.

Sutton-Smith, B. Play, creativity, and moving. In E. Han & W. Preising (Eds.), *Human movement.* Schorndoff, Germany: Verlag Karl Hoffman, 1976.

Svendson, M. Children's imaginary companions *Archives of Neurology and Psychiatry,* 1934, *2,* 985–999.

Tannenbaum, P. H., & Zillmann, D. Emotional arousal in the facilitation of aggression through communication. *Advances in Experimental Social Psychology,* 1975, *8,* 149–192.

Tomkins, S. S. *Affect, imagery, consciousness* (Vol. 1). New York: Springer, 1962.

Tomkins, S. S. *Affect, imagery, consciousness* (Vol. 2). New York: Springer, 1963.

Tomkins, S. S. A theory of memory. In J. S. Antrobus (Ed.), *Cognition and affect.* Boston: Little, Brown, 1970.

Tower, R. B. Parent's self-concepts and preschool children's behaviors. *Journal of Personality and Social Psychology,* 1980, in press.

Tower, R. B., Singer, D. G., Singer, J. L., & Biggs, A. Differential effects of television programming on preschoolers' cognition, imagination, and social play. *American Journal of Orthopsychiatry,* 1979, *49,* 265–281.

Trilling, L. *The liberal imagination: Essays on literature and society.* New York: Viking, 1950.

Tucker, J. *The role of fantasy in cognitive-affective functioning: Does reality make a difference in remembering?* Unpublished doctoral dissertation, Teachers College, Columbia University, 1975.

Turner, J. D. *An investigation of the role the imaginary companion plays in the social development of the child.* Unpublished doctoral dissertation, Miami University, 1972.

U.S. Commission on Civil Rights. *Window dressing on the set: Women and minorities in television.* A report of the U.S. Commission on Women Civil Rights, 1977.

Watt, J. H., & Krull, R. An examination of three models of television viewing and aggression. *Human Communications Research,* 1977, *3,* 99–112.

Werner, H. *Comparative psychology of mental development.* Chicago: Follett, 1948.

White, B. L. *The first three years of life.* Englewood Cliffs, N.J.: Prentice-Hall, 1975.

Winn, M. *The plug-in drug.* New York: Viking, 1977.

Witelson, S. F. Sex and the single hemisphere: Specialization of the right hemisphere for spatial processing. *Science,* 1976, *193,* 425–427.

Appendix 1:
Behavioral Variables

I. The Nature of the Project

This study involves two major phases:

A. *Direct Observation of the Spontaneous
Play Behavior of Preschool Children*

This phase requires a number of careful recordings of exactly
what the child does and says during specific time periods on a
number of occasions. The emphasis is upon careful reporting and
recording without interpretation or evaluation. The protocol of
the play behavior during the sampling period then becomes a
basic source of data for further analysis in a number of ways
described. By having separate observers record the behavior of
each child at a given period we increase the chances of accurate
recording.

B. *Ratings by Independent Judges
of the Protocols of Play*

Here the task is to read and reread the protocol also trying to
recall (if the rater was also an observer) the actual scene and

appearance of the child and then to rate the behavior along certain preestablished dimensions. These rating scales represent schemes for categorizing the natural flow of a child's behavior for purposes of comparison with its behavior at other times under other circumstances, before or after certain experimental interventions, etc. Our goal in setting up these particular ratings is to choose specific behavior categories that may have important theoretical interest. As long as we have the records of the children's behavior in detail from at least two observers we can always go back to them and score them along additional scales as these are developed or suggested by the research of other investigators.

II.   **A Critical Feature in Observing and Recording Is Thoroughness.**

We need as much detail as possible on what the child does and says during the 10-minute observation period. This recorder should try to be as impersonal as a camera—this is no time for analysis and interpretation. Psychology is too full of people who jump to interpret without looking carefully at what actually goes on. Recording then should give a moment-to-moment account of the child's movements around the room, its comments, and the specific emotions displayed. In the case of emotions try to be objective and limited—don't assume that because a child pounds on a block he or she is angry. The child may be laughing and *that* is the emotion to record. The interpretation of underlying anger can come later if at all during ratings. Just indicate if the child laughs, cries, whines, moves slowly, hits another child, breaks a toy apparently intentionally, etc. Examples of *10-minute duration* recordings of the same child at the same time by two different observers are appended here as examples. Read them carefully and look at their similarities and differences. The care of recording is important because the protocols may later be rated by persons who have not actually observed the children as you have.

Work in *pairs* so that we always have at least two independent records for each child at each observation period.

Write the observations out carefully on the protocol sheets making sure you record the child's name, time and date of observation. Remember to write your own name on the protocol as well. Use ink if possible because others may be reading your protocol. It would be best if you could retype your protocol afterwards but this will not be required if you are not a good typist.

Record how child is dressed, general appearance, any mannerisms. Important that you and your partner observe the *same* child at the same time. Do not observe a child during a structured period (e.g., snack, group singing). The children will be rated eight times—twice during four separate two-week time intervals.

III. Instructions for Ratings

There are several types of ratings that are to be done in this study. The scales are presented in the following with definitions of each scale point from one to five with five representing the "high" end of the scale. Review the protocol carefully looking for examples of each level. Naturally the child may change from time to time. We are interested in your evaluation of the overall pattern and predominant direction of its behavior with respect to each dimension. Don't be afraid to use a full range of scores rather than sticking conservatively to the middle. After rating a few protocols you may want to go back and revise earlier ratings based on broader experience with more children in the group. Under no circumstances must you consult with your partner until *after* your rating is set down, however; the ratings must be completely independent. If you do have some strong reservations after both of you have done your ratings then write a little note and attach it to the rating sheets.

SCORING CRITERIA—PLAY OBSERVATIONS
SCALES FOR FIRST PHASE

1. Imaginativeness in Play

Score

1. Is extremely unimaginative in play. Introduces no pretend elements into the play situation. Extremely stimulus-bound by the play materials.

2. Is slightly imaginative in play, occasionally introducing fleeting pretend elements into play situation, but does not stay with any pretend situation for very long. No originality in pretend situations. A few pretend elements added to otherwise very stimulus-bound play. Picks up pretend elements from others but adds little of own to same.

3. Shows a moderate amount of pretending in play, but not very original or removed from the actual stimulus situation. Little organization or consistency of pretense or role-playing. No voice changes or simulated vocalizations.

4. Shows a substantial amount of pretending in play, spontaneously creating make-believe situations, showing some originality in pretending, following out sequences of plot. Some organization and consistency in pretense or role-playing, including some simulated vocalizations.

5. Shows high originality in the ways toys and play material are used. A very high number of pretend elements in play. Is able to go well beyond what the play stimuli in themselves suggest. Multifaceted focused play, divergent thinking shown from routine games or activity.

2. Positive Affect

(Note that *mild surprise, interest,* and *joy* are viewed as positive affects and scored high.)

Score

1. Shows no interest or pleasure in the toys, play, or other activities; much tangential behavior, conversations with observer, teacher, and others; critical remarks about toys or activities; no smiling, laughter, or evidence of pleasure in playing.

2. Shows only mild pleasure and interest in toys or activities; much looking around and/or desultory manipulation of play material. Occasional smiling or laughter.

3. Shows moderate interest, pleasure and enjoyment of activities and toys; communicates easily about the play activities; somewhat lost in quiet enjoyment, some smiling and/or laughter during activities; some animation.

4. Shows deep pleasure and interest in play activity, smiling or laughing frequently. Expresses frequent pleasure, describing it spontaneously or manifesting it in the content of play or through the "voices" of play objects.

5. Shows extreme delight; laughing, singing, smiling; thoroughly enjoying self, reluctant to leave play situation; interested and curious about environment—explores it with delight or enthusiasm; seems to show mild surprise and interest in novelty.

3. Persistence Summary Score

Score

1. Shows brief or little attention to or absorption in activities; aimless wandering, high distractibility, many questions to teacher; responding

to noises or talk of children in room. Hyperactivity with no real interaction with play material.

2. Engages in superficial play with toys and play material while looking around the room, staring passively, talking to teacher, or wandering aimlessly. Changes toys and/or activities frequently.

3. Responds with moderate interest to the toys or play activities. Changes activities two or three times during the 10-minute segment. Some distractibility. Some responses to outside stimuli such as noises and the talk and play of other children.

4. Shows good absorption to play activity, very little response to outside stimuli, change of activity once or twice during 10-minute segment; no tangential behavior or conversation pertaining to activities other than the one at hand.

5. Shows intense absorption in play activity; stays with one activity for most of observation period, oblivious to outside stimuli, may not even respond to direct questions from teacher or children not included in the play situation at hand.

4. Aggression Toward Others

Physical Aggression

Aggression as defined here refers *only* to aggressive acts directed at other children, adults, or property. Aggression that is built into a make-believe game which doesn't "hurt" anyone is *not* scored here, e.g., a child banging two toy dolls together as if "they" are fighting. A "play fight" between two children simulating characters, e.g., Batman and the Joker, in which they hold their punches or simulate slow motion fighting, is not scored. But a child who suddenly charges on another and hits him or her hard in the back without "pulling his punch" would get scored for aggression even if the child shouts, "I'm Batman!"

Score

1. Nonaggressive activity. At no time does the child strike or push another child, knock over toys or blocks (except in the context of a game) intentionally or engage in any direct physical acts suggesting hostility.

2. Child is restless and moves around room carelessly bumping into others' toys, occasionally disrupting others' games or play space.

3. Child shows at least *one* clear incident of banging or wrecking *own* toys or those of others or kicks an *object* in anger or frustration. No direct attacks on other children are scored here, however.

4. Child shows at least one clear incident of pushing, shoving, or attacking another child physically, snatches other's toys or combines disruption of play with physically menacing behavior or shows *several* instances of attacking objects or property.

5. Child shows at least *two* instances of physical attacks on others, disruptions of games, attempted destruction of property.

5. Interaction: Peers

Interaction occurs when a child has *contact with a peer* through conversation or play activities. Interaction differs from *cooperation* in that a child can be *contacting* many children within the observation period without cooperating in a game or construction, or other play activity. *Interaction* can also mean the seeking of attention through such comments as "Look at this," "Give me that!" "Watch me jump," which solicits contact. *Interaction* implies contact. It can be both positive or negative. High score is given for a meaningful relationship. The bossy-child syndrome scored high for *interaction* but perhaps scored low for *cooperation*. You will find that a high score in interaction usually is given to a child who is seeking a warm, friendly relationship.

Score

1. Does not interact with peers. No opportunity to elicit this behavior. (N.A.-1)

2. Shows reluctant and timid interaction with peers only as a result of peer solicitation. Displays uneasiness in this interaction—tries to avoid contact.

3. Participates more readily in activities with peers although does not actively seek the company of a peer. Responds well to peers, but does not initiate activity during this interaction.

4. Readily engages in and finds satisfaction in activities with peers. Seems comfortable and at ease in the company of peers. Shows spontaneity in these interactions. Builds intimate friendship with a peer.

5. Initiates and maintains highly meaningful and satisfying relationship with peers. Seeks attention, companionship, and trust with his peers. Maintains effective peer group as well as single peer relationships.

6. Interaction: Adults

(See foregoing for explanation.)

Score

1. Does not interact with adults. No opportunity to elicit this behavior. (N.A. = 1)

2. Shows reluctant and timid interaction with adults only as a result of peer solicitation. Displays uneasiness in this interaction. Whining and complaining to adults—tries to avoid contact.

3. Participates more readily in activities with adults although does not actively seek the company of an adult. Responds well to adults, but does not initiate activity during this interaction.

4. Readily engages in and finds some satisfaction in activities with adults. Seems somewhat comfortable and at ease in the company of adults. Shows spontaneity in these interactions.

5. Initiates and maintains interction with adults—chatters, shows adults own work, no signs of dependency.

7. Cooperation, Helping, and Sharing with Peers

Cooperation occurs when a child helps another child to build something, or to hold an object, or in cooperating in taking an *active, sharing, service role.* For example, to be rated as *cooperative* a child's behavior indicates more than mere contact; i.e., child helps another child in sharing a game either by assuming a role or assisting in a construction in order to enable a game to be mutually satisfying. For example, a cooperative activity occurs when two or more children are sharing a mutually satisfying end-product or sociodramatic game, a construction or activity for the teacher, e.g., cleanup, collecting toys, distributing food.

The following are examples of *cooperation:*

1. Your subject gives materials to another on his own intitiative or in response to a request ("Would you want my crayon?" "Here let me hold this for you!").

2. Your subject participates in a game that needs the subject's cooperation, i.e., holding hands in "Ring-around-a-Rosy."

3. Your subject actively assists in block building with others, i.e., helping to construct an "airplane," or a "garage," etc.

4. Your subject assists in cleaning up.

5. Your subject assists in role-playing in games such as "house" or "pirates" in order to carry out a story line, assuming roles such as "Mommy," "Daddy," "Captain Hook," etc.

6. Aids another child in distributing or collecting materials, or in dressing or undressing, etc.

Score

1. NA—(1) No opportunity presented to elicit this behavior.

2. Show no cooperative or helping behavior. Refuses to cooperate in play or in other interactions with peers; fails to obey instructions and requests of peers. Shows negative affect when a peer issues a request.

3. Shows a moderate amount of cooperation and mild interest in helping. Cooperative behavior is usually not spontaneous; depends on external peer suggestion or physical stimulus.

4. Shows slightly more cooperation and desire to help. Begins to initiate own cooperative behavior. May offer to share materials for a game.

5. Cooperates willingly and enthusiastically; exhibits spontaneous helping behavior toward peers. Seeks out situations where child can be of service to peers.

Cooperation, Helping, and Sharing with Adults

(See foregoing for explanation.)

Score

1. NA—(1) No opportunity presented to elicit this behavior.

2. Show no cooperative or helping behavior. Refuses to cooperate in play or in other interactions with adults; fails to obey instructions and requests of adults. Shows negative affect when an adult issues a request.

3. Shows a moderate amount of cooperation and mild interest in helping. Cooperative behavior is usually not spontaneous; depends on external adult suggestion or physical stimulus.

4. Shows slightly more cooperation and desire to help. Begins to initiate own cooperative behavior. May offer to share activities or materials with adults. May assist teacher who needs help in moving or carrying something.

5. Cooperates willingly and enthusiastically; exhibits spontaneous helping behavior toward adults. Seeks out situations where child can be of
service to adults. Brings materials over to share with teacher or other
adult.

Mood Instructions

"Moods" rate the display of emotions listed as variables 12–15. The *degree of
intensity* of the emotion displayed should be the primary factor in rating and
the *duration of the display* should also be considered in the assessment.
Ratings are as follows:

1. *Not at all:* No indication of this mood during the observation period.

2. *Slightly:* Some indication of this mood. A *mild* interaction. Short
duration (a few seconds). Perhaps a fleeting display of the emotion.

3. *Moderately:* A *definite* display of the emotion. Can be of short
duration, or extend over a longer period of time if the display is a
relatively mild one. For example, if the child is frowning, pouting, or
droopy during part of the observation, the child would be rated
Moderately Sad (3); or if the child whimpers or cries for only a brief
moment, the child would be rated *Moderately Sad* (3).

4. *Very:* A *display of strong emotion* over a period of time (at least a 30-
second incident) or a *mild display* of emotion over the entire 10-minute
observation. For example: if the child is frowning, pouting, and droopy
over the *entire 10-minute period,* the child would be rated *Very Sad* (4);
or if the child cries for a shorter period, the child would be rated *Very
Sad* (4).

5. *Extremely:* A display of *strong* emotion *most of the observation period*
or a display of *intense* or *extreme emotion* over a period of time (at least
a 30-second incident). For example, if the child cries during most of the
observation period, or has sobbed *intensely* for a minute, a rating of (5)
would be given.

Mood

The rating of the child's mood is somewhat more difficult and unusual. There
are six moods to be evaluated. Because each child's moods may fluctuate
from time to time and vary widely in even 10 minutes, it is important to rate
each child *on each mood* for the observation period. Note that a rating of 1
indicates *minimal* occurrence of the mood and a rating of 5 indicates a strong
manifestation of the mood. Try to rate in terms of the intensity as well as

Mood Check List

			Score		
Mood	1 Not At All	2 Slightly	3 Moderately	4 Very	5 Extremely
Fearful-Tense		pacing up and down, tapping feet or fingers	biting nails, wringing hands, pale eyes wide	cold, sweaty, squirming	facial trembling, body trembling body rigid, tremulous or quaver voice
Angry-Annoyed		shrug, like comment	frowns	stamps feet, bangs table, shrill voice	clenched fist, clenched jaw, red face, menacing posture, glaring, yelling, says "I'm mad!" etc.
Sad-Downhearted		looking down at floor	frowning, pouting, droopy	lips quivering, voice quivering, dropped shoulders, hunched position	crying, sobbing
Fatigued-Sluggish		leaning slouched, whining voice	feet dragging, plodding	eyes half-closed, heavy lidded, yawning	head on table, head bobbing, sprawled out in chair or on floor
Liveliness, Excitement		some bouncy activity but mostly quiet	a good deal of movement but no jumping or running	some running, jumping, hand-clapping, movement around room	considerable spontaneous movement, shouting, rapid shifts of activity
Elated, Pleased, Joyful		some smiling but generally quiet but not unhappy seeming	more smiling, some laughter, but mostly quiet	laughs several times, seems pleased and smiles when not simply absorbed	much laughing, smiling, clapping hands. Remarks like "Wow!" "Great!"

frequency of the mood. Thus, if the child seems sad and downhearted to the point of tears for 1-2 minutes but then cheers up for the balance of the observation period you would still rate the child 4 or 5 on the scale. You could also rate him 4 or 5 on positive affect if for the balance of the 10 minutes the child is laughing and joking. It is not likely you will get such extremes, however. Remember to rate each child on all moods, however. Wherever possible try to give the highest weight to the most predominant mood.

Appendix 2:
Sample Observation Protocol

Code Number _____

Date _____

Play Research Project
Observational Record

Dorothy G. Singer Child's Name _____ Sex ____
Jerome L. Singer Observer's Name _____
1976-1977 Observation Period 1 2 3 4

Physical Appearance and Clothing

Ten-Minute Sample

Time Begun _____ Time Ended _____

Start writing here:

Sitting at the play kitchen corner, playing with phone. Looks over at Dan (observer) and then at me. Looks over to the other kids. *"Ring, ring. Sweetheart you should be home now, dinner's ready. I want to know if you'll come how now."* *"Yeah."* She hangs up. Playing phone with other girl. Hangs up a mop on the hook. Holds a cake pan and looks around the room. *"I was gonna make some."* Starts taking the pots out of the cabinet. They are playing house. *"I'll make it, sweetheart."* Smiling slightly, very involved in her game. Takes pot and puts it on the stove. Goes in the cabinets looking for stuff and putting other pots and pans away. *"I'm gonna take the baby for a ride."* Pushes cart around the room. Goes over to where the boys are playing. Looks at what the other boys are doing. Stands pushing the carriage back and forth. Not smiling, shuffling, appears restless. Picks up pocketbook that fell. Puts it over her shoulder. *"I know its apple pie."* Looks around the room (5′). Goes back over to the kitchen corner. Takes out pots, scrapes ladle across the pan. Looks at Observer. Scrapes the pan with the ladle. Does this approximately a dozen times. Watching O's write down what she's doing (6′). Goes back to cabinet, opens it, and puts that pot away, then another. Playing alone now. Puts the "tea pot" on the stove. Ladles a deeper pot. Stops and stares at Observer, again putting objects in the cabinet. Takes another pan out of the oven and puts it back in the cabinet. Not playing with any other kids. *"Two apple pies, two apple pies I made."* Teacher tells kids to "freeze" because some boys are being rough. Betty has the ladle in her mouth. "Freeze" is over, Betty gets the doll carriage again. (9′). *Do we have to pick up?"* to teacher. Teacher says no. Looking around, ladle in mouth. Looks at other kids. Goes back to kitchen corner. Betty is now playing the mother in a new game of house. *"Here's some lemonade" (2X) "I made some lemonade."* Smiles infrequently throughout observation, spotty periods of concentration during house game.

Appendix 3:
Imagination Interview

Code # _____

Child Interview

Child's Name _____ Sex ____
Date of Interview _____
Interviewer _____

1. What is your favorite game? What do you like to play most? (Write verbatim answer. Query if not enough information to score.)

2. What game do you like to play best when you're alone? What do you like to do best when you're all alone? Do you ever think things up?

3. Do you ever have pictures in your head? Do you ever see make-believe things or pictures in your mind and think about them? What sort of things?

4. Do you have a make-believe friend? Do you have an animal or toy or make-believe person you talk to or take along places with you? (If yes, say "Tell me about it").

(Feel free to reword any of these if the child does not grasp their intent. Try *very* hard not to accept an "I don't know" but to get the child to come up with something).

Total Score = (Yes with imagination examples for each item yields a maximum score of 4.)

Appendix 4:
Imaginary Playmate

Questionnaire

July 1977

Dear Parents:

We hope you've been enjoying your summer and have been managing to follow our suggestions for a few minutes of activities with your child each day.

We would like some more information about your child. We are interested in imaginary playmates, such as invisible friends, stuffed animals, dolls, etc. that your child plays with. As far as psychologists know, for many children, having an imaginary playmate is part of a normal developmental phase. Please answer the following questions and return this page as soon as possible in the enclosed, stamped envelope. Keep in mind that any information remains confidential and your child is identified only by a code number. Thank you for your cooperation.

Sincerely,
Jerome and Dorothy Singer
Co-Directors
Family Television Research and
Consultation Center

Your Name _____ Child's Name _____

1. Has your child *ever* had an imaginary companion?
    Yes _____ No _____ More than one _____
    Even if answer to the above question is *no, please return this page.* This
    information is important to us.

2. Did this imaginary friend appear only once, more than once, or is it a
    steady companion?
    Only once _____ More than once _____ Steady companion _____

3. Does your child talk to the imaginary companion?
    Yes _____ No _____

4. What is the sex of the companion?
    Male _____ Female _____ Neuter _____ Don't know _____

5. Is the companion older, younger, or the same age as your child?
    Older _____ Younger _____ Same Age _____ Don't know _____

6. What name does this imaginary companion have? _____

7. Can you give a reason for the name? _____
    _____

8. What age was your child when you first noticed an imaginary
    companion? _____

9. Does anyone other than the child ever share the imaginary companion?
    Yes _____ No _____ Who? _____

10. Is the imaginary companion human or animal?
    Human _____ Animal _____ Other _____

11. What activities does your child and the imaginary companion engage
    in?
    _____
    _____
    _____

12. Describe the imaginary companion as fully as possible. _____
    _____
    _____
    _____

Please check next to any of the TV characters below that your child has *ever* pretended to be.

_____None

_____Romper Room Teacher

_____Mighty Mouse

_____Spider Man

_____Mr. Rogers

_____Batman

_____Superman

_____Wonder Woman

_____Sesame Street

(Specify)_____

_____Other

(Specify)_____

_____Fonzy

_____Donny Osmond

_____Marie Osmond

_____Emergency

_____Bionic Woman

_____Captain Kirk

_____Six Million Dollar Man

_____Brady Bunch

(Specify)_____

_____SWAT

(Specify)_____

Appendix 5:
Language Variables and Sample Definitions Code Book Language Analysis Television Research Project—1976

(Developed by
Mrs. Rhoda Brownstein)

Contents

1. Total number of words

2. Total number of utterances

3. Mean length of utterance

4. Total number of sentences

   a. Declarative sentences
   b. Imperative sentences
   c. Interrogative sentences

5. Total number of exclamatory utterances

6. Total number of nouns

   a. Proper nouns
   b. Common nouns
   c. Predicate nominative

7. Total number of pronouns

   a. Personal pronouns
   b. Impersonal pronouns
   c. Possessive pronouns

8. Total number of adjectives

   a. Attributive adjectives
   b. Predicate adjectives

9. Adverbs

10. Total number of present tense verbs

11. Total number of past tense verbs

12. Total number of future verbs

13. Total number of conditional tense verbs

14. Total number of onomatopoetic utterances

15. Incidence of repeated utterances

16. T.V. characters—people

17. T.V. phrases or sayings

18. T.V. products

19. T.V. slogans—jingles—used in advertising

1. *Total Number of Words*
All vocal and verbal expressions are counted individually as words. Included are:

Exclamations, such as "Oh!" "Ouch!" "Hey!" etc., each counted as (1).
Onomatopoetic sounds such as animal sounds, motor sounds, etc., each counted as (1).

For example:

"Ss—Ss—Ss" [snake] (3)
"Grum—grum—grum [motor] (3)
"yo...yo...yo..." [code 808] (3)
"Meow!" "Meow!" [cat] (2)

2. *Total Number of Utterances*
The total number of utterances made by the child during the observation period. *Utterances* is defined for the purposes of this analysis as "any stretch of talk by one person, before and after which there is silence on the part of that person" (Harris). It is not identical with "sentence" because a great many utterances consist of single words, phrases, incomplete sentences, etc. Complete sentences are also included in this category.

Count (1) for each *utterance.*

For example: (from Code 808)

"Can you get me there?" (1)
"Look you see me jump." (1)
"And you can read this book... (1)
"Do it—go backward." (2)
"Ruff." (1)

3. *Mean Length of Utterance* (MLU)
The average length of the child's utterance is measured in words (as defined above in 1; total number of words). This is derived by totaling the number of words in each utterance and dividing this total by the total number of utterances made by the child during the observation period.

For example:

(Code 808) $\dfrac{\text{Total No. of Words}}{\text{Total No. of Utterances}}$ = MLU = 4.4

$$\frac{75}{17} = 4.41 = 4.4$$

4. *Total Number of Sentences*
A sentence is defined for the purposes of language analysis in this study as "either a verb alone, a verb accompanied by one or more nouns, or a configuration of this kind to which one or more coordinate verbs have been added." (Chaffee, 1972, p. 98).

For example:

"Look." (Nouns is implied: *You* look)
"See?" (*Do you* see?)
"Hey, I wanna go up there." (Code 808)
"I'm 3 years old." (Code 808)

A. Total number of *Declarative Sentences*
A *declarative* sentence that makes a statement.

For example:

"Here's chocolate milk." (Code 656)
"He's going down the road." (Code 603)

Appendix 6:
How to Keep Your
Television Log

Maintaining the television log requires only four simple steps.

The essential first step is to record all of the programs that your child watches during each two-week sampling period. Simply circle the listing of the show. *For example:* Turn to the attached sample log page. On it you will see six programs circled. Those are the shows the child watched during the time span covered by that page.

Your child may watch programs that are not listed on the log form, such as specials and replacement programs for shows that have been cancelled in midseason. To solve this problem, we have left spaces at the end of each day's listing on the log form. Write in any shows your child watches that are not listed. *For example:* Turing again to the sample log sheet, you will see that the hypothetical child watched a Charlie Brown special and a show called "Marcus Welby, M.D." that had not been listed on the regular log form.

You may have noticed the letters and number to the right of the circled programs on the sample log page. They merely tell *where* a show was watched, *with whom,* and *how intensively.*

Where: for each program your child watches, you should indicate whether your child views it at home or away from home. If the child watches the program at home, mark an H to the right of the program listing; if the child watches it away from home, mark an A. If your child watches away from home, please ask the parent there what was watched when you pick the child up or ask by phone. *For example:* On the sample sheet, the symbols tell you that all of the programs were watched at home except for the *"Jackson Five Cartoons"* at 5:00 p.m.

With Whom: These are four symbols you can use to record with whom your child watches each show. The symbols are (with what they refer to in parentheses):

P (parent or parents)
O (other adult such as baby sitter or grandparent)
S (sibling = brothers or sisters [S = brother,
    S = sister]
C (other child such as a friend or relative)

Thus, referring again to the sample page, we can see that at 5:00 p.m. the hypothetical child watched only with another child or children, whereas at 8:00 p.m. she/he watched with at least one parent and at least one sibling. It is important to note that if no one had watched with the child, *none* of the symbols would have been used. Conversely, it is conceivable that all four might be used at one time.

How intensively: The last step requires you to estimate with what degree of concentration your child watches each show. The choices are:

1 = hardly watches the screen or involves him/herself in the program though remains in the room where it is being shown.

2 = occasionally watches the program but overall concentrates only for a small portion of time on it.

3 = watches the screen about half of the time.

4 = occasionally moves away from the screen but otherwise concentrates on it.

5 = watches with great concentration during almost all of the show.

For example: The sample sheet shows that the child watched the *"Jackson Five Cartoons"* with great concentration (5), the "NBC News" with poor concentration (2), and "Marcus Welby, M.D." with almost none at all (1). Note that this does not tell how long a child watches a program; it only tells how intensively the child watches during the time she or he is in a room where a television is on.

These four steps, essential to the television log, should require only *five* or *10 minutes* to complete each day.

Some Additional Suggestions

1) If the child watches two shows simultaneously by switching back and forth, *for example:* The sample log sheet shows that at 7:30 p.m., the hypothetical child watched part of the *"Muppet Show"* and part of

"Adam 12", please circle both shows on the answer sheet and mark in the appropriate symbols.

2) If you sleep late on Saturday or don't happen to be around when the child is watching, you can still get the necessary information by asking another adult who was present, an older sibling, or the child. Then you can fill in the log yourself. An older brother or sister, or the child will feel very important if given an opportunity to share in the task.

Sample Television Log

Code # _____   P = parent(s)   S = brother(s), sister(s)
                       O = other adult(s)   C = other children

(1) hardly watches; (2) occasionally watches; (3) watches half the time; (4) turns away occasionally but watches most of the show; (5) watches almost the whole show

Monday, February 6, 1978

Morning

5:45	(8) Davey & Goliath		7:30	(11) Mighty Mouse
				(13) MacNeil/Lehrer Report
6:00	(3) Agronsky and Company			
	(4) Man to Woman		8:00	(2,3) Captain Kangaroo
	(5) News			(5) Flintstones
	(8) Conn. Woman			(8) Good Morning America
				(11) Tom & Jerry
6:10	(2) News			(13) German
	(7) News			(20) Today
				(49) Child Development
6:30	(2) Sunrise Semester			
	(3) Face the State		8:30	(5) Archies
	(4) Not for Women Only			(9) Medix
	(5) Education Update			(11) Wacky Races
	(7) Listen & Learn			(13) News
	(8) Little Rascals			
			8:45	(13) Vegetable Soup
6:45	(11) Little Rascals			
			9:00	(2) To Tell the Truth
7:00	(2,3) News			(3) Mike Douglas
	(4) Today			(4) Phil Donahue
	(5) Quick Draw McGraw			(5) Green Acres
	(7) Good Morning America			(7) Stanely Siegel
	(8) Munsters			(8) Phil Donahue
	(9) News			(9) Joe Franklin
	(11) Banana Splits			(11) Munsters
	(13) Lilias, Yoga & You			(13, 49) Sesame Street
7:30	(5) Bugs Bunny		9:30	(2) With Jeanne Parr
	(8) Dusty's Treehouse			(5) Bewitched
	(9) PTL Club			(11) I Dream of Jeannie

10:00	(2,3)	Here's Lucy
	(4,20)	Sanford & Sons
	(5)	Partridge Family
	(7)	Movie
	(8)	Ryan's Hope
	(9)	Romper Room
	(11)	Get Smart
10:30	(2,3)	Price is Right
	(4,20)	Hollywood Squares
	(5)	I Love Lucy
	(8)	Edge of night
	(11)	Abbott & Costello
11:00	(4,20)	Wheel of Fortune
	(5)	Movie
	(7,8)	Happy Days
	(9)	Straight Talk
	(11)	Lucy Show
11:30	(2,3)	Love of Life
	(4,20)	It's Anybody's Guess
	(7,8)	Family Feud
	(11)	700 Club
11:55	(2,3)	CBS News

Afternoon

12:00	(2)	Young and the Restless
	(3)	News
	(4,20)	Shoot for the Stars
	(7)	The Better Sex
	(8)	12 o'clock Live
	(9)	News
	(13)	Zoom
12:30	(2,3)	Search for Tomorrow
	(4,20)	Chico and the Man
	(7)	Ryan's Hope
	(9)	Topper
	(11)	News
	(13)	Electric Company
1:00	(2)	Dating Game
	(3)	Match Game
	(4)	Gong Show
	(5)	Midday
	(7,8)	All My Children
	(9)	Movie
	(11)	Open Mind
	(20)	Insight

1:30	(2,3)	As the World Turns
	(4,20)	Days of our Lives
	(13)	Electric Company Special
2:00	(7,8)	$20,000 Pyramid
	(11)	Magic Garden
2:25	(5)	News
2:30	(2,3)	Guiding Light
	(4,20)	Doctors
	(5)	Bugs Bunny
	(7,8)	One Life to Live
	(11)	Popeye
3:00	(2,3)	All in the Family
	(4,20)	Another World
	(5)	Abbott and Costello
	(9)	Ironside
	(11)	Jetsons
	(49)	Zoom
3:15	(7,8)	General Hospital
3:30	(2)	Match Game
	(3,5)	New Mickey Mouse Club
	(11)	Banana Splits
	(13)	Mister Rogers
	(49)	Hodgepodge Lodge
4:00	(2)	Tattletales
	(3)	Dinah
	(4)	Marcus Welby, M.D.
	(5)	Journey to the Center of the Earth
	(7)	Edge of Night
	(8)	Brady Bunch
	(9)	Movie
	(11)	Dastardly & Muttley in Their Flying Machines
	(13)	Villa Alegre
	(20)	Gong Show
	(49)	Sesame Street
4:30	(2)	Mike Douglas
	(5)	Popeye & Friends
	(7)	Movie
	(8)	Star Trek
	(11)	Droopy Dog
	(13)	Sesame Street
	(20)	PTL Club

5:00	(4) News		7:30	(2) Muppet Show
	(5) Spiderman			(3) That's Hollywood
	(11) Tom & Jerry			(4) In Search of
	(49) Mister Rogers			(5) Hogan's Heroes
				(7) Hollywood Squares
5:30	(3) Mary Tyler Moore			(8) The Price Is Right
	(5) Flintstones			(11) Baseball
	(8) Odd Couple			(13) MacNeil/Lehrer Report
	(13) Mister Rogers			
	(49) Electric Company		8:00	(2,3) Young Dan'l Boone
				(4,20) Little House on the
6:00	(2) News			Prairie
	(3) News			(5) Cross-Wits
	(4) News			(7,8) San Pedro Beach Bums
	(5) Brady Bunch			(9) Penn State Highlights
	(7) News			(13,49) Upstairs, Downstairs
	(8) News			
	(9) It Takes a Thief		8:30	(5) Merv Griffin
	(11) Please Don't Eat the			
	Daisies		9:00	(2,3) Movie
	(13) Electric Company			(7,8) NFL Football
	(49) Child Development			(9) Nine on New Jersey
				(13) Movie
6:30	(5) I Love Lucy			
	(8) ABC News		9:30	(2,3) Maude
	(11) Honeymooners			(9) Newark & Reality
	(13) Zoom			
	(20) NBC News		10:00	(2,3) Rafferty
	(49) Family Risk Manage-			(5) News
	ment			(9) Meet the Mayors
				(11) News
7:00	(2,3) CBS News			
	(4) NBC News		10:30	(9) New York Report
	(5) Brady Bunch			
	(7) ABC News		11:00	(2) News
	(8) Concentration			(3) News
	(9) Bowling for Dollars			(5) Fernwood 2 Night
	(11) Odd Couple			(9) Life of Reilly
	(13) Once upon a Classic			(11) Odd Couple
	(20) Journeys to the Mind			

Use Lines Below for Any Programs Not Listed

Time	*Channel and Name of Show*	Codes

If you need more space, use the back of this sheet.

Appendix 7:
Play Protocol Analysis Chart

February, 1978
Dorothy G. Singer
Jerome L. Singer
NSF-TV Research

Child's Code # _____ Sex ___

Observation # _____

Date _____

Scored by _____ Group Category _____

I. *Play Environment*
   A. *Indoor*
      Bounded Space 1 = 100% bounded
      2 = 50% bounded
      3 = less than 50% bounded
   B. *Outdoors*
      Bounded Space 1 = 100% bounded
      2 = 50% bounded
      3 = less than 50% bounded
II. *Who is playing*
   A. Alone(1 = thoughout period)
      (2 = more than 50% alone)
      (3 = less than 50% alone)
   B. Playing with one child predominantly (1 = same sex; 2 = opposite sex)
   C. Playing with more than one child predominantly (1 = same sex; 2 = opposite sex; 3 = both sexes)
   D. Playing with adult (No = 1; Yes = 2)
III. *Type of play*
   A. Physical-motor (none = 1; some = 2; predominant form = 3)

B. Exploratory activity with objects (none = 1; some = 2; predominant = 3)

C. Art forms (drawing, clay molds, bead, pegboard) (none = 1; some = 2; predominant = 3)

D. Ritual play ("Ring-around-the-rosy") (none = 1; some = 2; predominant = 3)

E. Language play (puns, silly talk, rhymes) (none = 1; some = 2; predominant = 3)

F. Games with rules (checkers, candyland, red light) (none = 1; some = 2; predominant = 3)

G. Dancing and singing (none = 1; some = 2; predominant = 3)

H. Make-believe play (none = 1; some = 2; predominant = 3)

I. Mastery play (none = 1; some = 2; predominant = 3)

IV. *Materials*

A. Water, sand, dirt (no = 1; yes = 2)

B. Large motor toys (bikes, wagons) (no = 1; yes = 2)

C. Exercise toys (swings, climbers, jungle gym) (no = 1; yes = 2)

D. Blocks (no = 1; yes = 2)

E. Art supplies (playdough, paints, etc.) (no = 1; yes = 2)

F. Miniature toys (plastic soldiers, cars, etc.) (no = 1; yes = 2)

G. Dolls (no = 1; same sex = 2; opposite sex = 3; both = 4)

H. Stuffed animals (no = 1; yes = 2)

I. Games and puzzles (no = 1; yes = 2)

J. Books (no = 1; yes = 2)

K. Dress-up clothes (no = 1; yes = 2)

V. *Who starts play?*

A. Subject initiates play (no = 1; yes = 2)

B. Subject follows another's lead (no = 1; yes = 2)

C. Subject terminates play (no = 1; yes = 2)

D. Subject disrupts a game (no = 1; yes = 2)

E. Turn-taking play with another (no = 1; yes = 2)

VI. *Aggression during play period*

A. Subject initiates attack or breaks toys, etc. (no = 1; yes = 2)

B. Subject reacts to attack by others with aggression (no = 1; yes = 2)

C. Subject withdraws, weeps, or cowers in response to aggression (no = 1; yes = 2)

D. Subject coped effectively, e.g., calls teacher, defends materials, etc. (no = 1; yes = 2)

VII. *Make-believe play forms*

A. *Themes*

1. Family games (mommy, daddy, house, shopping) (no = 1; yes = 2)

2. Occupations (doctor, teacher, baker) (no = 1; yes = 2)

3. Animal games (dog, kitty, house) (no = 1; yes = 2)

    4. Adventure (fantastic, superhero, spaceman, witch, ghost) (no = 1; yes = 2)

    5. Adventure (more realistic—cops, robbers, firemen at fire) (no = 1; yes = 2)

    6. Sports (baseball, olympics) (no = 1; yes = 2)

    7. T.V.-related variety and quiz shows (no = 1; yes = 2)

    8. T.V.-related family show characters (Fonz, etc.) (no = 1; yes = 2)

    9. T.V.-related fantastic characters (bionic man, etc.) (no = 1; yes = 2)

    10. T.V.-related commercials (jingles, Burger King Magician) (no = 1; yes = 2)

B. *Roles*

    1. Same sex role or opposite sex role? (same sex = 1; opposite sex = 2; both = 3)

    2. Mother (no = 1; yes = 2)

    3. Father (no = 1; yes = 2)

    4. Baby (no = 1; yes = 2)

    5. Sibling (no = 1; yes = 2)

    6. Grandparent, uncle, aunt, or older figure (no = 1; yes = 2)

    7. Doctor (no = 1; yes = 2)

    8. Nurse (no = 1; yes = 2)

    9. Teacher (no = 1; yes = 2)

    10. Animal (small or pet) (no = 1; yes = 2)

    11. Animal (large, fierce) (no = 1; yes = 2)

    12. Fantasy characters (no = 1; yes = 2)

    13. Hero (no = 1; yes = 2)

    14. Villain (no = 1; yes = 2)

    15. Aggressor in game (no = 1; yes = 2)

    16. Victim in game (no = 1; yes = 2)

    17. TV characters (no = 1; yes = 2)

C. *Transformations*

    1. (Degree of introduction of pretend or make-believe characters, materials time, space)

        1 = no major transformations

        2 = some transformations

        3 = many transformations (at least 3 transformations)

    2. *Divergent Activity or Novelty*

        1 = none

        2 = block is used for houses or building structures

        3 = blocks used as cakes, guns, etc.

D. *Reality versus Fantasy* (predominant trend)

    Extremely close to reality situations (playing house, going to visit grandparents) = 1 or 2

Moderate (going to far-away place, flying in plane with parents) = 3

Far removed from ordinary life situation (changes of characters, becoming fantasy figures, sports heroes, etc.) = 4, 5

E. *Time Perspective*

No references = 1

Short time spans in play themes = 2 (all events occur within few minutes as they would)

Implied long time spans (morning, noon, night) = 3

F. *Dynamic Themes*

1. Orality, hunger, basic deprivation (no = 1; yes = 2)
2. Cleanliness and toilet behavior (no = 1; yes = 2)
3. Separation fears, death, rejection (no = 1; yes = 2)
4. Dangers (disasters, monsters, illness, body mutilation) (no = 1; yes = 2)
5. Sexuality (boyfriends, marriage) (no = 1; yes = 2)
6. Sibling rivalry or jealousy (no = 1; yes = 2)
7. Parental conflicts (no = 1; yes = 2)
8. Power struggle; racial conflicts; social conflicts (no = 1; yes = 2)
9. Wealth accumulation or achievement (no = 1; yes = 2)
10. Religious themes (no = 1; yes = 2)

Appendix 8:
Family Interview Schedule

Child's Code #: _____
Date of Interview: _____
Parent (M, F): _____
Interviewer: _____

1. Private home _____ Apartment _____
2. Location of child during interview _____
   Location of interview in home _____
3. No. of TV sets & locations _____
   _____

4. Is TV on?   No   Yes
                          ───────────
                          1   2

Home Observation
5. Home Rating
     1 2 3 4 5
6. Toys & games
     1 2 3 4 5
7. Books & Magazines
     1 2 3 4 5
8. Musical instruments & Stereos
     1 2 3 4 5
9. Rifle cabinet or other indications of weapons or hunting
     1 2 3 4 5

10. Marital status of parents   (1) _____, (2) _____
                                       single   married
                                       (separated;
                                       divorced)

Family Life Style
11. Members of family living in house (including grandparents, relatives, boarders)

_____

12. Number of rooms _____
13. Child have own room?   No   Yes
                                  _____
                                   1   2

Daily Routine
14. Child's wake-up time weekday   (1) before 6 a.m.   (2) 6–7 a.m.
                                     (3) 7–8 a.m.   (4) 8–9 a.m.
                                            (5) after 9 a.m.

15. Child's wake-up time weekend   (1) before 6 a.m.   (2) 6–7 a.m.
                                     (3) 7–8 a.m.   (4) 8–9 a.m.
                                            (5) after 9 a.m.

16. Mother's wake-up time weekday   (1) before 6 a.m.   (2) 6–7 a.m.
                                     (3) 7–8 a.m.   (4) 8–9 a.m.
                                            (5) after 9 a.m.

17. Mother's wake-up time weekend   (1) before 6 a.m.   (2) 6–7 a.m.
                                     (3) 7–8 a.m.   (4) 8–9 a.m.
                                            (5) after 9 a.m.

18. Father's wakeup time weekday   (1) before 6 a.m.   (2) 6–7 a.m.
                                     (3) 7–8 a.m.   (4) 8–9 a.m.
                                            (5) after 9 a.m.

19. Father's wakeup time weekend   (1) before 6 a.m.   (2) 6–7 a.m.
                                     (3) 7–8 a.m.   (4) 8–9 a.m.
                                            (5) after 9 a.m.

20. Do children watch TV regularly
     in early weekday AM?   (1) No or little   (2) yes
21. Children's favorite programs
     Weekday a.m. (1)   Weekend a.m.   (1)
                    (2)   (2)
                    (3)   (3)
     Weekday p.m. (1)   Weekend p.m.   (1)
                    (2)   (2)
                    (3)   (3)
     Comments re: TV habits (note any changes in past year, in preferences, time, interests, etc.):

22. Family eats together (weekday)   1 meal _____ 2 meals _____
                                                                        3 meals _____
23. Family eats together (weekend)   1 meal _____ 2 meals _____
                                                                        3 meals _____
24. Children or family watch TV while eating?
           1   2   3   4   5
        never   always
25. Who takes the child to school? _____
26. Who brings child home? _____
27. No. of hours child is in school _____
28. After school activities—typical day (any TV-viewing, free play, structured activities, lessons, etc.) _____

_____
_____

29. Supper time (1) 5–6 p.m.   (2) 6–7 p.m.   (3) 7–8 p.m.   (4) after 8 p.m.
30. Bedtime   (1) 6–7 p.m.   (2) 7–8 p.m.   (3) 8–9 p.m.   (4) after 9 p.m.
31. Bedtime routine   (1) Irregular?   (2) Regular?
32. Describe how child is put to bed, e.g. is there a bed-time ritual? (Do not ask leading questions but look for reading, story-telling, prayers, discussion, singing.) _____

_____
_____

Child's Sleeping Pattern
33. Sleep through night?   (1) Never   (2) Sometimes   (3) Usually
34. Nightmares?   (1) Never   (2) Sometimes   (3) Usually
35. No. of hours of night sleep _____
36. Does child come into parents' bed?
                                (1) Never   (2) Sometimes   (3) Usually
37. Does the child have visiting
    friends (in the daytime)?
                                (1) Never   (2) Sometimes   (3) Usually
38. Does the child visit other
    children (in the daytime)?
                                (1) Never   (2) Sometimes   (3) Usually

Weekend Activities
39. Activities with whole
    family   (1) Rare   (2) Moderate   (3) Frequent
    List:
40. Mother's activities with
    child on weekend   (1) Rare   (2) Moderate   (3) Frequent
    List:

41. Father's activities with
    child on weekend   (1) Rare   (2) Moderate   (3) Frequent
    List:

Joint TV Watching on Weekend
42. (F-child)   List:

    1   2   3   4   5
  never   regularly

43. (M-child)   List:

    1   2   3   4   5
  never   regularly

Family Viewing Style in General
    Get narrative account. Include following questions:
44. Who controls TV?   (1) Child   (2) Sibling   (3) Parents
                                                or adult
45. Are there conflicts?   (1) None   (2) Moderate   (3) Frequent
46. Resolution of TV conflicts (1) TV turned off
                             (2) Use supplementary sets
                             (3) Compromise—take turns
                             (4) Parents' preference prevail

Family Activities (parents with child)

	never	occasion-ally	some-times	often	regu-larly
47. Visiting relatives to-gether	1	2	3	4	5
48. Shopping	1	2	3	4	5
49. Park, picnics, zoo, out-ings	1	2	3	4	5
50. Museums, galleries, con-certs	1	2	3	4	5
51. Movies	1	2	3	4	5

Sports Interests of Family

	never	occasion-ally	some-times	often	regu-larly
52. Father a participant? List sports:	1	2	3	4	5
53. Father a spectator? List sports:	1	2	3	4	5

54. Mother a participant?   1   2   3   4   5
    List sports:

55. Mother a spectator?   1   2   3   4   5
    List sports:

56. Child a participant?   1   2   3   4   5
    List sports:

57. Child a spectator?   1   2   3   4   5
    List sports:

58. Father's sports in-   (1) noncontact sports, e.g., tennis,
    terest mainly in: baseball, hiking, swimming, bike
                         riding, jogging
                  (2) contact sports, e.g., football,
                         hockey, wrestling, boxing, judo
                  (3) no sports interests
59. Mother's sports interest   (1) noncontact sports
    mainly in: (2) contact sports
                  (3) no sports interest
60. Child's sports interest   (1) noncontact sports
    mainly in: (2) contact sports
                  (3) no sports interest

Television Viewing Habits
61. Family, regular TV-view- (1) Never, or rarely, watches TV
    ing with child   together
                  (2) Moderate   (3) Frequent
62. Examples of regularly seen shows, child and family together:
    (1)
    (2)
    (3)
63. Examples of shows (or categories, e.g., cartoons) child regularly watches
    alone:
    (1)
    (2)
    (3)
64. Examples of mother's favorite TV shows:
    (1)
    (2)
    (3)

65. Examples of father's favorite TV shows:
    (1)
    (2)
    (3)
66. Examples of TV specials seen in last year:
    (1)
    (2)
    (3)
67. Hobbies or interests of mother:

68. Hobbies or interests of father:

Family Stress Situations
69. Have there been major illnesses, bereavements, family problems, etc., in the past year, with children, parents, or grandparents?
    (1) Minimum (2) Moderate (3) Major
70. Arguments between children?   1   2 3 4   5
                                   never   very
                                                      frequent
71. Arguments: physical vs.   1   2 3 4   5
    verbal   mostly angry   mostly blows
                               comments   and hitting
72. Any parental arguments witnessed by children? (1) No (2) Yes
73. Parents ever disagree about child-rearing?
    (1) Minimum differences   (2) Moderate differences
        (3) Major differences

Discipline and Punishment
Examples of discipline, with brief descriptions:

74. Restriction?   (1) Rare   (2) Moderate   (3) Frequent
    Father: Mother:

75. Psychological?   (1) Rare   (2) Moderate   (3) Frequent
    Father: Mother:

76. Scolding?   (1) Rare   (2) Moderate   (3) Frequent
    Father: Mother:

77. Physical?   (1) Rare   (2) Moderate   (3) Frequent
    Father: Mother:

78. Reward pattern—praise and affection? (1) Yes (2) No
79. Reward pattern—any material reward? (1) No (2) Yes

Child Behaviors
80. Physical aches & pains   1   2   3   4   5
81. poor habits, e.g.,
 toilet, messiness, care-
 lessness   1   2   3   4   5
82. Fighting, noisy, stubborn-
 ness, possessiveness   1   2   3   4   5
83. Worries, fears, doubts   1   2   3   4   5
84. Shyness, seclusive,
 solitary, passive   1   2   3   4   5
85. Importance of TV in home in terms of use and interest
 (1) Minimum (2) Moderate (3) High
86. Parents' involvement with child's schoolwork and/or activities
 (1) Minimum (2) Moderate (3) High
 Describe:

87. Does parent or other adult in the family enjoy "rought & tumble" play
 activities, bear hugging, wrestling, play with child?
 (1) Minimum (2) Moderate (3) Many
 Describe:

88. Number of hours father views TV each week _____
89. Number of hours mother views TV each week _____
90. Number of hours child views TV each week _____

Comments—Open-Ended:
(Parent's interests, view of life, affection, discipline, religious values or
ethics, self-sufficiency, etc.) Use reverse side to complete.

Appendix 9:
Television Character
Recognition Test

Rules of administration: Preschool children
1. This individual test should be given in a quiet place away from others who may interfere or be taking the test at a later time.
2. The examiner should be pleasant and encouraging.
3. To motivate the subject to do the child's best, praise should be given generously. Such comments as the following have been found effective: *"Good! You are doing well,"* etc. However, praise can be overdone. Many individuals know when they are beyond their depth and are not deceived by unearned praise. The sensitive examiner will soon learn the optimal amount of encouragement to elicit maximum performance.
4. Do not indicate whether or not a response is correct. If an incorrect response is made, encouragement should be given. If a subject says, *"Did I get that one right?"* say *"That was a good answer."*
5. It is not permissible to show the subject the printed stimulus names.
6. Stimulus names may be pronounced aloud more than once by the examiner. Do not introduce any stimulus words not on the score sheet. When a character's name is given, do not mention the name of the program it is from.
7. The subject may take any reasonable amount of time per item to make a selection. However, after approximately one minute, the subject should be encouraged to make a choice. Say: *"Try one. Point to one of them."* Always secure a response. Do *not* record "no response" or "don't know." There is no penalty for guessing on this test.
8. Some of the subjects, especially young ones, may point to one corner on plate after plate. It is therefore necessary to repeat frequently, *"Be*

sure to look carefully at all four pictures. "If the child continues to do this the examiner should point to picture No. 1 saying, *"Look at this one";* then picture No. 2 saying *"and this one";* then to picture No. 3 saying *"and this one";* then to picture No. 4 saying *"and this one."*

9. When a subject spontaneously changes a choice, record the final response.

10. For subjects who use the pointing response, precede each stimulus word when starting the test with one of the following: *"Put your finger on   ." "Can you find   ?" "Show me   ." "Point to   ." "Where is   ?"*

11. When a name is given in quotation marks it indicates the name of a television program. Precede the name with *"Can you find someone from the television program called   ?" "Point to someone from the television show called   ."*

12. Two passes are to made through the test book. After completing the book once turn to plate 1 and continue asking the names on page 2 of the score sheet.

Introducing the Test

Introduce the test by saying:
"I want to play a television picture game with you"
Turn to the example and say:
"See all the pictures on this page."
Indicate this by pointing to each in turn.
"I will say the name of somebody on this page and then I want you to put your finger on the picture of the person or television show I have said. Let us try one. Put your finger on   ."
When a subject makes the desired response, turn to the next page and say:
"Fine! Now I am going to show you some other pictures. Each time I say a name, you find the picture of that person. When you are not sure you know the person I want you to look carefully at all of the pictures anyway and choose the one you think is right. Point to   ."

With very young children, additional trial series may be necessary to establish the desired pointing behavior. In such cases, ask other names on the example page.

With very immature subjects, the examiner will need to establish the pointing response by saying *"Put you finger on   ,"* and at the same time placing the child's finger on the correct picture. After a few trials the tester may take the lead by pointing and then encouraging the subject to do likewise. The length of time required to establish the desired pointing behavior will vary from child to child. The example plate may be repeated. However, if the desired response has not been established after a number of trials, the test should be discontinued.

TABLE B
Television Character Recognition Test

	Pass One				Pass Two		
Plate No.	Name	Key	Resp.	Plate No.	Name	Key	Resp.
1.	Yosemite Sam	(1)	___	1.	Mr. Magoo	(2)	___
2.	Hardy Boys	(3)	___	2.	Marlin	(1)	___
3.	John Boy	(1)	___	3.	Gong Show	(4)	___
4.	Lamont	(3)	___	4.	David Hartman	(2)	___
5.	Woody	(1)	___	5.	Big Bird	(3)	___
6.	Police Woman	(2)	___	6.	Mr. Spock	(3)	___
7.	Tom	(3)	___	7.	Gene	(1)	___
8.	Aquaman	(2)	___	8.	Batman	(1)	___
9.	Herman	(1)	___	9.	Animals, Animals, Animals	(2)	___
10.	Magic Garden	(3)	___	10.	Viki	(2)	___
11.	Kotter	(2)	___	11.	Bob	(4)	___
12.	Emergency	(2)	___	12.	Barney	(1)	___
13.	Scooby Doo	(4)	___	13.	Jabberjaw	(2)	___
14.	Alice and Raymond	(2)	___	14.	Donny and Marie	(3)	___
15.	Tom and Jerry	(1)	___	15.	Wilma	(2)	___
16.	Sandy	(4)	___	16.	Alice	(4)	___
17.	Bill	(2)	___	17.	The Fonz	(4)	___
18.	Pepper	(4)	___	18.	Bionic Woman	(3)	___
19.	The Partridge Family	(1)	___	19.	The Stevens' Family	(4)	___
20.	Wonder Woman	(1)	___	20.	Nancy Drew	(3)	___
21.	Oscar	(2)	___	21.	Mister Rogers	(3)	___
22.	Little House on the Prairie	(4)	___	22.	Barney	(1)	___
23.	Starsky	(3)	___	23.	Steve	(4)	___
24.	Alfalfa	(4)	___	24.	Porky	(3)	___
25.	John Chancellor	(3)	___	25.	Chuck Scarborough	(4)	___
26.	Caroscolendas	(4)	___	26.	Charlie's Angels	(2)	___

Author Index

Numbers in italics denote pages with complete bibliographic information.

Subject Index